T0293764

Ollie has written the authoritative guide to retail transformation – packed with wisdom that is a testament to his own deep experience. Every retailer struggling to change their business will get something from this book.

Ian Shepherd,
Chair, Bensons for Beds, Author, Former CEO, COO and CMO

This book is a refreshing change from the usual theoretical guides, offering a practical and pragmatic approach to navigating the challenges of modern retail. Oliver presents a witty and engaging narrative that keeps you hooked while he captures the challenges faced by the retail industry today and underscores the need for swift, decisive action. Essential reading for any retail leader looking to not only survive but thrive in today's fast-paced environment.

Paula Bobbett,
Chief Digital Officer, Boots UK

I feel that defining what we need to do to evolve our business is only half the battle. Where most businesses fall short is in their inability to successfully transform. To implement their ideas, their new strategy, their new direction of travel or whatever the big idea is. Ollie does a great job of highlighting in a very practical way, why transformation is often ineffective, and what businesses can do to deliver change and transformation more effectively in the future.

Martin Newman,
Consumer Champion, Advisor and Author

This book will help you navigate your path through the journey of change using a simple and clear framework, brought to life with compelling stories and examples. It's an essential read for anyone delivering transformation, wanting to be confidently set up for success.

Janice Southway,
Former Transformation Director, ASOS

I have over 12 years' experience leading retail transformations, yet every time I talk with Ollie, he brings a new perspective and challenges my thinking. This book provides a wonderful introduction to transformation, giving a clear and concise view of what it means to lead a transformation, and how to do it well! It offers real, practical tools to help navigate through change that will be useful to both new and experienced transformation leaders.

Laura Ross,
Head of Customer Transformation, Holland and Barrett

In retail, the only constant is change. But how do you make it happen? Oliver Banks has penned an important book to help you. If you're in retail, read this, study it and apply its many lessons to help guide you to drive real, lasting, transformational change.

Mike Doherty,
Demand Clarity Inc., Co-author, Flowcasting the Retail
Supply Chain

This book is a comprehensive guide for anyone navigating the complex world of transformation. Oliver's style is very clear, digestible and actionable, with lots of good examples and processes to follow. The framework and the scoring aspect is a brilliant touch, it's very practical and will be invaluable to readers. It is a transformative approach to transformation itself. A must-read for change management professionals and those leading transformation.

Miya Knights,
Retail Technology Magazine Publisher, Author, Consultant

'How?' 'Where do I start?' If these questions give you pause, then you've picked up the right book. Oliver Banks helps you to understand, through this personable and insightful read, a new way of seeing and working, and kits you out for leading and navigating your journey of transformation. Easy to read, with concise chapters, valuable summaries and conversational narrative. It's more than just a one-time read, it will be your trusty reference guide to keep picking up.

Claire Lewis,
Process Improvement Manager, Iceland Foods

Driving Retail Transformation is an upbeat, straightforward guide to every step of bringing about change in a retail organization. Whether you've done it before or embarking on your first change programme, Ollie's advice, tips, and reminders will be a helpful co-pilot along the way.

Holly Steele,
Technology Director, Creed Fragrances

Oliver Banks' book stands out with its impeccable structure and compelling readability. I especially appreciated how he expertly unpacks complex topics of the day; making them technically robust for pros, yet accessible for everyone keen to tackle the challenges of change within the retailing industry. His step-by-step account of the biggest challenge facing all retailers, the need for leaders to embrace vision, manage change and execute flawlessly at speed in business transformation, is a really enlightening and enjoyable read. A valuable reference for the industry facing irrefutable competitive challenges on so many fronts.

Gary Newbury,
Retail Supply Chain Transformation Strategic Advisor

It is hard to think of an industry that is transforming more fundamentally than retail. Although there are many books that will tell you what is changing, there needs to be one that explains HOW. I can think of no one better than Oliver Banks to deliver the knowledge, frameworks and experience to guide us through the mechanics of our much-needed retail transformations.

Carl Boutet,
Chief Strategist, Studio RX and Guest Lecturer, McGill University

Far too many transformation initiatives fail to fulfill their promise. In *Driving Retail Transformation*, Oliver Banks delivers an urgent and compelling call to action, packed with highly pragmatic advice.

Steve Dennis,
Strategic Advisor, Keynote Speaker, Best-selling Author

This book is like condensing a whole degree in strategic change management into one book. Oliver Banks's guide to retail transformation is both an enlightening read and an invaluable toolkit. Seamlessly blending strategic insights with practical advice for every stage of transformation.

Joe Murray,
Former CEO, Internet Fusion Group, Worldstores

DRIVING
RETAIL
TRANSFORMATION

How to navigate
disruption and change

OLIVER BANKS

First published in Great Britain by Practical Inspiration Publishing, 2024

© Oliver Banks, 2024

The moral rights of the author have been asserted

ISBN   9781788605281 (PB print)
        9781788605809 (HB print)
        9781788605304 (epub)
        9781788605298 (mobi)

Every effort has been made to trace copyright holders and to obtain their permission for the use of copyright material. The publisher apologizes for any errors or omissions and would be grateful if notified of any corrections that should be incorporated in future reprints or editions of this book.

Want to bulk-buy copies of this book for your team and colleagues? We can customize the content and co-brand *Driving Retail Transformation* to suit your business's needs.

Please email info@practicalinspiration.com for more details.

For Sarah

Contents

About the author

Oliver Banks helps retail leaders drive transformation and realize their strategic goals. He's the founder of consultancy OB&Co and helps retailers and brands to deliver change to improve customer experience and increase profitability.

Originally a Chartered Engineer and cocktail mixologist, he blends a logical, systematic approach with energy and left-field thinking.

Formerly at UK retail grocery giant, Tesco, he led multiple change programmes, increasing effectiveness and efficiency across stores, online operations and the supply chain.

Since founding OB&Co, Banks has kick-started transformation projects with global retailers and brands; creating innovative propositions, unlocking new revenue streams, expanding internationally, integrating acquisitions, plus defining, simplifying and realizing ideal operating models. Collectively, these initiatives have delivered over £100m of net new annual profits for clients.

He's one of LinkedIn's Top Voices for Retail and among the world's top retail influencers, recognized by global retail news and insight firm, RETHINK Retail, and retail media outlet, the Retail Technology Innovation Hub. He hosts the popular podcast, the Retail Transformation Show, delivers energizing and insightful keynotes, and thoughtfully advises and consults on navigating transformation and the ever-evolving retail trends, guiding retail leaders towards a bright future.

Preface

Transformation is arguably an overused word. It evokes a range of emotions, both positive and negative. And making it happen is challenging, complex and hugely rewarding.

This book is not focused on the 'what' of transformation. If you're looking to be prescribed the precise and exact answer to the future of retail, this isn't the right book (and in fact, that book doesn't exist or would be quickly out of date!).

This book aims to explain the 'how' of transformation. You'll learn *how* to approach a transformation, *how* to discover the why for your change, *how* to find the optimum solutions and *how* to turn an idea into reality.

My aim in writing this book is to help you drive your transformation through to success, delivering meaningful value for your customers, colleagues and business. I will equip you with an approach and techniques to define the transformation goals and how you can achieve them, empowered by a strong mindset, practical skills, guides and tools, and cross-functional teamwork.

This approach suits any particular type of change and can be applied across all categories. Your learning will apply in physical retail, ecommerce, omnichannel and anything in-between.

You may be surprised to discover that *digital transformation* is a term that I'm allergic to. In fact, I promise that this is the only time you'll see those words together in this book. We live in a digital world now. Very nearly everything has a digital element to it. However, the danger with this term is that it encourages us to think exclusively about IT and digital technologies, and in turn, become very focused on technical solutions. Even if technology is a big part of your solution, it's not everything. This term puts blinkers on us and those around us, and we are likely to miss or underestimate critical elements such as people and process.

Transformation impacts the whole business, along with customers, suppliers, partners and potentially the wider world too, and therefore I'd encourage you to use this simpler term from now on.

As a consultant and advisor, I help companies, teams and individuals navigate the changing retail industry, identify their place in the competitive landscape, and adapt their business and operations accordingly.

Transformation is a journey and I'm here to help you navigate the way to reach your destination and successfully achieve your goals.

Oliver Banks
2024

A few side notes

This book is based on my experiences, observations and research, as well as discussions I've had over my career. Transformation is complex and there are many ways to achieve the same result. Additionally, what works in one situation may not be guaranteed to work every time. What I present here are the key themes that I have found most successful in guiding individuals, organizations and transformation initiatives.

This book includes case studies and real stories of transformation, although companies and names have been removed or changed for confidentiality purposes.

Foreword

Tracey Clements

SVP CEO bp Europe: Mobility and Convenience. Former Managing Director, Tesco, COO, Boots and CEO, One Stop.

'The pace of change has never been faster.' '70% of change programs fail.' 'Customers are changing faster than ever before.' 'We must transform or die.' During my near 30 years in retail, I have heard all these sayings, and many more. They are all true. What I have also learned, during my career with the UK's largest retailers, is that successful transformation is all about the how, the leadership of change. In my journey from Programme Manager to COO, CEO, MD, and SVP I have been involved in and led successful and unsuccessful transformations. The learning experience has been key to my personal career and leadership journey. I was therefore delighted when Oliver told me he was writing a book on exactly this topic. In fact, my two favourite subjects coming together; retail transformation and leadership.

I first met Oliver when I had the great privilege of leading the Operations Development team at Tesco. Having started my career as a retail consultant I had just returned to a head office role following four years deep in the operations of the convenience store business at Tesco. Leading a team of talented MBA's, former consultants, Lean 6 Sigma Black Belts and engineers was a pivotal experience. During that time, we oversaw a substantial number of projects and programs that supported the transformation of the Tesco business, which was known, at the time, as not only the market leader in the UK, but also as the leading innovator for customers. It was always clear to me that Oliver would have a phenomenally successful career and drive profound change for organizations. I have followed his journey with interest, listened to his hugely insightful podcasts and was delighted to see him awarded the recognition of becoming one of LinkedIn's 'Top Voices for Retail'. What a privilege (and a thrill) to be asked to write the Foreword to his fantastic book on retail transformation!

Driving Retail Transformation is a must-read book for anyone in the retail sector. The book is organized fundamentally around the Retail Transformation Steering Wheel, an incredibly useful tool, which focuses on the key activities, elements, capabilities, skills and characteristics needed to deliver a successful transformation initiative.

Oliver deeply understands that business strategy and transformation plans are not the same thing, and that it is critical they align. He sets out a clear approach to transformation that ensures all the key considerations are made when launching a program. His insight comes from deep personal experience, a huge dose of pragmatism and a deep understanding and appreciation for the six Ws of change (What, Why, hoW, Who, Where, When). In my experience, transformation programs fail when they don't consider the six W's and they don't adequately prepare for the journey of retail transformation.

He has deep respect for defined processes and the use of data, but also understands the human element of all change programs and preparing for how that change impacts people is key to success. The right mindset for change trumps the best Gantt chart in my experience.

I particularly enjoyed the sections on the psychology of change, the leadership of change and the reminder that no matter how senior or successful you are that remaining close to the front line, and your customers, is key. Accepting you may have to have an honest look at yourself and a recognition that you must recognize your own biases to change are key.

I wish you every success on the transformation you are embarking upon. You're making the right first step, simply by reading this book.

Introduction
The ever-evolving world

Once upon a time, the world moved slowly. Stability and consistency meant that change happened rarely, and at a snail's pace. For years, decades and even centuries, life remained the same. You lived in the same place, secured a job-for-life, with a lifestyle akin to your parents.

However, in today's world, significant shifts and disruptions happen regularly and at lightning speed. These changes impact all aspects of life as we know it, for both businesses and individuals. And interestingly, one of the critical shifts in recent years has been that it's now consumers who drive the pace of change, not businesses.

Perhaps these shifts are created by the adoption of new technology systems, innovative digital devices, or the growth of a new channel. These technology-based developments have rebalanced the power to consumers and enabled people to vote with their wallets. But it's not just technology factors. The demand for more sustainable and ethical business practices is increasingly being driven by consumers, too.

Consumers set the direction and dictate
the pace of transformation.

The rise of the internet and ecommerce, along with globalization and cross-border fulfilment, means that consumers have vast choices in front of them; there is more choice than ever before. And all from the convenience of a handy smart device. And to serve their demands, a seemingly never-ending group of businesses locked in a 'survival of the fittest' competitive battle.

Therefore, the corresponding challenge from customers, to all consumer-facing businesses is simply: 'keep up, or we'll move on'. This challenge alongside disruptive forces in the market drives the need for transformation.

So, are you ready to rise to the challenge? Of course you are, hence why you're reading this! But you also probably know that change is hard. So, this book aims to arm you with the skills, mindset and confidence to take on the challenge of change and transformation.

The future will happen, one way or another.
And it will happen to you, not with you, unless
you intentionally take action to transform and evolve.

The causes of the changing world

We regularly hear that the pace of change is accelerating. But why do we experience this and what does this tell us about how the future will evolve further?

Five broad factors contribute to the changing market for consumer-facing businesses. For each of these, reflect how they have and are impacting your business. And continually assess how future changes could provide new challenges or opportunities.

1. **Generation-based life experiences:** Each generation grows up and experiences a slightly different world through global and local events. These changes, in turn, shape attitudes, behaviours and even skills. These all play into an evolving consumer mindset over time. Whilst I believe there are many factors that shape our own individual personality, there are trends and attitudes which can be influenced. External factors shape us all through world events, politics, societal shifts, economic buoyancy, media and the increasing rise in consumer technology. Even aspects like preferred social media platforms tend to shift by generation. Also, remember that these changes, in particular, can be slow to come

to fruition as it takes time for these altered behaviours to reach a critical mass.

How will global events, economic factors, cultural shifts and other changes impact future consumer mindsets and shopping behaviours?

2. **How we live:** The global trend of urbanization, which sees more people moving into cities or other metropolitan areas, looks set to continue. By 2050, 69% of the world's population will live in cities, compared to 56% in 2022.[1] This trend is represented across all geographies and all income groups.[2] Other factors changing how we live are the rise in work-from-home lifestyles and portfolio careers. These changes also have follow-on implications, for example, how personal transport in urban areas will change the future of life, work and shopping.

    What impact will the current lifestyle shifts will have on your categories, your channels and your future business?

3. **How we relate to each other:** We're more connected than we've ever been, mostly enabled by the smartphone or other digital devices. We're increasingly being bombarded by notifications or messages. We also consume more content than ever before, with a seemingly insatiable desire for more. But it's not all about technology. How we relate to, and communicate with, each other is driven by factors like the evolution of inclusivity, diversity, social mobility and even organizational hierarchies in businesses.

    Which changes have shaped your customers relationships most, and how will this affect their relationships with brands and businesses?

4. **The rise of technology:** New technology-based innovations are continually launching. These advances can drive change themselves, or they can act as a catalyst for other changes discussed already. Whether we're talking about better-connected, smarter devices, further AI-powered enhancements, robotics or other technology, we can be sure that these shifts will continually impact consumers and consumer-facing businesses.

    Which consumer and business technology changes have impacted the retail market most for you, and which are set to add more disruption?

5. **Focus on caring more:** As a collective society, we seem to be increasingly aware of our own wellbeing and the broader impacts

of our actions. Looking inwards, we take more care of ourselves as we focus on mindfulness, wellness, health and nutrition, with the overall wellness category forecast to grow 9.9% per annum.[3] Looking outwards, we show more empathy to others and are more considerate of aspects like inclusivity, driven by movements like Black Lives Matter and recognition of disabilities, sexuality and gender. Meanwhile, at a macro view, we recognize and worry more about the impact of environmental factors, ethical business behaviours and social justice.

What are your customers starting to care more about and what they will care about in the future?

These aren't hard and fast rules. Consumers are individuals. And individuals are, well, individual, so expect exceptions to the rule. However, these five elements are driving significant change to the retail and consumer-facing market.

Consider how these will form and shape expectations and shopping habits, and how they impact both customers and colleagues. In addition, also consider the category and geography level specifics to get a closer idea of the specific shifts and evolutions that face you and your organization.

Transform or die

In a highly competitive, consumer-led market, it remains a business's prerogative to transform to keep up and, hopefully, stay ahead of competitors.

However, there is a choice. You could choose to *do nothing*. To stay static and desperately cling to the hope that consumers, competitors and the world will also choose *not* to change. If you think that's what's going to happen, good luck.

But I'm sure we can all think of what happens next for companies in any industry that fail to keep pace with the broader market. History is littered with plenty of examples of retailers who have failed to keep up and fallen by the wayside.

Meanwhile, the retail winners will be the companies and brands that adapt and evolve. Apple transformed from industry laggard to innovative technology leader. WHSmith refocused their growth into travel hubs like train stations and airports. M&S have excelled in transforming their food offering. Starbucks refocused on customer experience to turnaround poor performance. Amazon are always evolving; expanding to new categories and channels, disrupting through new business models and continual operational improvements.

Whilst there are plenty of companies that have failed to evolve, there are fortunately endless examples of positive change, improvement and reinvention.

The decision is clear: transform or die. And the choice feels simple.

It's about 'what' the transformation is, right?

If it's obvious to transform and evolve, the next factor is that it must be about *what* that specific change is, right?

To explore this, let me share three (real) strategies that different companies have laid out. And my question to you is: which strategy leads to success?

Company strategy #1

'Our growth plans require us to have the right structure, talent and determination to transform our business and achieve the financial objectives we've set for the company.'

Company strategy #2

'Our goal remains to continue to solidify and extend our brand and customer base. This requires sustained investment in systems and infrastructure to support outstanding customer convenience, selection, and service while we grow.'

Company strategy #3

'Our mission is to provide our customers with the most convenient access, delivered through multiple distribution channels such as our stores, mail, kiosks and digital devices. We believe we offer customers a value-priced experience, combining the broad product depth of a speciality retailer with local neighbourhood convenience.'

So, which approach is destined for success? They all seem feasible and sensible. But what would you think if I told you that two of these three companies were out of business soon after communicating these sensible-sounding strategies? What went wrong? (Find out who these strategies belonged to at the end of this Introduction.)

There are usually numerous reasons for any business failure. But simply deciding on the 'what' to transform is not enough to prevent failure.

We must be clear on the 'why' to transform to ensure it tackles a real challenge and seizes a meaningful opportunity, and that we're focused on the highest priorities, which may be relevant to sections of or the whole business.

Additionally, we must deliver on the 'how' to bring the transformation into reality and ultimately to ensure that we achieve the purpose or goal of the change. This is where is starts to get hard.

Transformation is hard

A meaningful and successful transformation initiative may include many different aspects. From a compelling, attractive proposition for customers, a new technology stack or a viable market for a new business unit. Delivering on time and to budget is an expected goal and strong stakeholder support an essential enabler. You must carefully navigate all the challenges that inevitably crop up along the way. Delivering successful transformation relies on many factors, influencing the 'stars to align' or getting those proverbial 'ducks in a row' are often used analogies alluding to the difficulties experienced.

Additionally, each transformation initiative is entirely unique. It involves a bespoke set of activities to deliver a better outcome. With different starting positions and situations, as well as varying capability levels, even when two separate companies pursue similar goals, it will result in different journeys.

There is no defined path to follow. No precise set of instructions. No exact prescription.

When you realize that this unique piece of work has many failure modes and opportunities for error, the chance of delivering a successful transformation feels slim.

'70% of transformation efforts fail.'

McKinsey & Company[4]

Change is hard. The risk of failure is real. We can't shy away from this fact.

But it definitely doesn't mean it's impossible. I believe it's always possible. No matter the challenges facing a specific company, there is still time to pivot, improve and change for the better. To do this will take the very best of you, and those around you. This very best will need a blend of hard work, smart work and careful work too.

- ▸ **Hard work:** We're not talking about working long hours here. Sure, there may be instances where this is required to prepare for major milestones or other deadlines. Hard work means that we do what it takes to make it easy for others, even in the face of difficulty, especially for changes impacting vast numbers of people. It means persisting to achieve the desired result, even if we don't want to do the work or find it complicated or difficult. Hard work means that we do the work if it's the right thing to do. Even the activities and elements that you don't like or don't know how to do, yet!

- ▸ **Smart work:** This is about being clever with understanding the problem, defining innovative solutions and delivering the change. Consider the current situation and the future too, looking from different people's point of view. Smart work requires you to think of more effective and efficient ways to solve problems and approach change.

- ▸ **Careful work:** Work must be full of care. Transformation has the possibility of causing an immense impact for different groups. This impact could be good or bad, so it needs delicate handling. Of course, silly mistakes must be avoided, and this level of diligence should go without saying.

In Figure 0.1, we see when hard work, smart work and careful work align, it's more effective for driving transformation. We experienced this alignment during the pandemic as we saw the Covid effect on retail transformation.

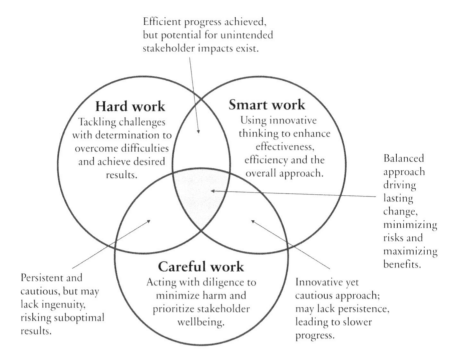

Figure 0.1: Bringing together hard, smart and careful work

The Covid effect

The Covid-19 pandemic, which spread across the world in 2020, was horrendous for many reasons. However, it also showed our capability for change and what can be achieved, both personally and professionally.

I'm sure we can recall various examples or experiences where 'years of change' were delivered in just a few weeks or months. It took a Herculean effort to ready each consumer-facing business for social distancing, new cleaning policies, significant surges in online orders, updated working practices and increased digitization across the whole enterprise. And all of this in a completely unique environment where nobody had relevant experience relative to the next person.

We should not forget the brilliant lessons learned from the Covid effect on change:

> ▶ **Focusing on what mattered most:** The Covid pandemic provided an important catalyst for change. A burning platform that offered no opportunity to *not* change. Businesses clearly recognized that

safety was the paramount objective in terms of minimizing the risk of infection and contamination. Did a given initiative promote or improve the safety of customers and colleagues? If yes, brilliant, crack on. If not, then let's stop it or pause until later, unless it represented significant and urgent value creation for the business. Continuous media coverage reinforced the focus on safety and examples were regularly shared about what other companies were implementing in terms of plastic guarding, traffic light entry systems or order collection processes. All companies were focused on the same objectives.

▶ **Reacting with urgency:** The fast-spreading pace of Covid meant that change was needed quickly. Whilst some shortcuts were taken to boost speed or bypass bureaucracy, generally we found ways to deliver change sensibly. Changes were delivered when they were ready, resulting in an escalating momentum to encourage a mentality of getting things done.

▶ **Getting things done:** The retail industry has many experienced operators who are excellent fire-fighters when faced with a problem. The industry excels in acting quickly and managing short-term task lists or consistency through compliance based operational tasks. When the pandemic emerged, these attributes allowed retailers to react quickly and make changes at speed.

▶ **Working together:** With a clear and shared goal, collaboration and teamwork became essential, and not just within the company. We also witnessed great examples of different organizations working together to overcome critical challenges such as logistics or labour availability. Organizational silos and hierarchies were knocked down. Essential resources were shared across teams, people found ways to communicate with the right people, and traditionally admin-heavy or slow governance processes were rapidly streamlined.

▶ **Progressing through the unknown:** Working in a 'VUCA' environment became commonplace. VUCA stands for Volatile, Uncertain, Complex and Ambiguous; this military term describing the chaos of war became standardized across commercial industries. We learnt together. We made progress, and we found a way.

> Delivering the significant changes in response
> to the Covid pandemic proved that every
> company can transform and evolve.

Was this colossal effort to become Covid-ready sustainable? No way. Since the pandemic, we've seen and heard others, or perhaps ourselves, suffer from symptoms of fatigue or burnout. The mental strain and relentless changes coupled with the emotional turmoil and horror pushed people over the edge.

The Covid effect taught us that we can apply the skills to change when we put our mind to it, but the long journey must be viable. We can't rely on a global crisis to help our transformation efforts.

The transformation skillset and mindset

Given the complexity and challenge of being able to deliver a transformation initiative successfully, we require specific skills. The good news is that these transformation skills can absolutely be learned. However, like all skills, they truly come to life when put into practice.

But the ability to drive transformation is not based only on a skillset. The right mindset is also vital. That mindset is open to consider the world in a different way. It is flexible and determined. It can be expansive and creative, but it must also critique ideas and dive into the details. Without this transformation mindset, it will be near impossible to successfully apply the skills and therefore deliver change.

However, transformation can and should be a team game where different individuals, skills, viewpoints, backgrounds and mindsets come together. A diverse and closely integrated team can ensure all aspects are covered with a range of perspectives, experiences and capabilities. Then, by collaborating effectively and working with the appropriate team, you can drive successful retail transformation.

What's in this book

Considering the future survival and prosperity of the business hinges on evolving with consumers, I urge you to actively transform. Given the complexity and challenges of doing so, this book aims to ready you with the skills, mindset and confidence to lead your organization through the challenge of transformation, along with a flexible and dynamic framework to keep your transformation on track.

Transformation is a journey, for you, your colleagues, your customers and your stakeholders to improve customer and colleague experiences, boost business performance and profitability whilst creating a positive and lasting impact on the world. Given this journey, we'll be using the metaphor of driving a car throughout the book, so buckle up.

Looking at what's coming up, in Part 1, Chapter 1 we explore how retail is evolving and the key themes that are ever-present in instigating transformation. Then in Chapter 2, let's dive deeper to understand the challenges of transforming. In Chapter 3, you'll discover the Retail Transformation Steering Wheel, a framework to apply to all your transformation efforts.

As we move into Part 2 of the book, Chapters 4 to 16 expand on each section of the framework. These can be approached in any order, so if you already feel a particular challenge which you must focus on, start there first.

Finally, in Chapter 17, you'll be ready to critically assess your own transformation and ultimately improve how you're approaching any change initiative.

There are two Appendices. Appendix 1 gives you the criteria to assess your performance on the Retail Transformation Steering Wheel. Appendix 2 explores what to do when a transformation needs rescuing.

How to use this book

Use this book to help you prepare for and drive change. But I understand that you're busy with many topics whizzing around your head, so I aim to make it easy to digest this book whilst you keep the plates spinning.

Depending on your role, you may be applying the learnings directly to the transformations you're running. Or if you're a leader, then use the ideas and activities to prompt and guide your teams who are actively working on the transformation initiative.

Each chapter is kept short, and you might want to read whole chapters in a sitting. Chapters conclude with a short summary of what's been covered. Although, if you want to go even deeper, there are additional optional resources to help go further, including podcasts, videos, quick reference guides and templates. You can access these by scanning the QR code below or at DrivingRetailTransformation.com/extras.

Keep this book to hand as a reference guide for regularly assessing the health of your transformation and to refresh your understanding as you look to successfully steer transformation initiatives.

Whilst I believe that all companies can complete the journey of change and all people can navigate the path, it must be intentional. Transformation and change do not happen by chance. They must be purposefully driven. You must choose if you're ready to do this. This book will prepare you to make this choice and successfully drive meaningful retail transformation.

Change vs. transformation and other terms

Before we set off fully, let's clear up some important points of terminology.

What's the difference between *change* and *transformation*? In short, nothing. I believe that they're interchangeable terms. There is, however, a spectrum of differing sizes of change and transformation, as discussed below.

Fundamental transformation is a shift of significant scale and often referred to as a 'big bet', marking a major change to the business model, proposition or operating model. Examples include targeting a new sector, launching a repair service, designing a radically new store format, automating a fulfilment centre or starting to operate via a new channel. These large-scale changes are likely to take more time, effort, cost and focus to deliver.

Incremental transformation is a set of smaller improvements and is often targeted specifically at a section (or subsection) of the organization or customer base. Examples include simplifying stock control processes, adjusting reporting dashboards, tweaking the online checkout flows or optimizing warehouse layouts. Incremental transformations are generally quicker and less-resource intensive than fundamental changes. That's not to say they're easy, though! However, despite the smaller scale, changes still represent a meaningful impact especially when calculating the cumulative effect of small shifts.

A wise strategy involves blending both fundamental and incremental transformation. The fundamental shifts are revolutionary changes that redefine the business to access long-term opportunities, while the incremental changes offer continual refinement and improvement, contributing to secure and predictable growth in the short and medium term. Attempting multiple fundamental transformations concurrently risks overwhelming, distracting and confusing an organization and its people. This emphasizes the need for a balanced, thoughtful approach which allows organizations to experiment with and benefit from the more radical innovation of fundamental transformation and drive steady progress and continuous improvement enabled by incremental changes. We'll dive deeper into different types of transformation in Chapter 6.

Another point of terminology to quickly align on is *project*, *programme* and *portfolio*.

A **project** is a unique, one-off change initiative to address a specific problem or seize a particular opportunity. For example, improving labour productivity for unloading trailers at a fulfilment centre. Some projects may not be transformative, for instance, preparing for Christmas or other peak trading periods which are often seen and managed as a project in retail businesses. A project is typically well-defined, with clear start and end dates and may form a building block for a larger transformation initiative.

A **programme** is a larger initiative aligned to a particular goal or part of the organization, such as improving overall supply chain productivity, and may include a co-ordinated collection of projects. Programmes are typically more ambiguous than projects, especially initially, with more open-ended timelines. Programmes are often considered as defined, structured transformation initiatives.

A **portfolio** is the company's ultimate collection of all current projects and programmes, which exist in a complex ecosystem. When important decisions must be made, such as allocating capital expenditure for the company, the entire portfolio should be considered. Effective governance and portfolio management is crucial to effectively transform businesses and avoid overwhelming the organization through excessive change. The collection of transformation initiatives forming the portfolio ultimately delivers the company's strategy.

How you apply transformation to your company or brand will vary in scale and the framework and learnings from this book are still relevant to help you deliver change. Driving successful transformation relies on good project and programme management skills, but not exclusively these capabilities. There are many other facets, as we'll discover on the way.

Which approach belonged to which company?

If you're wondering which strategies belonged to which companies, the first was from Toys'R'Us[5] (2017), the second was Amazon[6] (1997), and finally, the third strategy was from Blockbuster[7] (2008).

What are you thinking and feeling based on this?

PART 1

DRIVER OR
PASSENGER:
IT'S YOUR CHOICE

Chapter 1
Retail is evolving,
with or without you

The act of shopping continues to change. Thousands of years ago, retail was centred around marketplaces with local traders selling wares. Since then, we've been though many different forms of retail: over-the-counter shops, self-serve stores, mail order, catalogue shops, in-home shopping parties, television shopping channels, hypermarkets, shopping malls and out-of-town shopping parks to name a few.

Then, this thing called the internet came along. And with it, it brought ecommerce, soon followed by social media, smartphone apps, on-demand video, livestream shopping, virtual consultations and digital environments, which together open the doors to a potentially infinite number of digital universes and corresponding commerce opportunities. And these will continue to shift and shape the act of shopping.

These shifts are a mix of evolutions and revolutions. They gradually change retail. However, they are not and cannot be fully controlled by one single person or company. Recognize that there are many factors that are forever changing the industry. These shifts are out of your circle of control, as popularized by Stephen Covey.[8] They might be within your circle of influence. But they absolutely present you with a number of opportunities. In this chapter, we'll explore the factors that are the primary catalysts for retail transformation, starting with external elements which impact the business or customer, then moving into aspects within the organization's control.

Customers have more choice than ever

In modern retail, customers have an endless opportunity of choice. Transport and technology open a world of shopping opportunities. Literally.

There are retailers specializing in every category and specialism that exists. Equally, retailers can expand their ranges to cater for any eventuality. The potential scope for a one-stop-shop retailer is vast, when one retailer's range extends from grilled chicken[9] to truck grilles[10] (for your very own 18-wheeler; yes, really). And why stock just one electric toothbrush if you can sell over 4,000 different options?[11]

Inevitably, with an enormous range and comprehensive choice comes the risk of major customer confusion. The clarity of proposition and relevance to customers is more crucial than ever. In days gone past, this was never an issue. Customers want to be clear what they can to buy from you. Sure, they might like a little surprise 'treasure hunting' from time to time, but within reason.

Ecommerce opens near limitless choice for retailers. Where should you buy your next TV from? Who genuinely understands the category and can advise on the various technologies available? Or who is just keen on selling high volumes at low prices to maximize profit?

The reasons why an individual customer should choose any particular retailer are complex and dynamic. Maybe it's about the lowest price, expert advice, quality, experience, trust, environmental credentials, ethical values, returns policies, convenience... the list goes on.

The retailer's role is to clarify the reasons why a customer should choose to shop with them. Along the customer journey, it's essential to demonstrate a mix of values and value which undeniably appeals to that single individual customer at that precise moment. And bear in mind, that mix might be totally irrelevant, or even repelling, to another would-be-customer.

This focus on the customer is no longer optional. Fortunately, there are plenty of examples of companies who major on customer centricity and have become wildly successful, including IKEA (for continually inspiring customers with stylish, functional, affordable and convenient home furnishings), Nike (for hosting running clubs and other exercise-based community events whilst being inclusive to all ability levels), and Canada Goose (for helping customers choose the perfect winter jacket by accessing opportunities like with cold testing rooms with temperatures as low as –25°C or –13°F).

> *'Commercially successful brands over a sustained period are those that are customer-centric.'*
>
> *Martin Newman*[12]

So, appealing to the right customer segments in the right way is increasingly an important success factor. And many retailers have huge opportunities to continue to evolve here.

Your customers, colleagues and business operate across multiple channels

The concept of channels has emerged in the last 15–20 years, especially as ecommerce grew in presence and market share. The truth is that channels have always existed.

Rewind the clock way back again; a retailer or merchant may have sold their wares through markets, direct from their workshops or via travelling salespeople. They may have received customers' orders through messengers who paid for and collected orders. Fulfilment may have been instantaneous, or at an arranged collection point or even home delivery. All of these are examples of how retailers were working in multi or omnichannel ways back then, in the same way that retailers operate today.

Terms like 'omnichannel' or 'unified commerce' often bring much confusion. There is no clear definition with tangible aspects and, if there was, it would likely become outdated quickly due to rapidly developing technical capabilities. Many innovations claim to 'enable omnichannel' or offer the tantalizing goal of becoming 'seamless', whilst new trends in this area emerge continually, allowing you to be ever-present.

Yet, omnichannel doesn't mean being present and active across *all* channels at once. It means being clear on which channels you do actively choose to operate in, and you've made it simple for customers to shop across these. Additionally, recognize that your brand may passively exist on other channels as customers share feedback and viewpoints, with or without you. So as your channel mix changes, so too does your own personal definition of omnichannel.

Consumers live across multiple channels, regularly switching between devices, apps and even mindsets. And your prospective customers want you to be omnichannel because it makes their lives easier. They can spend less energy and less brainpower to shop with you. And, therefore, it's less likely that they'll fall between the cracks of your different channels and take their custom elsewhere.

However, it's not only your customers who strive for an omnichannel approach. You and your colleagues are also living and working in omnichannel ways. Switching tasks and tools with a desire to simplify and streamline. As a result, your business will naturally work in omnichannel ways too. Jumping from face-to-face interactions, to emails, to video conferences, to messages, to terminal computers, to smartphone apps and more. You're operating model exists across multiple channels and these too are evolving continually.

Don't fight omnichannel. And don't over think it either. There is no one definition of omnichannel; you can forge your own meaning that makes sense in your world and for your customers and colleagues.

Do consider how omnichannel is changing for your customers, your colleagues and your business. Do think about how you can stay flexible as the meaning evolves, experimenting to find what's best. Consider how you can offer multiple routes to achieve any particular mission, so people have the choice of what works best for them. Allow and even encourage cross-channel switching in a sensible and coherent way. Often, the best omnichannel retailers keep it simple. After all, nobody wants complicated instructions or lengthy onboarding processes about how to shop or work with you. We all desire simplicity.

Customers strive for simplicity and convenience

In the omnichannel world, people are still looking for ways to streamline life. Humans are naturally minded to find the easy way of doing things. And shopping is no different. We, as consumers, don't want to travel long distances for tasks like shopping. We don't want to overthink our purchases and certainly don't want to think about the act of purchasing and paying. We want to minimize the amount of time and effort in any way possible. We seek to avoid the undesirable frictions in any and every experiences.

As a result, convenience is a major consumer driver. The industry sees many initiatives focused on driving convenience and simplicity. Back in 1916, Piggly Wiggly[13] opened the first self-serve grocery store, allowing customers to freely browse and pick their shopping. The introduction of the barcode into Sainsbury's supermarket operation in 1973[14] sped up the checkout process and revealed business productivity and data benefits that quickly expanded to the wider industry. Amazon's 1-Click innovation in 1997[15] made it simple and quick for existing customers to place new orders. The supermarket space race of the 1990s and 2000s aimed to open new sites and get as close as possible to the customer. More recently, innovations for checkout-free 'frictionless' stores, ultra-fast deliveries and subscription services aim to make the process of shopping easy. They quench the desire for convenience but it's also important to consider social aspects too.

People are naturally social creatures

When the Covid-19 pandemic hit, online channels saw massive growth. However, what surprised many after the pandemic subsided was the resilience and resurgence of physical retail stores.

Humans' desire for social interaction was highlighted and many shared their delight at the return of simple interactions. Stores that bring people together build community. Whether it is a technology retailer hosting workshops about taking perfect smartphone pictures, a sports retailer offering yoga classes or running groups, or bookstores creating reading clubs. Coming together to indulge in interests and passions is a draw for many consumers.

Digital channels are also looking to focus on these natural aspects. Social media and evolving web technologies are designed around community and interaction. Online forums, groups and even whole digital universes are centred around conversation and connection.

Maslow's Hierarchy of Needs[16] teaches us that our psychological needs are interlinked with social interaction and recognition. It's what humans start to think about once we've satisfied our ability to keep ourselves alive and sustain a lifestyle.

Therefore, many retailers have a huge opportunity to bring in elements of social interaction and community and integrate into operations. Building relationships with consumers helps encourage loyalty and protect from the fierce competition in the industry.

Fierce competition is coming from all angles

Retail has always been competitive. In populated areas, you'd see your competitors across town, over the road or even next door. But as choice and channels explode, the competitive landscape is becoming unclear and confusing.

Traditional competitors are working across different channels and may be focused on a different channel mix and therefore a different omnichannel vision compared to you.

Large multi-national corporations are looking to expand into new territories, flexing their muscles by bringing technical might and deep pockets to invest in success. With a proven business model, they're looking to 'rinse and repeat' at scale.

Meanwhile, barriers to entry are arguably lower than ever, especially in digital channels. So small companies and brands pop up from nowhere, like guerrilla fighters, looking to snatch away your market share.

And then there are the disruptors. Those that would not have traditionally existed or been considered as competitors. Think of companies such as Netflix, Airbnb and Uber. Usually enabled by effective use of new technology, they're approaching your market and your customers in a different way.

Also think of those partner brands that are moving to sell via a direct to consumer (DTC) model. They know the market intimately and have incredible brand presence and reputation.

Finally, recognize that other non-competitive companies could expand into your category at any moment. Even if they don't, it's likely that your customers' expectations are being evolved through their experiences elsewhere. These non-competitive companies are raising the bar for you, even if you don't directly see them doing it.

Simple questions are valuable to challenge us to continually rethink and reconsider competitive positioning. What alternatives do your customers have? Who are your actual competitors? What do they do and how do they pitch themselves? What do they stand for and what are their values? What are your customers expecting, for both the shopping experience and from your brand?

Also consider what these competitors are thinking right now and how they'll react. How are they looking to evolve and put you out of business? Because that's the conversation that they're having.

The retail market is fiercely intense and viable competitors come in all shapes and sizes, approaching from every direction.

Whilst there are many external factors to react to, there are also many aspects which are more within retailers' direct control.

Sustainability is not optional

The rise in sustainability awareness and appreciation is well documented. And more consumers are demanding, not just desiring, that retailers and brands focus on minimizing their environmental footprint and impact on the world. Aspects like the circular economy, recycling, reuse, resale, refill and repair are crucial conversations for every company.

Sustainability is not just about environmental considerations though. Business ethics and working practices are increasingly under the microscope as environmental, social and governance (ESG) factors take a more prominent role. ESG ratings and reports are increasingly being used by investors as they allocate capital, so this becomes a more high-profile topic for leaders and boards.[17]

Visibility and intrinsic evaluation of these topics is increasing among consumers, investors and governing bodies. For some people, these issues will be less important than other values. However, the trajectory shows that for many, these will quickly become table stakes. Sustainable operations and practices will be the basics of being in business.

I believe this is absolutely right and that sustainability, in the bigger sense of the word, is not a path you *could* follow. It's a path you *must* follow for long-term success.

Unlimited data is not what you need

The data revolution opens many opportunities for retailers. The sheer volume of data collected allows for high levels of business optimization and detailed forecasting. Although arguably, the industry has too much data to use fully.

There are many different types of data: product data and attributes, customer and order data, operational and financial performance, people information, to name only a few. With these types, there are numerous formats and sources too.

It's easy to imagine data as a set of numbers, sitting in a dashboard, spreadsheet, database, data warehouse or a data lake. This is only the quantitative data. Sales data, stock holding, website traffic and much more. It's tangible and undeniable.

Retail is awash with qualitative data, too. Customer research, comments and feedback are the most notable here, and this is captured in an organized way via surveys, reviews or emails, and in disorganized ways via conversations with colleagues, calls to customer service centres or via social media. This qualitative data is richly valuable but harder to gather and interpret at scale.

The vast volumes of both quantitative and qualitative data must be carefully managed. Data requires cleaning and organizing before making it available to the right people at the right time and in the right format.

As the volume and value of data increases, someone must be responsible and own the data, ensuring effective data governance to guarantee trustworthiness. Incorrect data could easily lead you down the wrong path and encourage poor decisions.

But the data is not actually what you need (unless you're just looking to unleash the inner geek!). You're more interested in what the data is telling you: the insight. Even this is not what you really desire. Above all else, you're looking for what you and your organization should do differently next time and how that will affect the future. Transforming how you use data and how you take action is a valuable avenue for retailers.

The ultimate purpose of data is to
actively change the future for the better.

Strained supply chains looking for best of both worlds

The pandemic and other global events have exposed retail's global supply chains for the world to see. They highlighted the complex and disconnected ways of working which led to availability challenges on many fronts. This led some retailers to over-index on stock, only to be met with a cost-of-living challenge and reduced demand.

Consumer focused supply chains must find the appropriate stock flow models, balancing just-in-time and just-in-case. The benefits of a lean and light-touch stock operation are clear, but fragile in nature. Yet, the comfort of a large stock holding is a financial burden which many can't justify.

The challenge is to develop supply chains which bring both resilience and agility. Local sourcing, a distributed supply base, better transparency and visibility, and enhanced collaboration are some of the routes that allow consumer focused supply chains to better serve customers.

Business diversification as standard

Business diversification has always been a strategy to drive growth when the original market becomes saturated. Additionally, classic wholesale-based retail (i.e., buying items from other companies in bulk to sell to consumers) is an inherently low margin game. So, looking at other business models seems an appealing way to grow profits in a low-risk way.

Large retailers have expanded into new categories naturally, over many years. However, enabled by technology, marketplace and dropship models are quickly becoming an attractive way to expand categories and range without the investment or risk of stockholding.

Whilst wholesale retail is low margin, there remains an opportunity to develop your own products or even develop your own brands which allow more headroom for growth and profitability. Additionally, offering related and relevant services can bring in higher margins.

Brands and other companies value the opportunity for building awareness with retailers' customer base. As a result, more retailers are offering media networks and services, including advertising and promotional activities, which offer additional revenue at a high margin.

Meanwhile, we're also seeing retailers like Amazon, Walmart, JD.com, THG and many others establish inherent business-to-business (B2B) services. From content creation to warehouse operations, to full-on retail-as-a-service offerings. Scaling the existing operating model capabilities and offering these as a B2B service is another low-risk way of expanding the business.

And finally, retailers expand beyond the traditional realms of retail. Banking, payments, cloud computing, healthcare and even movie and TV production are some of the radical ways that retailers are diversifying into other industries.

By 2030, Bain & Company forecast that 35% of retailers' revenues and 50% of profits will originate from non-classical markets,[18] including elements such as technology solutions, fulfilment services, financial services, entertainment, advertising and media networks, and B2B services.

Business diversification is a tried and tested way to open new markets and new growth opportunities. However, they also pull the company in different directions, split or shift the focus, and can lead to misalignment of strategies or priorities.

'One team' remains a dream

I forget how many times I've heard the term 'one team' from different companies. It's a phrase that has even made it into our vocabulary when talking about corporate culture. But it remains frustratingly out of touch for many companies.

'One team' is a goal to create alignment across the organization. It's a recognition that the company is being pulled in different directions. It is a subconscious admission of functional silos.

Functional silos represent a number of bad business behaviours. Internal conflict and infighting. Communication breakdowns and misunderstandings. Unique language and acronyms. Duplication of work and capability. Unproductive ways of working and process waste. Competing metrics. Confusion. Winners. Losers.

I'm sure that none of those will surprise you. Yet they continue to exist.

There are many reasons that 'one team' visions have not been realized. Often, it's because the business model and operating model are not clear.

Different teams don't understand the various roles and responsibilities across the organization. Business diversification adds even more fog to the situation.

But above all, the primary challenge for 'one team' goals is to define the reason for being.

The reason for being

A clear purpose can drive the entire organization forward. It gives the business direction and meaning.

As the workforce evolves, employees are looking for roles that clearly support a meaningful goal. And the employee's engagement will exponentially grow if that purpose aligns with their own personal values. Plus, it will help define relevance for your customers too.

However, the concept of defining a purpose can be confusing and result in a hollow set of words that amounts to nothing but hot air. And people see through hot air with ease. Purpose and values must be more than pretty words, artistically displayed on walls at head office. Instead, consider the question that a wise person once taught me.

> *'What do you want to be famous for?'*
>
> *Anja Madsen, former CEO of the Danish retailer, Fotex Group*

Defining what makes you famous is an excellent way to discover your purpose or 'North Star'. Perhaps this will be an excellent reputation for customer service (Zappos, shoes), encouraging customers to actively touch and feel fresh products in store (Lush, fresh cosmetics), designing the most environmentally-friendly products and supporting relevant causes (Patagonia, outdoor clothing) or offering trusted advice backed up with extended guarantees (Richer Sounds, consumer electronics). Additionally, a clear purpose will make sure that your teams are aligned. If your executive team cannot agree on this at a corporate level, there will never be agreement on transformation plans or strategy at executive level or throughout the company. However, purpose is also a valid conversation to be had at different levels of the organization, each zooming into what the relevant team will be famous for, both internally and externally.

It won't be an easy conversation but moving towards agreement is an important process for a team to go through. It's a way of exploring thoughts and feelings from different perspectives and experiences. This may take a few attempts, but that alignment will cascade through the organization and will be more prepared to stand the test of time.

Once you finally do have agreement, use this statement of intent as an aspirational goal that all decisions can be measured against.

Discovering this purpose or reason for being is empowering and should give meaning to your retail organization as if it were a living organism.

Retail organizations as living organisms

In an ever-evolving world, businesses must act like living organisms. Sensing and reacting to the outside world and striving to achieve its meaning of life.

Psychologist, Abraham Maslow has defined a pyramid of needs for humans to work through in pursuit of satisfaction and fulfilment. So, what would be the hierarchy of needs for a living retail organization?

Building off Maslow's theory, in Figure 1.1 we see similarities for how a retail business should focus attention, especially when it comes to considering what transformation will enable greater achievement for any specific company. As time passes and business performance evolves, a retailer can move up or down the levels of the hierarchy, resulting in different focus areas and requirements.

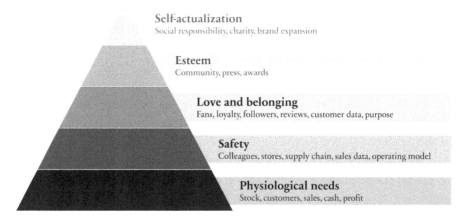

Figure 1.1: Retail's Hierarchy of Needs

Starting at the base of the pyramid then moving upwards, we have:

- ▷ **Physiological needs:** These are the basics of remaining alive in business. An ongoing flow of stock and customers are key to generate revenue. Cash and profit round out the most basic needs as the lifeblood of the organization.

- ▷ **Safety:** Like a person seeking a roof over their head, retail strives for a safe and secure life. Across stores and the supply chain, the team of people within a retailer must feel safe and secure before they are overwhelmed with fear and exhaustion or decide to pursue other avenues. A business also needs a robust operating model along with a basic flow of data that allows it to pivot against future dangers.

- ▷ **Love and belonging:** As we move up the pyramid, we seek customer loyalty and winning fans. Customer relationships, feedback and data become important, as do public proof of this customer love in the form of followers and reviews. And external collaborations and partners help to expand the love for the brand.

- ▷ **Esteem:** Nearing the top, presence in local communities as well as positive recognition in the press. Awards for the company or the specific products become more of a focus now.

- ▷ **Self-actualization:** At the crest, we aspire for corporate fulfilment through social responsibility initiatives, such as charity partnerships. Additionally, expanding the brand to take on new meaning or serve a higher purpose to the world.

By considering a retailer as a living being, we can see how companies pursue different targets depending on where they are in the pyramid. And if a retail organization were alive, it must focus transforming and evolving as the world around it continues to change.

The only constant is change

As the wider world evolves, so too must retail and therefore retailers. Whilst it's comfortable to stay in the status quo, realistically and deep down, we know that's not a valid approach.

It was the Greek philosopher, Heraclitus, who observed around 2,500 years ago that 'change is the only constant in life'.

And change doesn't seem to be stopping anytime soon. Quite the opposite in fact, the pace of change is accelerating. Figure 1.2 demonstrates this well as we see the accelerating pace of adoption for new technologies and innovations, and how consumers are taking charge.

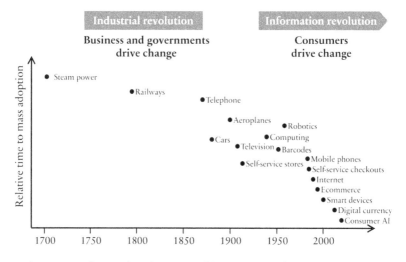

Figure 1.2: The accelerating pace of innovation adoption, increasingly driven by consumers

However, in day-to-day life, we don't often see change as single examples, as Figure 1.2 suggests. Instead, we observe a stream of small changes. Evolutions. Even major revolutionary shifts tend to occur slowly and almost by stealth.

These relatively small shifts seem manageable. And they are. If they are handled with intent. You can't simply cross your fingers and hope that your organization will evolve alongside the wider world. You can't leave this to chance. You must actively drive your transformation.

What we've covered

- ▷ Many factors are changing the game in retail, and many of these are out of your control or influence.

- ▷ The evolutions and revolutions in the wider industry will impact you and force you to make changes.

- ▷ We can bank on continual transformation and an accelerating pace of change.

Chapter 2
The danger of leaving change to chance

One of the elements I love about the retail industry is that we all are customers. We all do shopping of one sort or another. And we all have an opinion. We know when we have a wonderful experience. We definitely know when we don't.

Therefore, as consumers ourselves, we naturally understand that shopping is changing. And we see that the retail industry is evolving.

But change doesn't happen by chance. At least, not a change that we want. It's takes intentional action to transform a business, a team, ourselves or anything. When faced with an ever-evolving market, we must intentionally change; we can't leave change to chance. Yet, most of us struggle to adopt to change or transformation and actively resist it.

> *'The world as we have created it is a process of our thinking. It cannot be changed without changing our thinking.'*
>
> *Albert Einstein*

Humans have evolved to resist change

Many people struggle with adapting to change. It brings strong emotions: fear, excitement and confusion to name but a few. People feel discomfort at the idea of a change, even if they dislike the current situation. Varying emotions are felt by all stakeholders of the change, both the originators and teams involved in the change as well as the recipients of the change who will be impacted in some way.

A change represents the unknown. We understand how things are today. We also recall and reminisce how things used to be. But if the future is unclear or uncertain, it is usual to feel worried or even fearful. This is a natural feeling and a positive side of our evolution. This fear of the unknown, and the resulting behaviours, originated with our ancient ancestors to keep them safe, rather than potentially being eaten by bears or wolves when venturing into dark caves. It meant our ancestors took caution when exploring new territory and could assess any risk of danger before taking preventative action to stay alive.

But in the modern world, life is often much safer and it's unlikely that we need to explore dark caves. Nevertheless, the same feelings, emotions and psychology happen when we sense the unknown in all parts of life. And in a business setting, this fear of the unknown means we don't want to expose ourselves to danger. This can keep us from making mistakes, but also prevents us from exploring and ultimately finding a better way. To transform, we must find a way to overcome the fear of the unknown.

Another fear to overcome is the fear of failure. Failure means we lose control, we become uncertain, and the future becomes unclear. Elements we value and crave, such as job security and positive relationships, are put at stake. In turn, this could turn our world and life upside down. Instead, it seems much safer and simpler to not open ourselves up to the chance to fail. Maybe someone else could take the lead and expose themselves to any dangers, then we'll know it's safe to follow. However, we all experience the same feelings of not wanting to make a mistake. Not wanting to expose ourselves. Not wanting to put our life and safety at risk. Not wanting to fail. The fear of failure is connected to the fear of the unknown. And, again, it stems from our primitive brain trying to avoid danger and death. It also presents itself in modern life as a way of preserving the status quo.

Another hangover from our prehistoric selves is our love of energy. When precious, essential resources such as food have been historically hard to come by, we don't like to expend energy needlessly. It makes us inherently lazy as a species, only choosing to burn calories when absolutely essential. However, when we're considering transforming in a business or retail setting, this reluctance to invest energy also provides resistance to change.

People become reluctant to put in the extra effort that is so often needed to make a transformation successful. This effort is often required from the originators of the change as well as the recipients of the change. Plus, to get other people to buy in to the change at any time, we must ease their fears of the unknown and of failure. Doing this and finding the appropriate solutions that drive the business forward needs a blend of hard work, smart work and careful work. However, all three of these require us to burn more calories and to simultaneously use our heads and hearts; something we are pre-programmed to avoid.

Organizational dynamics add resistance to change

As the 'low hanging fruit' changes are increasingly fully picked, it means initiatives become more complex. More business divisions are affected. Solutions become more technical in nature. And the likelihood is that no single person is an expert in the entire scope of the change. Meanwhile, business challenges can be deeply embedded, and the visible symptom is further removed from the ultimate root cause. And when you consider the temperamental and fragile nature of some businesses, any change effort has many opportunities to fail and little room for error.

Fortunately, it is definitely possible to motivate ourselves to spend the required energy when we're working on and improving something we are passionate about, for example, our colleagues, our customers, our organization and our business.

And when we're considering how to propel what we're passionate about, we all have a view on what's best. This view or opinion is formed from a host of different inputs. For example, what information people are privy to, their experience and personal demeanour all play in to forming opinions. So, invariably, when we look around the board room or the wider team or the whole company, these opinions differ. Quite wildly sometimes. Yet all are aligned, in as much as everyone *feels* they know what is best.

However, as I'm sure you have experienced, these differences in opinions can lead to conflict. They spark new disagreements or reignite old debates. But whilst some people like or even enjoy conflict, others can't stand it and will back away from these scenarios. Although, if individuals have backed away, it doesn't mean their opinion has changed, so the conflict still exists in an underlying form. If managed effectively, conflict can be healthy. It encourages us to consider different perspectives, to learn from new insights and to challenge us to find the genuinely best solution. But not all conflicts go down this path and there is a risk that the conflict escalates into a bigger issue or evolves into a prolonged war between individuals or functions. Unfortunately, either of these can detract from the change effort. The primary aim is forgotten. The discussion devolves into an argument with the aim of winning. The attention is on the conflict, not the actual goal.

Conflict can also arise if there is a feeling that part of the business, a team, or even an individual will lose. Maybe the change benefits one functional area more than another. Perhaps, for example, it's hugely positive for consumers but seems to show a negative impact from a financial perspective, for example. Or delivers strong operational performance but means that colleagues are not treated in an ideal way. Whichever way this perceived win/loss falls, it means there is a fear of failure, a difference of opinion and more conflict arises. This moves the initiative away from the original target or goal.

That is, if there is an original goal. Another challenge that forms resistance to change is a lack of purpose behind the change. Perhaps the change is to adopt a sexy, new technology. Maybe it's following a move by a competitor. Or it could even be a pet project or brainchild from a senior leader. With these examples, the goal has often not been identified or clarified. The real problem may have not been understood clearly or may be hidden entirely. However, an unclear or illogical goal causes confusion, a lack of direction, low motivation and results in varying opinions about what's best. Additionally, without a clear goal for the transformation, it's likely there is strategy misalignment.

When strategy misalignment occurs, the business comes across as disjointed and muddled. Questions will be raised over leadership from colleagues, from customers and from shareholders. 'I thought we were meant to be focused on this?' 'Why are they not thinking about this key challenge?' 'Do they even know what they are doing?' These types of questions are quick to be raised but incredibly tough to dissipate. They suggest a breakdown in trust and loyalty and can cause many organizational issues and business challenges. And whilst it seems so obvious that transformation efforts should be aligned to the strategy, it's not guaranteed. However, to realize the strategy, it's likely that change is needed; however, it must be the right change. But that 'right change' can only truly be identified through listening to customers, colleagues, stakeholders, shareholders and the business. And this requires huge efforts (and therefore expending energy on hard, smart and careful work) as well as a zoomed-out view of the full situation.

'In business, what's dangerous is not to evolve.'

Jeff Bezos,[19] Founder of Amazon

'We've always done it this way' or 'we've tried this before and it didn't work'. These are perhaps the classic phrases to highlight the resistance to change at a personal and organizational level which are said or thought when the current situation is seen as acceptable. This can happen if the challenge is not understood or recognized across the wider business or by customers and other stakeholders. It could be a sign that the challenge isn't actually a problem but it's more usual that the wider, zoomed-out view is not appreciated by or visible for everyone. Either way, this feeling of nostalgia for the current set up is also a warning sign that there is fear of the unknown. A feeling that the current position is still somehow tenable. A feeling that maintaining the status quo is the best outcome.

The status quo is the default direction

Humans are wired to maintain the status quo, so any time we're uncertain, that's the default decision. The status quo seems safe. We understand it. Perhaps we're happy with the current performance and we don't want to 'rock the boat' and add an element of the unknown. If the business is in a growth phase, sustained future positive results from maintaining the status quo may seem tempting, especially to shareholders who are looking for consistent, stable delivery year after year.

However, the status quo suggests perceived stability, but offers declining fortunes. Without change, the current positive trends will fade as competitors catch up and consumers raise their expectations. Meanwhile negative trends will gather pace and drag performance down faster. The attractiveness of the status quo decays, rapidly.

Ultimately, staying with the status quo will impact the business more over time. Competitors who continue to evolve will catch up and ultimately take the lead. Meanwhile, as customer demands are fulfilled by these competitors, the expectation bar will be raised. Suddenly your proposition won't measure up and customers will vote with their feet, their fingers and, most importantly, with their money. When that happens, the status quo will not be such an attractive position for stability and certainty.

Deep down we know this. But when we're making decisions, the status quo is always the default option. If there are multiple options on the table and a decision cannot be made, the status quo is the selection option. If a decision is required and it's not made, the status quo is the selected option. If there is disagreement or conflict which rages on, the status quo is the selected option. The status quo is an inevitability. Always. Unless we take the chance to change.

The term 'burning platform' is often used to visualize the need to move on from the status quo, suggesting a painful moment where we must progress, take a leap of faith or come to an untimely end. However, we rarely encounter genuine situations where there is *no way back*. The Covid pandemic was one of these rare occasions, and even then, there were companies that clung onto the status quo. Therefore, we must be careful that expectations set by a 'burning platform' do not lull us into a false sense of security where we assume change will happen and the status quo will not be the default direction.

Even if the status quo feels uncomfortable due to poor results, diminishing market share, poor customer experience or any downward trajectory, it retains control. Unless there is an intentional decision to transform away from the status quo, we stay put. If we can't decide exactly how to change, we stay put. And if we cannot develop or deliver the change and transformation, we stay put.

To be better than the status quo, we must be intentional to transform and overcome the challenges of developing and delivering transformation.

The challenges of change

Our journey away from the status quo is, unfortunately, not an easy one. There are risks, complications, and difficult decisions.

Research into failed projects and transformations suggests many different root causes for the failure. Usually, it's a blend of these reasons which makes it harder to spot and diagnose before it's too late.

Broadly, there are four areas which cause issues.

1. The challenge

You probably already know there are multiple challenges in the business. You sit in meetings, read reports, have conversations and through all these mediums, you'll discover a variety of problems or potential opportunities.

As a leader, it's easy to feel responsible for taking on all of these challenges.

In fact, William Oncken, Jr. and Donald L. Wass wrote about this originally in a 1974 article for the *Harvard Business Review*.[20] They describe how challenges are like monkeys which jump onto your back for you to deal with, delivered to you by the original owner (who often happens to be a member of your team). As you progress through your day, more and more monkeys jump onto you and suddenly you're dealing with other people's problems all day long.

Now consider the various businesses problems and challenges, or should I say 'monkeys', jumping on you. They gather faster than you can disperse them. You quickly collect a whole troop of monkeys. But with too many on your back, where do you start? How many monkeys are even on your back? Which is the dominant, alpha monkey? Now add in an element of communication where you describe the monkeys on your back whilst colleagues and team members describe the monkeys on theirs. Now how many monkeys are there? Are any monkeys missing?

With so many challenges, it's easy to get confused about which are most important and what the business impact is. And equally, smaller issues are confused for larger ones. Meanwhile, some people can feel like it's a badge of honour to take direct responsibility for more and more business problems, demonstrating their personal worth within the company. It's also tempting to take on more monkeys and expand the scope in exchange for the opportunity to deliver more business value, but this is at the risk of stretching too far and creating exceptionally high expectations.

But the monkeys are only the visible symptoms, not the origin. Without discovering the source, more issues will continue to arise and solving the visible symptoms is akin to putting a band aid on a more severe issue. So, like a doctor examining the patient, it's crucial to investigate and identify the root causes and discover the underlying issues. It's these issues that the transformation should focus on, not the visible challenges on the surface.

We cannot find a solution if we
do not know the challenge.

Understanding the challenges, root causes and aligning on priorities is often a task I speak with consulting clients about. There are many challenges and many opportunities so it's easy to become confused and even overwhelmed. And this can happen at all levels of an organization too.

The key to overcoming this is to clarify the challenges you face along with their root causes and understand the business priorities, strategy and guiding principles. Once you understand this, you can assess how you'll find the solution.

2. The solution

With a clear understanding of the challenge, if you discover that there is no viable way to solve it, then you'll never move away from the status quo. When it comes to defining and developing the solution, there are many factors which must be tackled.

First, does the solution solve the precise problem? Whilst it sounds obvious, it's an easy mistake to make, especially when it comes to technology solutions. With technology solutions, especially off the shelf options, it might be that it partially solves the specific problem but leaves critical aspects unsolved. This may be unavoidable based on the specific situation, but it should at least be an intentional direction where you know there is a mismatch between the problem and the solution.

This mismatch between the problem and the solution can also be created due to insufficient requirements or specifications. This results in an undesirable situation where the change does not deliver the benefits expected. A lack of requirements, or clarity of those requirements, can also mean that the users of the solution would have expected it to work in a particular way. Plus, it's also possible to focus so much on the solution that drift or scope creep occurs so that the deliverables expand uncontrollably to a point where they are no longer focused purely on the problem.

As more teams from across the business get involved, it's essential to ensure there is a good level of understanding about the solution. Many and differing assumptions will be made about what's achievable or what's in scope. But in turn, this results in different expectations being set across the organization.

Another challenge is that the solution doesn't fit within the wider operating model. The operation becomes disjointed, making it complicated or clumsy to understand or use. For example, in a retail store, this might mean having to swap between different tools, systems or applications or missing critical cut-off points such as ordering deadlines. Having to regularly switch tasks or tools breaks up the rhythm and adds an annoyance. This makes the solution harder to use and essentially increases chances that adoption will never meet expectations.

Without clarity on the solution, it's also possible that the transformation impacts the wider business. Maybe this impact is recognized and an early impact assessment is possible. However, an effect could be unknown but still present. An example might be additional steps which are introduced later in the buying process, consuming extra resources which need funding to be built into the business case. Another example is that there could be a change to warehouse inbound check procedures which delay pick processes and therefore deteriorates product availability. Or supply chain changes which impact the transfer of stock ownership between entities, impacting finance's accounting practices and business cashflow. Whatever the impact, customers or frontline colleagues will not be able to explain exactly what has happened, but they will experience the effects. These impacts must be factored into the business case and communicated clearly to avoid any surprises.

It's also critical that reasonable assumptions are used to make sensible business decisions. Over-promising and under-delivering is a sure-fire way to disappoint stakeholders and miss business expectations. This burns trust and it will be harder to win people over in the future and show that you have a realistic solution that doesn't negatively impact customers, colleagues or the business.

3. Mindset and leadership

People are integral to change but arguably present the toughest challenge. And 'people' include yourself! Your mindset, in particular, and those of others leading transformation initiatives, is essential to encourage positive transformation, but it can cause an invisible, psychological based issue at the heart of your approach. There are several aspects of your mindset and emotional state which can cause challenges.

- ▷ **Fear:** We've already discussed the fear of the unknown and the fear of failure and these concerns may arise at any moment for you. In the heat of the moment, you may instinctively respond with the fight, flight, freeze or fawn[21] response. And outside of the immediate instinctive response, you may recognize the symptoms that fear presents: worry, anxiety, distraction, tense muscles, difficulty sleeping and others too. These negative feelings may also draw you into feeling the imposter syndrome.

▷ **Imposter syndrome:** The feeling that you're not good enough to lead or architect such an important initiative can be common. Perhaps you feel like you don't know what you're doing. Maybe you're concerned that you'll be 'found out' as the imposter. Or that you shouldn't be leading such a crucial strategic play. Imposter syndrome can trigger many follow-on issues and can significantly impact your confidence.

▷ **Confidence:** A lack of self-esteem or self-belief shows. It may mean that you shy away from important topics and conversations. Or perhaps you don't present your case clearly in debates. It could also prevent you from sharing your relevant opinions and perspectives when there is conflict. This lack of confidence can wear you down and may provide additional stress to test your resilience.

▷ **Resilience:** Personal resilience is a measure of how robust you are to challenges. If defines how you respond when you face a barrier. And in the world of change and transformation, it's certain that you'll encounter barriers and obstacles; you just won't know what or when they'll appear. So, resilience will be continually tested, and you should strengthen this characteristic to deal with the various challenges, conundrums and complications ahead, or risk being overwhelmed.

▷ **Being overwhelmed:** This feeling will perhaps be present or familiar already, with many topics and conversations on your mind. Some need your active involvement, consuming headspace. Some cause you worry and stress, depleting energy and resilience. In the complex world of retail, the ability to deal with vast numbers of activities is important and so is the ability to work out which ones matter most. Which monkeys should you focus on first? The ability to resolve issues is often enabled by an optimistic, positive viewpoint.

▷ **Positivity:** Given that change is hard at the best of times, a suitably positive mindset will help to see a way though. Without this, it's easy to see the doom and gloom of a situation and allow all these mindset challenges in. However, it's critical to note that there is a valid place for negativity too. It allows us to critique our own thoughts and importantly see the cracks in the status quo. Plus, it will keep us safe when the odds are unlikely. The challenge for the transformation leader is to be able to switch between a positive and negative outlook. Recognize that the glass can be half full and half empty at the same time.

Beyond your own mindset, and the mindset of others playing leading roles in transformation, there are other people-based issues. Change management is a topic that is easily misunderstood, in my experience. All the people involved in or impacted by your change will face a number of different emotions, all at different times. John Fisher's Personal Transition or Change Curve[22] is a fantastic guide to the rollercoaster of feelings and thoughts that people go through when they are the recipient of change. However, the reality is even more challenging, and emotions can be more volatile when presented with the true experience of change implementation, as shown in Figure 2.1.

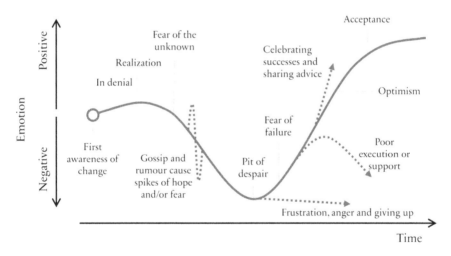

Figure 2.1: The realities of execution add turbulence to Fisher's Change Curve

The other significant people-based challenge that can block or restrict transformation is organizational silos. All organizations have them and it's a common wish to overcome them. Silos are natural in an organization that is set up in different functional divisions. The metaphorical silo walls are constructed to allow individuals and teams to specialize alongside other people with similar skills. Silos enable personal development, people movement and career development in an organization. But the same walls restrict communication and working relationships. They deter collaboration. They lead to different priorities and therefore different preferences on resource allocation. Ultimately, they give rise to longer term conflicts within a company. And when more transformation initiatives are increasingly complex, requiring more involvement from the wider business, organizational silos are an escalating challenge.

Example: Breaking down silo walls

Working with a historic retail organization, I was developing a new operating model which inevitably required cross-functional collaboration. In one instance, there was reluctance to collaborate between two different teams. People told war stories about 'them', why they were so difficult to work with and how it would all be a waste of time. Meanwhile, the other team felt exactly the same way. Both sides suffered a mental block preventing them from working with each other.

Through an initially tense workshop and additional small discussions, we started to name many of the challenges and discovered that they were mostly caused by historical issues which were now irrelevant. We agreed simple, immediate fixes to the current ways of working as well as arranging team-building activities to develop relationships. At that stage, we could then start to discuss the new operating model productively.

Where are mental blocks causing issues between people or teams in your organization?

---

4. Progress and execution

The challenges presented by a lack of execution are perhaps the most frustrating for transformation leaders. They give a thought of 'what could have been'.

> *'In real life, strategy is actually very straightforward. You pick a general direction and implement it like a hell.'*
>
> Jack Welch, Former Chairman and CEO of General Electric[23]

Initiatives can get bogged down and a lack of progress makes it more likely that the transformation will lose momentum and dissipate to nothing. There are many reasons for a lack of progress and execution, including:

- **Lack of direction:** This could be that the goal isn't clear or hasn't been communicated to the people that must understand it. The direction helps formulate what happens next.

- **Unsure of next steps:** When someone isn't sure what to do, the easy answer is to do nothing. It conserves energy and there is the assumption that another person is taking the initiative.

- **Unclear ownership or responsibility:** If it's not clear who is meant to own a task or activity, the chances are that it will 'fall through the cracks' and be forgotten about.

- **Invisible or unreasonable expectations:** Excessively high expectations, or expectations that have not been communicated or understood, is a path to future disappointment and frustration for everyone.

- **Communication breakdown:** A lack of execution can come around due to the right people not talking to each other. Dependencies become disjointed and miscommunication is too simple.

- **Lack of capability:** Progress can be denied simply because there is a lack of capability. Or a lack of skills can mean that acceptable work of a good quality takes longer to complete.

- **Waiting on others:** Equally, work gets held up waiting. Nothing happens, wasting time until, for example, the next governance meeting is held or a key resource is made available.

- **Resource availability:** With many plates spinning at once, it's likely that some individuals or teams will be in high demand. People, finance and other resources often depend on a prioritization alongside other initiatives.

- **Switching priorities:** Execution can lose energy and momentum if the direction is refocused to other priorities. The history of priority changes is quickly forgotten which leads to a perceived lack of progress toward execution.

- **Scope creep:** Initiatives get delayed and can seriously lose their momentum if the scope is too broad or is open to ongoing adjustment, usually scope creep. Taking on too much ironically leads to delivering less positive change.

▷ **Conflict:** Earlier in the chapter, we discussed how ongoing conflict can continue. It distracts from the main aim and if it means decisions are not made, the status quo lives on.

▷ **Firefighting:** Finally, it may be that many issues and problems have risen their ugly heads, and at a faster pace than they can be resolved. If this happens, some change initiatives fall into a doom loop where even more problems raise their heads. Time is spent solving problem after problem. Monkeys overwhelm you. Maybe you know this as 'whack-a-mole' or 'death by a thousand cuts'. Either way, a multitude of problems can stop a transformation dead in its tracks.

Example: A lack of confidence, clarity and progress

A financially strained company needed to cut costs to drive profit. There was a particular transformation to streamline the business that had been spoken about for a long time but had yet to make any progress. This was causing increasing frustration in executive meetings as it felt like a missed opportunity that could deliver value.

Jim had been assigned to lead the initiative but in turn hadn't allocated any resource to the project because he personally felt it was the wrong decision and was ultimately confused about how it could work. I sensed Jim wasn't confident to admit this confusion. I worked with Jim to break down the challenge into smaller elements, gather the supporting data and define an approach for building the solution.

With this clarity, Jim could start to see how the initiative reduced costs whilst protecting essential elements of the operation. After this, he was energized and realized how he could deliver a meaningful operational cost saving, and that's what he did.

How many initiatives in your business are held up through procrastination or confusion?

With many potential challenges ready to disrupt the transformation, there is a genuine chance that the change succumbs to failure.

When transformation fails

When a transformation initiative does fail, the repercussions are far reaching. It's not just about wasted resources of time, money and effort, but there are other hidden consequences too. Severe impacts are felt by individuals involved in the change alongside the company culture. However, there are different categories of failed transformation:

- **Cancelled project:** Stopped due to insufficient benefits or value, lack of progress, company reprioritization, significant market realignment or others. Investments must be written off and there may be other implications, which are discussed in Appendix 2.

- **Paused project:** Similar to the cancelled project, but with the intention to resuscitate the initiative in the future.

- **Lost opportunity:** Slow progress means that the window of opportunity closes, for example, to capture market share.

- **Underwhelming results:** The transformation failed to deliver the expected results or impact, although the initiative isn't necessarily abandoned or cancelled.

- **Excessive resource burn:** Forecast resources, including time, money and people, are spent or require additional investment to continue.

- **The never-ending project:** The final (often hidden) type is when an initiative continues indefinitely, consuming resources without ever showing clear, meaningful progress or results.

Long-term transformation failures waste company resources as the return on investment is never realized. Time, money, effort, people and other resources are all painfully lost for the business. However, there are other impacts to beware of too, including adverse effects on people and culture. When transformation fails, the status quo lives on. Whether you like it or not.

Embracing failure as a learning opportunity

It's drilled into us that failure is a bad outcome. Of course, nobody sets out with this objective. However, a failed change is not necessarily all negative. I'm sure you've heard of phrases like 'fail fast' and 'fail forward'. This idea is centred around the fact that the earlier the transformation fails, the lower the impact to the business. Recognizing and accepting this failure allows the company and individuals to learn lessons, move on and refocus on other high priority initiatives.

Intentional experimentation is a vital approach to learning about new customers, categories, channels and markets or when ambiguity exists. A series of genuine experiments should expect a significant failure rate and the learnings gathered from these occasions should be celebrated.

Whether an intentional experiment or not, when you discover that the solution is not appropriate, it's important to confirm this quickly and stop. Effective stakeholder discussions and using proof of concepts or tests help accelerate the time taken to discover if a specific solution is or is not viable. Be sure to take learnings from this concept as well as the transformation journey before returning to the 'drawing board'.

> Failed change should not be considered a failure
> if it's not the right solution for the company.

Alternatively, it's disappointing if a viable transformation fails due to a poor approach or execution. Learn how the transformation lost its way and what could have been done differently next time.

All of these learnings are essential to capture and critical to recall and apply at relevant occasions in the future. It is especially important to capture learnings quickly before the team disbands or individuals move on. When this happens, attention rapidly refocuses on new topics and the detailed memories and lessons are quickly overwritten, leaving only emotion-based impact.

The emotional impact of failed change

The emotional impacts of a failed initiative are often hidden from view and not considered. But they're there and in the face of a failure, you should consider the specific and individual actions to overcome these issues.

- **Frustration:** It can be incredibly frustrating for those involved in, sponsoring or benefitting from the change, especially if the causes are out of their control. During transformation, it's not only the company investing; individuals also invest blood, sweat and tears. So when failure arises, it creates disappointment, anger and strong negative emotions.

- **Distraction:** Aside from the lost resources invested in the initiative, failure can divert attention from key business operations or other transformation efforts. This is accentuated by unclear or conflicting communications, gossip and rumours. Additionally, consider the emotional turbulence from the change curve, as discussed earlier.

- **Confidence:** It's easy for individuals to let the weight of a failed transformation rest on their own shoulders. I've certainly felt this at times and seen it in others. It makes you question your capability. It destroys confidence and tests personal resilience, affecting optimism, motivation and wellbeing. There is a mental-health impact of failed transformation which can be further exacerbated when people who are against the change proclaim 'I told you so.'

- **Degraded trust in strategy:** Visible failure prompts scepticism and concern about the company's strategy. Rebuilding trust takes time and is hard. Meanwhile, there may be declining customer loyalty, increased colleague turnover, concerns over job security and resistance to future transformation efforts.

Even during experimentation, these emotional impacts can still be present. Clear communication and expectation setting help minimize them but nevertheless, keep an eye out for these.

The risk of failure is ever-present in a transformation. There may also be micro failures within the journey that conjure the same feelings but on a lesser level.

Always look to take specific lessons and learnings from failures. Additionally, never take success for granted, even if all the signals are positive. Continue to take intentional action to drive forward until the initiative is formally closed and set to business as usual.

Failed change is certainly not a fun place to be in, even if it is the right decision. But does this mean successful transformation is all good?

The danger of transforming

Is all change good? Hopefully so! It should deliver genuine value relative to the resource investment required. Otherwise, why are you doing it?

Transformation, whether if fails or succeeds, can distract attention from the main business at all levels. The team involved in the transformation are focused on this. Key resources may be tied up supporting the project or programme. Board meetings invest time discussing the change when there are plenty of other important topics worthy of their attention. Frontline teams or impacted individuals can be distracted by the potential impact they'll have to deal with. And other people become distracted simply by observing. All of this means time and headspace is not spent on other topics which could help drive business success and growth.

A busy schedule of change and transformation can even be so distracting for the wider business that it can become overwhelming. This in turn can lead to procrastination, confusion over priorities and can mean people behave like a 'rabbit in the headlights'.

Transformation is tiring too. Energy is invested in hard work, smart work and careful work. And what happens when we spend all our energy? We risk burnout and exhaustion. And this can be felt at an individual, team or company level.

In fact, you may recall after the high velocity of change initiatives during the Covid pandemic, coupled with long hours and emotional turmoil, many people suffered the effects of burnout at all levels in organizations, from frontline colleagues through to executives. Additionally, customers were subjected to continually changing government rules as well as dealing with different policies in their place of work, shops, restaurants and when travelling, so also felt overwhelmed and burnt out.

So, transformation should not be a journey that you start lightly. To overcome the dangers, consider the basics first and make sure that the organization is working as it is meant to.

Getting the basics of retail right

Despite the ever-evolving retail environment, at the most fundamental level, retail largely still depends on the same success factors. Let's review the fundamentals briefly.

Customers are looking to purchase products and services. They seek a trustworthy company offering a competitive price. They expect to be treated fairly with helpful and friendly service. They want to be able to buy easily and ensure the experience is relative to their excitement about the purchase.

Meanwhile, retailers and consumer-facing businesses are looking to attract customers to their products and services. These offerings are sourced and developed with good unit economics. Retailers strive to operate efficiently and consistently to drive profitability. They aim to offer a positive repeatable experience in the hope that each individual customer tells their friends and returns for repeat purchases, thus ensuring ongoing business success.

Yes, there are additional elements to add in, for example, keeping colleagues happy, building an environmentally sustainable business, fundraising or delivering shareholder value. Ultimately though, retail does not need to be overly complex. Yet we do tend to overcomplicate things.

Before you embark on the transformation journey, consider and challenge yourself and your organization. Are we getting the basics right? Is the business model and operating model working as expected? Can we accurately predict and deliver our future performance?

Perhaps after reviewing this, you need to refocus on those basics and know just what to do. Or maybe you determine that a transformation or change is necessary. Super. Read on and discover how to ensure that you:

- Focus on the critical challenges.
- Define the appropriate solution.
- Develop your mindset and leadership.
- Drive your retail transformation forward.

'It is not the strongest or the most intelligent who will survive but those who can best manage change.'

Charles Darwin, biologist

What we've covered

> ▹ People resist change and we aim to expend the least amount of energy. And both driving or being subjected to transformation is energy intensive.
>
> ▹ If you don't transform, the status quo wins and performance declines over time.
>
> ▹ Failed transformation is painful for the company as well as those involved and impacted by the change, but valuable lessons must be learned to improve in the future.

Chapter 3
The journey of retail transformation

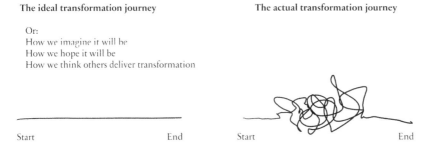

The ideal transformation journey

Or:
How we imagine it will be
How we hope it will be
How we think others deliver transformation

Start   End

The actual transformation journey

Start   End

Figure 3.1: The ideal transformation vs reality

Delivering transformation is more complex than it seems at first glance. Figure 3.1 illustrates the ideal versus the actual transformation journey. That's often the same for any journey; looking at a map or simply plugging your destination into a navigation system seems far simpler than the reality, where you must cope with congestion, blockages, delays or bigger externally driven impacts. From afar, you miss the intricacies of the landscape, signals, warning signs and other travellers.

Perhaps looking at the deceptively simple view of a transformation is positive, if we understood the true challenges ahead then that could only provide extra reasons *not* to move from the status quo. The challenges that lie ahead may be technical or cultural. They may be from internal factors within your influence or from the external environment beyond your control. Perhaps you'll face small deviations or a major roadblock.

Some of these we can predict at the start or early on, but others do not reveal themselves until the last minute.

All these challenges and deviations are hugely important in the moment and navigating them effectively will be the difference between successfully reaching your destination or not. And at the end of the day, what's important is that you reach your destination safely, securely, in time and with full confidence that it's the right destination.

Transformation is more than just the 'what'

It's easy when thinking about transformation to be carried away with the 'what' or the desired future state. It's a new seamless omnichannel solution. It's a cutting-edge automation. It's a reorganization. It's expanding into a new trending channel. Or chasing down the next big thing. Additionally, the temptation to get carried away with the solution tends to be stronger when it's a sexy, new technology-driven solution. All of these are the 'what': your destination. Think beyond the 'what'.

First, consider why you're wanting to change. What's the purpose of making the journey and expending all the energy and resources to get there. What are you trying to achieve? This is critical and I'm sure is something that you already know, just don't assume other people know too and don't forget to explain the thinking and aims. This will be a major factor to inspire people to get on board.

The 'how' is another crucial factor. If the journey seems unreasonable or unlikely, it will highlight the dangers to others and encourage them to stay put. But having a sensible way to reach the destination will build confidence and shows who must do what, and when that should happen.

The 6Ws (What, Why, hoW, Who, Where, When) are good friends on your journey of transformation and it's always worth falling back to these key questions to give clarity, especially for engagement, communications, onboarding and training.

We'll be exploring the 'why' and the 'how' in more detail later but at this stage, I can't encourage you enough to think beyond the 'what', however exciting it may be. Even if you're following a competitor or other benchmark company, these must be considered for your own specific situation because each transformation is completely unique and bespoke.

Transformation is bespoke

Your organization is unique; from the precise location you find yourself in through to your team and the new capabilities required on the transformation journey to your specific destination.

Perhaps it sounds obvious, but your unique situation requires a bespoke transformation. There is no one-size-fits-all answer, and it may even require a fully customized solution. Additionally, the approach, strategies and tactics you employ must also be tailored to fit.

This means you'll be beating down a new path. You'll face challenges where there is no pre-determined answer. It's easy to lose your bearings and get lost. Fortunately, being clear on your 'why' and 'how' will help guide you when you've been spun around, lost the track or encounter uncertainty. They will motivate and focus your attention towards completing your journey.

Organizations are not precise machines. And transformation is not a science. You cannot simply ask that a different team repeat the same 'experiment' at a different time, in a different place and expect the exact same outcome. Instead, that team and the leadership must be clear on what it takes to deliver a unique transformation.

What it takes to deliver transformation

Throughout this book, you'll learn how to lead and navigate your way through the transformation journey to deliver positive change. There are, however, four broad themes you'll need.

1. **The challenge:** We've already started to consider the 'why' or purpose of going on the journey, along with the root causes. Will it be worth the effort and expense? Or would the literal and metaphorical investment be better focused on a different goal or destination?

2. **The solution:** If the team understand and are fully aligned on the destination and the challenge, then you'll be off to a significantly good start. Often companies struggle to define and communicate clarity on the solution, so expectations and assumptions take over with confusion and misdirection following behind.

3. **Mindset and leadership:** Progress is delivered by huge numbers of people, probably more than you realize. The skill and will of

these people will be essential to deliver successful transformation, as will the change culture of your organization.

4. **Progress and execution:** As the saying goes, 'Rome wasn't built in a day', and similarly, your transformation will take time to develop, and to ramp to full effectiveness. Regular progress is achieved through completing activities and implementing tangible deliverables excellently.

With these four themes, you'll be ready to drive your transformation. Like driving a car, you'll want to monitor the diagnostics of your transformation to ensure you'll reach your destination without breaking down or suffering an avoidable drama.

The diagnostics of transformation

As you drive your transformation, you should continually check the health of your initiative and cross reference against the broader situation in the business.

But what's the best way of discovering the health, especially where there is no track history and when the situation can change regularly?

Tollgates, phase gates and formal reviews are often used for transformation. But these are infrequent and complex, plus can be perceived as a red-tape heavy processes to restrict progress and micro-manage. In some instances, they don't actively support the successful delivery of a transformation. Instead, enforcing compliance to a series of detailed measures.

This is like vehicles which must pass annual checks in the form of MOTs in the UK and other variants in different countries. With detailed measurements and plenty of inspections to be performed, it ensures a car is roadworthy and will hopefully remain so until the next assessment. The assessment results in a clear pass or fail, which is rarely the case in transformation. The assessment is complicated and not full proof. These vehicle assessments are the equivalent of a formal tollgate. So, to find the best solution, let's come out of the world of retail and transformation.

Analogy: Learning from newborn-baby health assessments

Maternity units have a huge responsibility to their patients: the parents and importantly, the newborn baby.

Prenatal monitoring is important but with the mother's natural support system in place, often no medical intervention is needed during pregnancy.

However, when a baby is born, it's critical to assess the health and rapid development as its' own life support systems kick in. Whilst many diagnostics and assessments exist, without any communication directly from the baby, and when speed is of the essence, doctors and midwifes need a quick and reliable way to check health, monitor progress and know when to intervene.

The APGAR score[24] was introduced in 1953 to do just this. Assessing five factors (activity, pulse, grimace, appearance, respiration, forming the acronym APGAR) on a simple scoring mechanism enables a super-fast assessment. The APGAR score can be quickly captured, recorded, communicated and then compared to future scores.

The score acts as an indicator for risk to life and suggests to medical professionals when they should intervene in this precious and tense moment.

The APGAR score works because it's standardized across the world, allows for easy communication, is quick to perform, becoming second nature to those in the profession. It can be easily assessed over time to see progress and will have been responsible for saving countless infant mortalities.

So, how do we break down the performance of the transformation in a similar way to how the APGAR score assesses a baby's health? How can we know when to raise an alarm bell or request further analysis, testing or observation? Let me introduce you to the Retail Transformation Steering Wheel.

The Retail Transformation Steering Wheel

The Retail Transformation Steering Wheel is your diagnostic measurement to assess the health of the transformation. This is your equivalent of the APGAR score.

The aim is to help you drive successful transformation, highlighting opportunities and discovering potential problems early so you can make the relevant intervention.

It's based on the same four themes we highlighted earlier, with each breaking down into smaller measures. These smaller measures will be explored throughout Part 2 of this book. Additionally, in Appendix 1, at the end of the book, you'll find specific questions to help you take a quick reading and assess your score against each element.

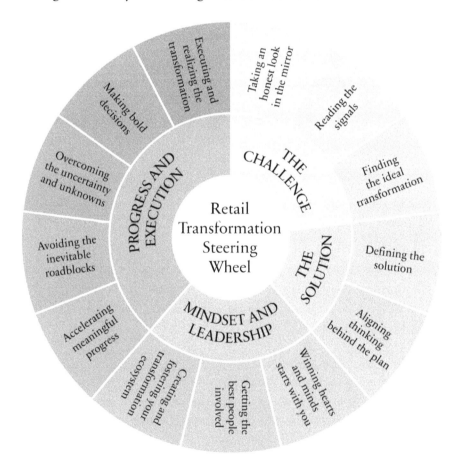

Figure 3.2: The Retail Transformation Steering Wheel

In Part 2, we'll explore each segment of the Retail Transformation Steering Wheel, starting with elements in The Challenge and working around clockwise. You'll learn how to identify and understand your transformation challenge (or opportunity) before discovering how to define, develop and deliver the transformational change.

This tool can be used at any stage through the transformation initiative's life and ideally on a regular basis. It can be used for any transformation, so whatever the 'what' of your transformation, you can use the same common assessment. With a clear and timely assessment, you'll know where to focus your attention.

This quick assessment will help you drive and steer the transformation along the journey (see Figure 3.2 and more details in Appendix 1).

Steering the wheel

When you're driving a car down a straight road, whilst you feel like you hold the wheel still, you're actually making a continual series of small tweaks. You read the road and make minor adjustments rather than waiting until you've nearly veered into a ditch before making a major swerve at the last moment. Transformation works best when you do the same. Don't wait to make the major swerve.

The Retail Transformation Steering Wheel will help you do this if you self-assess all areas quickly and dive deeper where relevant, taking actions that are specific to the situation you face.

Let's do your first self-assessment right now. Turn to Appendix 1 to find the questions and criteria or find an editable template online at DrivingRetailTransformation.com/wheel or by scanning the QR code below.

It's also important to consider that your transformation is bespoke. If you know there is a particular area that needs more or less focus based on your experience and situational awareness, then don't let this become an administrative blocker. Remember, it's a quick assessment to help you decide where, when and how to take proactive and remedial action. It's to provoke your thinking and help you drive forward and deliver your transformation in the right way.

Use the Retail Transformation Steering Wheel as you choose to be the driver.

What we've covered

- It's essential to consider the 'why' and the 'how' about your transformation, not just the 'what'.

- Delivering transformation is a unique journey and successful delivery depends on reason, clarity, progress and people.

- The Retail Transformation Steering Wheel guides you along the journey and encourages you to make frequent, small adjustments as you go.

PART 2
TAKE THE
DRIVER'S SEAT

Chapter 4
Taking an honest
look in the mirror

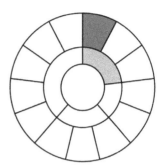

When does a transformation start? Is it the moment you name a project or programme? Is it the first time you schedule a meeting on this specific topic? Is it when you define a particular vision or problem statement? I'd suggest transformation starts way before. It's when you feel a pain point and decide this isn't acceptable, or when you first observe and consider a new opportunity.

At this inception point, reflect on the current state of the business and relevant parts of the operating model. Reflect individually and with peers and your team. Consider what got you to this point and where you have come from before.

If you've had your head down in the nitty gritty of the business and day-to-day trading or operations, you'll need to lift your head up. Look around and see how the landscape has changed. It's a common mistake to lose your bearings and become confused about where the organization is right now.

In response, it's time to take an honest look in the mirror, at where you've been and how you're currently placed to help understand the challenges in the business.

This honest look can help identify problems and opportunities for transformation. It can help you understand the status quo as well as see the intricacies involved in a topic. Unfortunately, it's hard to take an honest look in the mirror, so let's explore how to approach this.

Why would I not be having an honest look?

As a leader, you must overcome the 'curse of knowledge.' You look at the business with expert eyes. You think you know the problem areas. You think you know what's excellent, or not. You know the reasons and historical obstacles that have been overcome.

> 'The curse of knowledge: when we are given knowledge, it is impossible to imagine what it's like to lack that knowledge.'
>
> Chip Heath and Dan Heath[25]

Many take one of two views at this point:

View 1: The optimistic view. Wearing rose tinted glasses makes everything look nice. It's easy to excuse the ugly bits you're aware of; there's a reason they exist and you're confident that they're being resolved or are out of your control.

View 2: The pessimistic view. Alternatively, you see the situation more pessimistically (and some may try to defensively call this 'realistic'). You focus in on the challenge areas, especially those in functional areas that you're personally familiar with. The brain becomes hyper focused on the problems that you're already aware of. It's called the frequency illusion or the Baader-Meinhof phenomenon[26] and is a brain bias to keep your prehistoric-self safe.

Whilst you look at the business with reason and expertise, be that positively or negatively, the challenge is that your colleagues and especially your customers don't see or experience the same business. They're more literal and in the moment. There is no past comparison or excuse in their minds. They don't have the same expert knowledge. You must access this mentality too.

Additionally, if you're a senior leader, you'll almost certainly be prone to the 'red-carpet treatment.' Wherever you look in the business, for example, visiting stores or distribution centres, there is significant effort which goes into ensuring you see a polished operation and organization. The result is that you never see the true reality of the situation as your customer or colleague would see or experience on a normal day.

Example: The boss is coming

I was meeting Paula, a senior leader and had arranged to catch-up in a store, but we were travelling separately. I arrived first and introduced myself to Sean, the store manager. Sean was relaxed and we were talking freely. I was aware Sean and Paula had an existing, positive working relationship, so I mentioned that she was arriving soon.

Suddenly, Sean's eyes widened like he had seen a ghost. He was visibly shaken and immediately excused himself and quickly made a series of quick calls on his phone. Within minutes, store colleagues appeared from nowhere and were swarming over the front of the store and key selling areas. Tidying, replenishing and smartening the store to give the best possible visit.

Local store managers were also made aware that Paula was in the area, and they could expect a visit. I have no doubt that an equivalent flurry of activity started in multiple other locations.

There was no way that Paula would see the reality of the operation that day.

Although, I'm sure that local customers would have been delighted with the supreme shopping experience they received that afternoon.

Have you experienced similar situations? How are you avoiding this red carpet treatment?

Another factor obscuring the honest view on the business is experienced when continually working with the same people. With a consistent team, it's easy to suffer from Groupthink bias where the group finds itself in an echo chamber. So, when the same discussion topics come around multiple times, individuals, swayed by this bias, will reach the same conclusions. Inspired by the first person to share their point of view, any individual is more likely to rapidly converge on the same perspective. And as more members of the group agree, it becomes harder to consider any alternative. This is especially likely if the most senior person has shared their point of view first with others falling in line with agreement.

Finally, you might not be taking an honest look in the mirror because you don't want to see the harsh situation. Deep down, you know it's an issue. And it's a hard situation or fix that doesn't fill you with joy. You can't see what you don't want to see. It can extend to dismissing insights and intel from trusted sources. This is a state of denial.

By not taking an honest look in the mirror, you risk not understanding the true issues facing the business. This blind spot may cause you to ignore why, how and what you should be transforming.

Beware of the blind spot

As you drive a vehicle, you must be aware of your blind spot. You know it's there and there is increased risk. To get over this, cars come with sensors and additional mirrors.

As you drive your transformation, you also have blind spots, but last time I checked, built in additional sensors and mirrors are hard to come by.

You have blind spots as an individual and as an organization. It's hard to understand your own strengths and weaknesses. Brutal honesty is needed from yourself and colleagues at this point and this can only be achieved in a place of psychological safety. You'll need individuals who trust you will not use this honesty against them. No one wants to be thrown in front of the very same bus that they've just warned you about.

Questions to ask yourself, and to ask to others about yourself, include:

- If you were dramatically transformed into a superhero, what would your superpowers be?

- What would your primary customers say was your greatest strength?

- And what would those same customers say was the biggest pain point?

- What would your suppliers or partners say about how you operate?

- If you had a magic wand, what would you immediately change and why?

- What would it mean if that magic wand instantly changed the status quo?

▷ If you over index on a particular strength, how would that present itself as a weakness?

Ask these questions of yourself personally, and as an organization. Consult customers, suppliers and partners as they can be an incredibly useful and supportive source of feedback and ideas.

Additionally, as you look in the rear-view mirror, objects and events may appear closer than they are. Past wins feel like they occurred yesterday, when in reality they may have been years ago. The feeling of momentum lasts longer than the momentum itself, which can present challenges.

Taking an honest look in the mirror should be a group activity, not exclusively an individual one. Different people have different perspectives which give a broader and more rounded view, as long as they feel safe sharing those perspectives with you.

Uneducating yourself about the business

As you seek that honest view on the business, your customer experience and your colleague experience, you'll need to uneducate yourself to overcome the 'curse of knowledge', brought on by your experience and expertise. There are a series of activities which you can do to support this.

▷ **Listen directly to customers:** Could you listen to customers calling your customer service centre? Are there focus groups or community events that offer a chance to hear customers' point of view. Hear the words and phrases they use. Seek to recognize their aims and emotions.

▷ **Ask customers:** The obvious follow on is to engage in two-way conversation with your customers. Ask questions, seek to understand, be curious. What's really important to them? Why are they making the choices they do? What does a particular proposition/product/service/experience mean to them and as a wider aspect of their life? Use those 6Ws that we touched on in the last chapter and engage a range of real and independent customers, representing all your customer segments.

▷ **Ask colleagues:** Equally, speak to your frontline colleagues. Individuals who themselves are speaking to customers all day every day and delivering the operating model across the business.

Colleagues may also play the role of an internal customer, depending on what change you're looking at.

▸ **External benchmarking:** Time to go shopping! Engage enthusiastically with your competitors. Enjoy, don't critique their experience. Visit stores that cater for the same customers but serve in a different category. What is the baseline experience that customers expect? Recognize that these expectations are set by customers' broader shopping and consumer experiences, not just those within your specific category or competitor set.

▸ **Go undercover:** Like the TV show, *Undercover Boss*, where leaders don a disguise to experience the real status quo. Consider how you could avoid being recognized (maybe hold the wig though, usually just more of a casual look is fine), and perhaps travel a little further afield where your presence will be less expected. Experience the real shopping or working environment by listening, asking and observing.

'Thinking like an outsider… [means not being] wed to tradition, encumbered by internal loyalties or willing to bow to short term pressures.'

Carolyn Dewar, Scott Keller and Vikram Malhotra[27]

The aim at this stage is simply to listen and think like an outsider to learn, not explain or fix. Remember, you're looking to ease the 'curse of knowledge', not extend it. Personally, I have always found great opportunities and bright ideas through getting my hands stuck into frontline work, with or without the disguise. First-hand experience of walking a mile in someone's shoes becomes insanely valuable.

Walking a mile in their shoes

Discover the reality of your organization and the experience it gives to others by immersing yourself in the day-to-day operations.

Walking a mile in someone's shoes was originally a concept attributed to Native American tribes to empathize with another individual. We can extend this to understand how our operations work and deliver in real life. In the process improvement methodology, Lean Six Sigma, this concept is called a Gemba walk, derived from the Japanese for 'the real place'.

'The real place' can be in all and any parts of the organization, including stores, distribution centres, customer service centres, office functions and other specific elements for your business and operating model. This experience can be extended up or down the supply chain too, for example, collaborating with suppliers and partners to understand aspects like their product development, production facilities or recycling plants.

There are four stages to a successful walk.

1. **Plan your goals:** What are the specific objectives you want to complete and how will you achieve these. Then arrange the logistics of locations, times and days to check they align with these goals.

2. **Live in the moment:** Recognize what's happening and how someone would approach a particular issue. Resist the urge to investigate and fix things right now, unless there is a specifically urgent need, a major safety concern for example. Chances are that these issues have existed for an extended time already and may have been 'fixed' many times before. The trap of tackling issues as you go is that you'll be met with an endless list, in an unprioritized form, consequentially this will consume your energy and attention for unknown benefit. Also eliminate distractions to maintain focus.

3. **Record the experience:** Leave prompts about what you see, hear or feel to help you recall later on. When looking from someone else's perspective, there is a lot to take in. It's easy to become confused, muddled or overwhelmed. Try finding memory joggers to help revisit and refresh later on. Pen and paper is perfect, as are photos and videos. You might like to try short audio recordings too.

4. **Reflect:** Relive the experience with your strategic hat on and discuss with others. Often this is the stage that is easy to miss out. Perhaps you're fired up and want to fix things. Maybe you're worried that other plates need spinning, especially if you've been unavailable for a period. But to maximize the value from this time investment, share and review what you've found, and allow your team's collective brain make the mental connections and patterns to help you understand the reality and the root causes.

We've already touched on the importance of trust when taking an honest look in the mirror. It's entirely likely that people may (consciously or subconsciously) censor their views to avoid trouble or conflict. Or on the other end of the spectrum, people may exaggerate viewpoints about what challenges and opportunities exist. How someone feels may be factually correct and not representative. There are no simple rules or answers, and you should fall back on your experience and emotional intelligence, along with support from others, to help decipher.

You'll only experience a limited time period, in a single location. Colleagues, peers and your team can help extend this small scope but recognize this is a limited data set in a complex and ever-changing world. Supplement with supporting data and highlight a series of themes to investigate further.

Important skills and mindsets to use include:

- Empathy to see and feel things from other people's perspectives.

- Listening to people's opinions and thoughts. Let people keep talking to uncover the most valuable intel.

- Curiosity and intrigue to ask questions. How do you…? Who does…? Why is that…? What if…? These and more are handy prompts to understand more.

- Willingness to have a go and get stuck in.

- Avoiding making assumptions, use clarifying or exploratory questions instead.

- Recognize and have the humility to admit when you don't know a particular answer, yet.

- Openness to receive criticism about your actions, strategy or the organization in general. This is valuable feedback.

- Resilience to not let findings affect you, especially if you discover negative viewpoints; on the plus side, this demonstrates there are loads of opportunities to improve.

Walking a mile in someone else's shoes is a valuable observation and experience which will shed light on the challenges and opportunities for your organization. However, it might also tell you and others the uncomfortable truth.

The uncomfortable truth

This stage is highly dependent on your tenure in your current role or function. Often, new recruits are quick to point out the holes and challenges as they define their '90-day plan'. However, for those who have been in place for some time, perhaps suffering the 'curse of knowledge', this is a painful and challenging moment.

For those who have been in their current role for a while, it's natural to feel a mix of emotions and thoughts. 'It can't be that bad'. 'This can't be true'. 'It's a localized problem'. 'It's because of another department'. 'Why haven't I noticed this before?' 'Will I be found out?' Your team and other stakeholders will also likely be feeling this. The uncomfortable truth means people will feel threatened and our prehistoric brain takes over, looking to preserve life and deflect any potential damage.

It's easy for someone to be dismissive, discard the findings and put their head back in the sand. We don't want to accept the uncomfortable truth. Yet, it's inevitable that when you lift the hood on the inner workings, you'll see mess and disorder. That's real life unfortunately and it doesn't mean the status quo is acceptable.

To help ease acceptance of the uncomfortable truth, start early. Explain to others that you're taking an honest look in the mirror. Set the expectation that you'll find problems, and that you'll find opportunities too. Invite others to help you assess the status quo. 'We're all in this together' is a reinforcing mindset and message that will empower people and encourage trust. We're looking to avoid people feeling defensive or victimized, so they can be part of the solution.

After you've made your uncomfortable discoveries, consider how you will clarify and frame the problems for others to understand. Share your aspirations and the opportunity for changing. And mobilize any quick wins too to start building momentum.

> Crisis moments, pain points and discomfort
> fuel the transformation, but don't forget
> to steer towards an aspirational goal too.

Example: The uncomfortable truth with chaotic backrooms

Working with a client, we ran a series of activities to take an honest look in the mirror for store operations. A key finding was around the wildly inconsistent standards and organization in store backrooms, resulting in impacts to the customer-facing operation. This was a sensitive subject for store managers who were quick to blame the issues on various reasons, point the finger elsewhere or dismiss the issue.

To encourage acceptance of the uncomfortable truth and build support, we recognized and called out the various challenges as well as restrictions and root causes early on. Additionally, it was important to highlight the opportunities of what life could be like (and was like in some stores) if these challenges were resolved.

Quick win initiatives were delivered for an upcoming seasonal event. Ultimately, it started an energized programme across the organization to focus on stock levels, returns, productivity, equipment and training so that operations were streamlined, and stock could flow through the stores easily, improving availability, stock integrity and sales.

What are the uncomfortable truths which are being ignored in your organization?

Above all, don't skirt around the key issues, especially if you discover an elephant hiding in plain sight.

Calling out the elephant in the room

We've all been there. That moment where a big issue exists but nobody wants to confront it. And so, the elephant in the room goes unrecognized and undisturbed. But rather than blissful ignorance, it's better to identify the big issues.

Sometimes, this can be as easy as saying what you see. This breaks the ice and helps motivate the conversation.

There is, however, a fine line between revealing the uncomfortable truth and getting people's backs up. The latter then forms a stakeholder engagement mountain to traverse which is likely to impact the transformation at multiple future touchpoints.

Here are four tips to help call out the elephant.

1. What would customers say about this if they were part of the discussion? Listen to what they're saying or even bring them into the conversation; this can be especially valuable and insightful.

2. Gather feedback and testimonials from colleagues who are closest to the relevant issue. This will help clarify the issue, the impact and may hint at potential solutions.

3. Phrase it as an 'if' statement or query (e.g., if customer parcels were being delayed at this point due to slow processing, why could that be and which elements would need improving most?). This one is particularly useful if you're not sure about the exact shape and size of the 'elephant' in the room.

4. Simply say the situation as you see it, explaining the issue, impact and any alternatives. Refine the words and descriptions in time.

Calling out the elephant takes courage and may feel uncomfortable. But it earns trust and authority and helps focus on the right problems.

Once you have called out the elephant, the team can move on and investigate, analyse and address the issues with the status quo.

What we've covered

> Your transformation will rely on understanding the realities of the business, the operation and customer experience, but the 'curse of knowledge' might obscure the view.

> Different and diverse people have different and diverse perspectives, all of which are true but may be confusing.

> The organization must face into and accept the uncomfortable truth. People won't want to but it's refreshing and empowers change.

Chapter 5
Reading the
signals

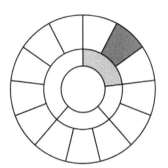

The digitalization of retail has exploded the volume and value of data. Effective use of the data can help drive huge opportunities for retailers. But what is 'data'? Simply put, it's information. And this information needs interpreting, which will allow you to read signals among the sea of data. These signals may be about what has already happened or an indication of what will happen.

Being able to read the signals, both on your own dashboard or control panel as well as when you look outward, will help you safely navigate the business through the transformation. In fact, being able to read the signals for the business is likely to be a huge opportunity to identify how the business is performing and diagnose issues.

These signals can be both the origin source of your transformation need and the proof you've transformed. Plus, setting up the signals properly might be, in itself, a transformation.

However, it can be a complex topic that dives deep into data science, statistics and advanced mathematics. Data, in the grandest sense of the word, can be a topic that some people truly fear and disengage with. It can cause confusion, it can be over relied on, and it can distract the business from the original intentions.

In a world with more channels, more customer engagement, more technology and more competition, you'll find that data is everywhere, and it's essential to read the signals properly.

Data is everywhere

We've seen a rapid evolution of the quantity of data collected, stored and used, driven through the rise of ecommerce and other channels as well as the digitalization of processes. Many retailers now have huge volumes of data, and sometimes more than they know what to do with. So, the data simply pours into a vast data lake and the challenge is how to filter, siphon and understand the most valuable data. The question then becomes about how to use the data.

Now we're talking about turning the raw data into insight. The insight is more important than the data. The insight tells us something, hopefully interesting. Maybe it's a trend over time, an intriguing statistic, a relevant and significant pattern or interaction. But knowing this is only the beginning. The question then becomes about how to use the insight.

Now, we're at the crux of the matter. Data is about action. Action to positively change the future.

There are two ways we can use data to drive action: reactive and proactive. Both are useful although we've traditionally been more focused on the reactive side.

Reactive data and insights are about sensing when part of the business is not functioning and highlighting the action to get back on track. 'Aargh, sales are down, let's take action to focus on driving revenue.' 'Aargh, a particular product is out of stock, let's take action to reorder and redeliver, or suggest an alternative.' Reactive data helps us understand when we're in trouble or starting to veer, allowing a chance to adjust.

Reactive data is historic, a view of the past. The event has happened already, and the data may already be out of date. Understanding the timeliness of data and the responsiveness of the reaction is therefore critical.

Proactive data and insight are about highlighting patterns and trends to make a forecast about the future. It allows us to speculatively take action to avoid future danger or take advantage of an opportunity. 'Ah, this product is selling well and will probably sell through at a faster rate than expected, let's reorder now.' 'Ah, this piece of equipment is showing signs that it may break soon, let's schedule preventative maintenance.' 'Ah, this customer is likely to be interested in these other products, let's make a recommendation.' Proactive data paints the picture of what we think is statistically more likely to happen and allows us to take early action.

Proactive data is a prediction, a view of the future. It's likely to come true, but not guaranteed. You have the ability to act based on chance and a forecast. The bigger the danger or opportunity, the more willing you should be to take proactive action.

For both types, the data does not need to be 1s and 0s only. Numbers are certainly a common and useful data type, but they can deter or repel some people who struggle with numeracy and data tools. Qualitative data is non-numerical and hugely valuable. Don't think of data as only numerical.

Whether your approach is for proactive or reactive data, recognize that data is everywhere and its insights will identify the best actions to help you to navigate the day-to-day business operations, strategic thinking and your transformation. The data will show what's working for the business and for your customers.

The customer is always right, right?

Customer data will reveal countless insights and potential actions. You must assess and prioritize which will be the right avenue for the business. It's drilled into consumers and retailers alike that the 'customer is always right'. But is that so? Should you listen and mindlessly do what customers tell you?

Contrary to popular belief, leading entrepreneurs will tell of the importance of *not* listening to your customers. That's not to say they don't care for their customers or don't want to hear customer feedback. Instead, they realize that innovation and customer delight cannot be determined by what a customer tells you.

> Surprise and delight will never happen
> if the customer is expecting it.

Customer feedback or customer experience metrics allow you to be reactive. Customer trends or behavioural analysis allow you to be proactive. The type of transformation that you embark on will determine the balance between reactive and proactive action.

Incremental transformation is more likely to be reactive to feedback and performance. Whereas fundamental transformation or reinvention will focus more on predictions and future opportunities. It's not exclusive but a definite pattern.

Another challenge with customer feedback is that they won't always tell the truth or the whole truth. The actions people take do not always align with what they say. They're not lying, consumers actively want to verbalize or communicate their ideal point of view. Perhaps this could be around sustainability, charity or price. This provides noise and confusion into the data. You must balance the one-off comments or customer behaviours in exchange for repeatable and representative commentary and behaviour.

Let's be crystal clear for a moment: your customers are crucially important for your present and future existence. They are of the utmost importance to you. However, from your customers' point of view, it's usually more of a one-sided relationship. It's likely that you are not as important to your customers as you think you are. When established companies fall into distress and close, there is often public outcry and mourning. That same public, however, were probably not present and making purchases as the pressure mounted, whilst there was still time. That established retailer just wasn't important enough for the individual consumer when they had the chance.

You must fight for every customer. Don't take them for granted. Don't expect consumers to choose you. And certainly don't expect loyalty; aspire to always be your customer's first choice. Retail expert Richard Hammond explains this excellently in his book, *Friction/Reward*,[28] and highlights the reasons flowing through a customer's head for and against shopping with you. Furthermore, those specific reasons vary for different customers so understanding the segments and attitudes as well as their shopping missions is essential.

How will you transform to ensure that there are effective and meaningful reasons for consumers choosing to shop with you? However, customers will not be able to explain this succinctly to you, and no score on an NPS (Net Promoter Score) survey will give any actionable detail. Customers can tell you what's right, but only once you let them experience it. The greatest idea remains hidden until it's delivered. You'll need to use instinct, intuition and insight to make sense of customers and consider the competitive choices that are open to them.

> *'If I had asked people what they wanted, they would have said faster horses.'*
> *Henry Ford, on the development of the first car, the Ford Model T*

Competitive trends

Similar to when you're driving on a road, stay aware of what competitors are doing. There are three key considerations.

1. **Don't blindly follow competitors:** Other companies may not be heading (or wanting to head) in the same direction as you. Relentlessly copying a competitor is not healthy, you've not come from the same place and you're not going to the same destination, so don't take the same route.

2. **Don't completely ignore competitors:** When customers have a rich choice of alternatives, it would be negligent to completely discard assessing competitors. Doing this would mean you could never understand why customers do or do not choose you.

3. **Don't obsess over your competitors:** If you're spending all your time looking at competitors you have taken your eyes off the road, and could forget where you're going. It's easy to dive into extensive benchmarking activities, keen to compare and leverage similarities and differences. Meanwhile, ignoring your own challenges and opportunities will not help you evolve.

Example: Taking your eye off the ball

For a team day icebreaker, after watching an expert demo, everyone took part in a head-to-head cup-stacking competition. I found it intriguing watching the behaviour and results for everyone.

Some people tried hard to replicate the expert skills, like they were a pro. Without practice, mistakes were made, and the performance was clunky.

Other people meanwhile were focused on innovating their own unique technique. They ignored what others had successfully done, and success was hit and miss as they searched for their own style.

Then, some were so focused on comparing progress with their head-to-head competitor, where the competitive victory was almost too important. This caused anxiety, leading to huge fumbles and further panic. Not a great approach.

And then there were those who watched and learnt from others, but when it came to their turn, were laser-focused on their own cups and their own performance.

Guess which approach was most successful and fulfilling? Which approach are you applying to your competitors?

Customer expectations are set by their overall experiences and perception of the market. Their experiences are not just within your category, but also extend to other retail segments, other channels and other consumer facing businesses, from hospitality services to utility companies.

Competitive benchmarking data can be useful within limits. Whilst this and other data can be interesting, is it actually telling you anything new or useful? Is the insight insightful?

Finding insightful insight

One of the main challenges with data and insight is that it often doesn't drive any action. And if it's not driving action, then it's not performing the core objective of changing the future for the better.

A key root cause for not driving action is that the insight isn't telling you anything new. Consider this: when was the last time you were genuinely wowed by an insight?

Is the data just proving what you already know? Are you looking for hard facts to act as evidence that supports your theory? Or is the insight not cut or displayed in a way that informs or educates you?

Curiosity is a core skill to hone in yourself and those around as you drive your transformation. To be more curious, seek a deeper reason for any given set of results by asking 'why?' Investigate the implications by asking

'If this happened, then what else happens?' Challenge the alternative with '… but this isn't so because…' These and other questions will help you to gain greater understanding and lead to genuinely insightful insights.

The ability to creatively blend non-obvious insights, in an analytical manner, allows you to identify new intelligence which may guide strategy or future innovations. For instance, Alibaba and MARS collaborated to discover that Chinese consumers who buy chocolate also enjoy spicy snacks. This inspired the Spicy Snickers bar, which was an instant hit that also cut product development timescales by over 50%.[29]

In addition, there are some insights which just feel wrong. You can't prove it right now but something 'smells' off about it. If the insight feels wrong, you must find the right balance between insight and instinct.

Balancing insight and instinct

How many meetings have you been in where the discussion has become purely opinion based? Equally, how many times have you seen odd recommendations or actions, purely because the 'data says so'?

Reactive data insights are factual but historic and could be out of date. Proactive data insights are forward-looking but predictive and uncertain. Meanwhile, your instinct or gut is based on your experience, outlook and what new intel you feed your brain. This can be both historic and future aware. However, no one else can truly understand or predict your instinct so it's important to share how you reach an instinctive conclusion with others to help develop people and explain the approach.

Your instinct is the output of your prehistoric brain. It includes your own experiences and lessons you've learnt from others. It's based on insights and research that you've processed before, as well as emotions you've felt and even your personal agenda to keep yourself safe and satisfied. It's impossible to frame or guess your instinct; but when you know, you know.

However, this gut feel both guides you and misdirects you. The gut expects a pattern, it expects situations and people to play out and behave in the same way that they have done before. And fears of the unknown and of failure creep in too. Additionally, in an ever-evolving market, it's possible that your instinct could be out of date and holding you back.

Both insight and instinct are relevant. The art is balancing them the right way at the right time, so you don't end up with mixed signals.

Understanding mixed signals

When you receive mixed signals, decisions get hard and it's easy to follow the wrong path forward. And mixed signals confuse a wider audience and can easily be interpreted in different ways resulting in diverging actions from different teams.

Mixed signals are, unfortunately, easy to receive. They're often a result of conflicting data although remember that one data set can be manipulated to show many different conclusions. Fortunately, with a careful approach, you can dissect these challenges to get a clearer read on the true signal, as Table 5.1 shows.

Table 5.1: Reading the true signals

Cause of mixed signal	Symptoms	Solution
Data is not clean	A significant number of outliers, a set of concurrent or relative data sources which mismatch the rest of the data.	Individual investigation is required to understand or eliminate erroneous data. Review data collection to check if unprecedented events or mistakes occurred when it was being collected.
Insufficient data	Volatile signal which jumps as more data is added.	Review the number of data points which will be relative to the measure. A rule of thumb is a minimum of 30 data points. Collect more data accordingly.

Instinct opposes insight	The data 'feels' wrong to you or someone else.	Clarify what aspect of the data feels incorrect and why that is. Review why you would expect another result. Seek a second opinion. Ensure data quality and analysis is fair.
Overlapping data segments	The data is very spread out or seems to have confusing patterns.	Consider what data segments could be overlapping and filter the data to get a clearer signal, there could be two or more segments muddled together. Be careful to ensure there is still sufficient volume of data points.
Inherent noise	There seems to be no pattern, trend or obvious conclusion. The standard deviation or other measure of spread seems large relative to the data.	Generate ideas about what could be causing the noise and investigate if this can be retrospectively measured. If not, consider restarting data collection.

Data quality is of upmost importance and data governance is an essential topic for many organizations to engage in. Understanding the variation and consistency of your data sources is important, and for that you may want to investigate statistical measures like variance and standard deviation, standard operating procedures (SOPs), measurement systems analysis (MSA) and gathering data over extended time periods (especially important for seasonal aspects in retail).

Being able to understand your data will be essential to decipher mixed signals. However, once you manage to understand and trust the data, you should ensure you have sensible metrics in place.

Be guided by sensible metrics

Retail businesses love good KPIs (key performance indicators). The KPI allows a comparison which appeals to the competitive spirit that exists within all companies. Whether that is comparison to a different team, store, group, country, or company, or whether it is comparison to a target, the KPIs quickly become the major focus for general performance. The right metrics allow you to understand the past, present and future performance and uncover the value of a transformation.

Metrics can help highlight challenges and transformation opportunities. They can also demonstrate the progress or performance of a given transformation based on the relevant goals.

First (and I need to get this one off my chest!), the 'K' that clearly stands for 'key' tells us that the metric is essential and stands out. It's not a regular performance indicator. It sounds obvious and I've been in many conversations where any metric is suddenly dubbed a KPI, which dilutes the focus on the actual KPIs.

Now let's explore the 'P'. A metric is designed to be a proxy for the desired performance or outcome. Challenge your KPIs (and any new metrics that get thrown in too) by asking what they hope to achieve and if that's the right outcome for the business. Then consider the different ways of how you could best achieve a positive KPI score but not meet the outcome. These are ways to game the system or manipulate the result and we must stop this risk.

Understand the difference between what your metrics
are designed to achieve and what they actually show.

And finally, the 'I'. What exactly is the metric supposed to be indicating? And based on what it suggests will happen, what action should be taken for the various outcomes?

Additionally, you'll know that in the urge to achieve a strong KPI score, the metrics can drive and alter the behaviours of individuals and teams.

In theory, this is great and positive behaviours focus on boosting the business in the desired direction. However, it's easy for the wrong metric to be assigned that can encourage wrong or unintended behaviours in a bid to achieve the answer. Humans, in our creative search to spend less energy on any given activity, seek ways to game the system. How can we get the best score with the minimum effort? But the best 'score' isn't what you desire, you're really looking for a positive outcome and performance, driven by the actions you're taking.

Leading and lagging measures can also be useful. Sales performance is the classic lagging measure; it's happened already, it's in the past, there is nothing that you can do to change that number. Leading measures give more visibility into future performance. For example, if you know that availability at a distribution centre is poor, you know you will soon see poor availability at the point of purchase and therefore reduced sales. The leading measure may still use reactive data, but it allows us to proactively consider what else will be impacted in the future. The warnings raised by leading measures (and the trend over time) should allow an ability to respond and act to drive better performance.

As your transformation develops, you'll want to ensure you have sensible metrics in place, for both the initiative and the whole business. Getting the ideal metrics in place can be transformative by itself. However, sometimes, the perfect metric doesn't exist, and you'll need to turn to proxies and educated guesses.

The proxy and the educated guess

You know the exact outcome that you want to achieve. But the data for that and therefore a desirable, obvious metric doesn't quite exist or isn't available. You'll need a proxy which is a relevant and useful stand in.

For example, consider that we want to understand how much profit was generated per store including nearby catchment areas, or per category on a daily basis. But this isn't immediately available due to complex cost attribution across the wider business. Instead, you use the sales volume, which is available. Although it's not a perfect representation of profit, usually it will suggest if the day has been successful.

However, in some instances, the ideal metric is too complex to be represented by a single proxy, for example, how many customers will make repeat purchases in the future. Instead, use a blend of data and educated guesses based on what you do know. An educated guess could be a result of a trend analysis, an extrapolation of historic data, or more complex modelling and simulation activity.

Latest developments in data collection, access, simulation, algorithms, machine learning and AI make the use of proxies hugely more accessible and predictable. Communicate clearly to ensure relevant people understand how and why these proxies are being used. It's also critical to remember the proxy is just that, a proxy. It is not the primary objective to obsess over, and it's also important to regularly reassess if it's still a valid stand in for that ideal but missing metric.

Then, with good quality data and sensible metrics in place already, it's time to determine what all this data is telling you.

The source of the challenge or opportunity

With multiple streams of data informing you about past and present business performance and giving you signals about the future, and when you've taken an honest look in the mirror, you'll be ready to define the challenge or opportunity which forms the reasoning behind the transformation.

At some point, we must determine that the status quo is no longer viable. If you monitor the signals and metrics, you should see this, but also be open to listen as well as share your perspectives. Your personal view can be essential as not everyone will have the same viewpoint or know what to look for.

There is likely to be an element of internal pressure. Missed expectations, failed targets, poor results all lead to pain and stress, often starting at the top and cascading down to all levels. This internal pressure can intensify if the external trends and intel oppose the business' direction.

The external view can include customer feedback and competitive advancements. New technologies, legal regulations, political situations and broader economic performance also form the external intel.

When you factor in these elements and consider the specific details, it's time for a pivot. You'll start to understand the symptoms or issues that the business faces which must be investigated and diagnosed further to help truly understand the specific challenges and opportunities.

Ask yourself: Is the transformation about
achieving growth or preventing loss?

It's time to set a new direction and a new destination and find the appropriate transformation.

What we've covered

> ▸ A vast volume of data exists, in many different forms, and it needs challenging to extract the true value.

> ▸ Listening to your gut is still relevant in the age of data, and you should be open to learning how to use both insight and instinct in balance.

> ▸ Deciphering the data and signals is only useful if you take intentional action to positively change the future.

Chapter 6
Finding the ideal
transformation

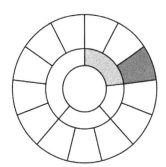

The word 'transformation' has many connotations and associated expectations. It also conjures up a range of emotions and feelings: hope, fear, anxiety, energy and more. And it's entirely possible that an individual could be feeling a whole mix of these positive and negative emotions all at once and they'll change over time too.

When we define a 'transformation', it's critical that we find a solution that meets and sets the right expectations. It must be big and bold enough to cover the business needs. It must be focused enough to guide the organization to a specific result. In addition, it should tackle the right opportunities and threats in a viable and meaningful way for the organization, the situation and the urgency.

Defining the goals for the transformation, and perhaps strategy, will map out the destination for your transformation journey. This stage may also raise big, existential questions to tackle. Who are our ideal customers? What does our brand mean? Why do we exist? These are important questions to face into and genuinely reflect on. However, often time is of the essence so you may need to start the transformation journey and adapt along the way. Whilst this may be frowned on by some, when you're up against it, this head start can make all of the difference. Consider how an ambulance is dispatched to an emergency before all the information has been shared about the situation. What's important is to make this an intentional decision, in full knowledge that you will stay flexible and adjust on the fly.

Once you understand the current challenges and trends, it's important to recognize the reasons and appetite for transforming, which are essential to find a transformation that's meaningful for you.

Confirming the why behind the transformation

By bringing together findings from your research and the business performance, you can assess if the status quo is viable or not. Valuable sources of intel to help you decide include:

- Discoveries from your honest look in the mirror.
- Intel from reading the signals, including financial or KPI data, customer research and external insight.
- The broader company strategy and existing transformation programmes.
- The North Star or purpose that guides the company.

By assessing these elements, you will identify and confirm if there is a genuine need to shift. You'll sense the urgency and importance relative to other priorities in the business right now.

This research should also suggest if a transformation will attract the right level of senior support and sponsorship. Winning this support early is a crucial indicator to prove that the status quo is not acceptable, and an alternative future is required. At this early stage, if stakeholders don't 'get' the need to change, the initiative is unlikely to be resilient to the trials and tribulations ahead. Alongside understanding the reasons for change, the organization must also have an appetite for change.

The transformation appetite

Transformation can mean different things to different people. It's a pre-loaded word, heavy with promise, possibility and peril. However, it's easy to throw around transformation as a buzzword in conversations about aspirational goals without too much consideration. The result is that many companies and people talk about their desire for transformation. The reality is that it's far harder to follow through to define and deliver meaningful transformation.

The idea of transformation can be exciting, heralding the start of a new positive era. However, it can also be threatening, an approaching storm which brings danger and uncertainty.

But after all of the talk, the reality is that a transformation requires significant effort and resources. We can't just state our desire and wave a wand to be magically transported to our ideal destination. The journey of transformation is essential. It's risky and rewarding. And it needs that blend of hard work, smart work and careful work to pull it off.

The start of that journey is to determine where you're going. And a crucial first step is to understand the actual appetite for transformation in your organization (remembering that it's easy and quick to sign up for the *idea* of transforming). Understanding expectations is also key. Are you looking to make smaller incremental changes that build up over time? Or are you thinking of big, bold shifts that fundamentally reshape your organization? Both are transformational. Neither is right nor wrong. But getting the appropriate level of transformation based on the need is critical.

Additionally, when you start to talk to others about the transformation, what will their expectations and assumptions be? Will their appetite for transformation match the business need, and their understanding of that need? Any mismatches at this stage will lead to future challenges and conflicts. Also remember that transformation conjures a fear of the unknown in people.

Clearly define what the company will find valuable versus a 'nice to have'. Assess the genuine desire for non-financial benefits. Whilst everyone may agree that 'soft' benefits are positive, they are easily deprioritized or discounted when hard decisions must be made. Approach these topics early as it's likely that different stakeholders will have opposing opinions on this.

The appetite for transformation may depend on if your organization is leading the industry or falling behind. In a leading position, the focus will be more on innovation and opportunity to extend the lead. Whereas severe disruption and declining performance will tend to make the appetite more acute for companies needing rapid improvement to catch up.

Example: An absent appetite leads to no transformation

The COO for a client was keen to develop a new business unit to move their business forward and alleviate concerns over falling profitability in the core business. It was difficult to get traction and time in board meetings to discuss ideas or approve investments, causing frustrations and wasted time.

It eventually transpired that the board were reluctant to switch business models, despite the very positive research and initial results of this disruptive transformation. The board struggled to explain why, but given the shift it would create, the appetite for this type of transformation never really existed. This had been accentuated by the board's lack of understanding for the new business and a corresponding fear of the unknown. The initiative was soon deprioritized in favour for a change programme to optimize the existing operating model.

To understand the transformation appetite sooner, the board should have been engaged earlier, in both formal and informal settings. Aspects like an overview of the financial plan, research findings or even plans for small pilots would have highlighted concerns and confusion earlier.

How will you assess the business's appetite for transformation as early as possible?

Defining the type of transformation that's right for you and your organization is essential so that you can approach the initiative in the right way and set the right expectations around the business.

Defining the appropriate type of transformation

As transformation is perceived as different things by different people, it's important to clarify exactly what we're talking about. There are six types of transformation (see Figure 6.1), each of which could be focused on any number of different topics. These six types are not in a sequence; they're independent of each other and can be approached in any order that suits your unique situation at any moment in time.

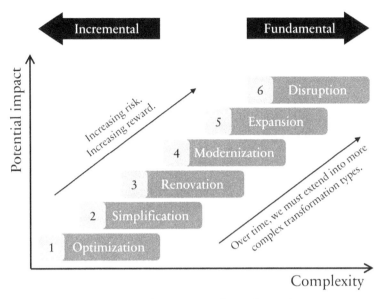

Figure 6.1: The six types of transformation

Using a standardized format for these types allows us to clarify expectations and guides thinking in subtly different ways. I'll also point out that when you get into the specifics of your precise transformation, there will be many more details than what I include here, especially with the benefits, risks and capabilities required. The boundaries between the types may also blur.

Type 1: Optimization

Optimization transformation improves business processes and operational outputs incrementally to gain efficiencies, cost savings or make marginal gains. Whilst each change is individually small, when a number of these optimization changes are collated, they can amass to form a meaningful incremental transformation. The goal is to enhance specific parts of the business and operating model.

Examples

▷ Optimizing processes to extend an order cut off time in a warehouse picking process.

▷ Enhancing a loyalty programme to increase the number of customers returning to store.

> Fine tuning the checkout process to increase conversion rate.

Who is it for?

> Optimization is for companies with an established operating model, who are now looking to improve efficiency and performance.

> Those looking to enhance their ways of working to deliver specific KPI or metric improvements.

> Companies that are looking to enhance their customer experience and eliminate the current niggles.

> Optimization can be a useful approach for retailers who are looking to build up their transformation capability or who are looking to establish a culture that is more accepting of change.

> However, a company should not be focused on optimizing a business or operating model that isn't working or where performance and results are far below expectations. Making smaller tweaks around the edge will not be sufficient to negate the current challenges. Instead, a more fundamental type of transformation will be needed.

What are the benefits?

> Improved efficiency and productivity across all relevant processes or operations.

> Reducing niggles and pain points from the customer journey or colleague experience.

> Motivational boost for colleagues, with increased confidence in the strategy and transformation.

> Improve relevant KPIs and metrics, including sales, customer satisfaction, working capital or other focus area.

What are the risks and pitfalls?

> Optimization will only improve the current model and will not account for significant shifts to the market or customer behaviour.

> Scope creep is a danger as it's easy to start to think about optimizing everything to perfection.

- Finding the right level of optimization is essential. It's likely that the 80:20 rule will hold for achieving most of the benefit relatively quickly, but the final improvements will be especially laborious, slow, hard and expensive to realize.

- It's critical that there is a reasonable payback for the time invested in developing and delivering this transformation. There is little point investing huge efforts and cash to shave off seconds of efficiency from a low frequency process. This is especially true once the 'low-hanging fruit' or quick wins have been realized.

- A large volume of optimization efforts needs careful coordination and communication as it's easy for the organization to be overwhelmed and confused. Change capacity will be important to track and monitor.

What skills and capabilities are needed?

- Data analytics, for both qualitative and quantitative data.

- Process improvement expertise, such as Lean Six Sigma.

- Critical analysis of benefits, efforts and costs for prioritization and viability assessments.

- Change management skills to implement new ways of working effectively.

Type 2: Simplification

Simplification is about implementing changes to boost productivity, reduce costs and streamline the business. Simplification is enabled by stopping activities or cost lines as well as improving efficiencies. Often, these changes are used to focus on rapidly boosting the financial performance, for example in the face of profit warnings or to fund unplanned growth activities, including pay rises, marketing efforts and other transformation initiatives. The goal is to reduce costs and improve profitability.

Examples

- Reorganization following significant growth or shrinkage in a particular part of the business.

- Reducing delivery frequency to stores to minimize logistics costs.

- Minimizing stock holding through reducing ordered quantities and looking to sell through existing stock on hand.

- Shutting unprofitable stores or propositions.

Who is it for?

- Companies that are struggling financially and must reduce costs, sometimes urgently.

- Removing unprofitable and non-value-adding parts of the organization.

- This is not usually a route for direct growth, although it can be used to fund other transformation initiatives or strategies which do deliver this.

What are the benefits?

- Reduces costs and unprofitable operations.

- Frees up cash and working capital to invest in other initiatives or deliver to the financial statements.

- Streamlining can release the pressure in the business to work on other transformation efforts.

- Stopping unpopular or unprofitable propositions can free up time and focus for the business and customers.

What are the risks and pitfalls?

- You cannot cost cut your way to growth. Whilst this will boost the bottom line, it's not often an approach that directly drives revenue growth.

- This is a short-term approach only. You cannot continue this approach for extended periods of time without impacting the company, culture and brand.

- This approach can unintentionally result in negative shifts to customer and business performance metrics, such as availability, customer experience or colleague satisfaction.

- Streamlining can dent morale and motivation, especially for colleagues but also customers, whilst forging a negative view on the company direction in the longer term.

- Making decisions without full appreciation of the implications. Unintended consequences and unforeseen on-costs or sales impacts can deliver a net-negative result for the company which can be especially brutal to those companies who are already struggling.

- Benefits must be realized and 'bankable' or the results of the change will only be conceptual.

- Timeframes for people processes, such as redundancies, can be longer than expected, especially for large workforces. It is also crucial to engage relevant unions and employee groups. There is often a sizeable management effort and emotional cost for facilitating these people processes.

What skills and capabilities are needed?

- Financial analysis and cost mapping.

- Process understanding and ability to investigate impact.

- Strong HR skills and understanding of relevant policies and procedures.

- Change management skills as this approach can be emotionally hard on all involved or impacted.

Type 3: Renovation

Renovations focus on repairing and upgrading specific parts of an organization. This provides a relatively small-scale transformation from a company level, but can be very meaningful when looking at the specific area. It can be driven by consumer demand, competitive development, or warning signals from within the company. The goal is to improve a specific and self-contained part of the business.

Examples

- Store refit or refresh programme which focuses on redeveloping a specific group of stores or departments within stores.

- Redesigning a product line to add new features or factor in more sustainable materials.

- Rebranding a sub-brand or own label product.

▷ Introducing new parcel handling equipment at a distribution centre to increase process throughput.

Who is it for?

▷ Retailers that have identified specific areas to improve or focus on.

▷ Brands that have detected a shift in consumer demands or requirements and must adjust to stay relevant.

▷ This may not be the right transformation for those who need a more sizeable shift in the business model or operating model.

What are the benefits?

▷ Achieving a specific objective for improving sales or another metric.

▷ Developing part of the business whilst avoiding impact to the wider business.

▷ Initiatives can progress as smaller entities without being slowed down by larger transformation programmes.

What are the risks and pitfalls?

▷ If many parts of the business are concurrently working on their own renovations, it could cause interference, confusion, overlap or duplication.

▷ Without clarity on the company's guiding North Star, multiple renovations could quickly cause divergence within the organization as different renovations focus on different objectives and goals.

▷ If the scope is too narrow, there could be negligible benefit at company level. But if the scope is too broad, it will strain resources and could stall.

What skills and capabilities are needed?

▷ Prioritization to ensure that the most critical elements are renovated first.

▷ Project and portfolio management, especially if multiple renovations are running concurrently.

▷ Expertise in relevant and adjacent areas of the operating model.

▷ Change management skills as those impacted by the trans-formation could see significant shifts.

Type 4: Modernization

This type of transformation is about overhauling all or large parts of the operating model. Often there is an aspect of technology or digitalization which enables the modernization. However, modernization is rarely only about technology; there will be knock on impacts to people, processes and other elements of the business. The goal is to upgrade essential parts of the business and bring in line with the latest industry standards and customer expectations.

Examples

▷ Replacing a critical legacy supply chain system and adopting latest integration practices.

▷ Making data more accessible with an analytics platform to collate and give access to intel.

▷ Overhauling the online or omnichannel customer experience to reduce friction.

▷ Introducing new modern payment methods or models which are more relevant for customers.

Who is it for?

▷ Businesses with outdated technology stacks which hinder progress and hold back other transformation efforts.

▷ Retailers facing industry disruption or where customer expectations are being raised quickly.

▷ Companies looking to adopt more modern ways of working.

▷ This would be an unsuitable approach for those needing quick changes or who are not ready to invest in new processes or technology.

What are the benefits?

▷ Up-to-date simpler operating models and processes for relevant areas of the business.

- Raising the customer experience in line with market standards or expectations, driving better sales and performance.

- Gathering more data and making it accessible, opening numerous future opportunities.

What are the risks and pitfalls?

- Potentially huge impact to the core business if the new solution is not fully functional as needed and to schedule.

- Especially with large systems, projects can be delayed by months and budgets overrun by millions.

- Rejection of change by people who feel that 'we've always done it this way'.

- The larger the scope, the larger the risks involved.

What skills and capabilities are needed?

- Ability to develop a strong operating model and clearly define and test new requirements.

- Relevant technical expertise on the current operating model and systems.

- Detailed planning for the switchover and significant change management for the transition, covering both technical and cultural aspects.

Type 5: Expansion

Expansion transformation is focused on growing the business in multiple ways to capture more market share. This growth could be to expand into new product or service categories, new channels, or expanding into more territories or internationally. Acquisitions, mergers and partnerships may also offer a viable way to realize the expansion. The goal is growth of the business into new areas whilst minimizing major rework to the business model, operating model, organization or technical architecture.

Examples

- Entering a specific country where you currently have minimal or no market share.

- Opening a new store network where previously there was only an ecommerce offering.

- Increasing the range with new product categories.

- Acquiring a company to absorb their customer base.

Who is it for?

- Retailers who have an established brand, proposition, reputation and operation in their current territories. The current territory should be working effectively and smoothly.

- Pureplay retailers who are looking to grow into more channels.

- Companies with sufficient finance and operational capability to stretch beyond the current scope.

- It's probably not the right move for companies fighting for survival or where the business model or operating model is not working or unprofitable. These companies should focus on consistent and predictable performance instead.

What are the benefits?

- Increased revenue and customer numbers.

- More resilience as the diversification across markets and categories reduces risk.

- A larger base for future growth initiatives.

- Improved efficiency through synergies and existing capability and capacity.

What are the risks and pitfalls?

- Entering new markets can take time to establish reputation. The business case should model various ramp-up speeds and set expectations accordingly.

- Expansion can open a number of potential growing pains, from lack of experience or strained bandwidth. This could include relevant recruitment, logistics and supply chain, currency exchange, reporting, new legislation and regulations, and more.

- May be likely to face a new competitor set who already has established market share and presence.

> ▷ If expansion is too far or too fast, it can detract from the core business, which still needs careful management and leadership to consistently produce results.

What skills and capabilities are needed?

> ▷ Effective market research to assess viability of the new expansion.

> ▷ May require recruitment for knowledge of the new category, channel or geography.

> ▷ Strong financial management and data analysis, especially if there is expected to be a halo effect or cannibalization of the core business due to the expansion.

> ▷ Effective change management to introduce the new areas and ensure that focus is reasonably split between the 'cash cow' of the existing core business and the new expansion opportunity.

Type 6: Disruption

The most extreme type is disruptive transformation. This involves significant changes to the business model and operation. Disruptive transformation is more likely to provoke a broader strategic discussion too as it seriously challenges the status quo. The fundamental nature of this type looks to disrupt the market, and possibly the core business too. It may include new products, new services and/or new customer segments. Like Expansion, acquisition may also be a viable approach to this type of transformation, especially if acquiring start-ups or operational capabilities and quickly scaling them to a disruptive size. The goal is to radically develop the current business.

Examples

> ▷ The limit here is based on your own imagination, so I'll share some specific examples to get started.

> ▷ Amazon launching B2B services, including FBA (Fulfilled By Amazon), AWS (Amazon Web Services), Just Walk Out technology or One payment method.

> ▷ Amazon launching Prime subscription services to consumers as a paid loyalty platform with many varied benefits included.

- Tesco moving into the wholesale market by acquiring wholesale specialist Booker.

- Pets At Home offering a range of pet and vet services in addition to retailing products.

- The John Lewis Partnership shifting to build and rent residential houses and apartments, whilst promoting their core retail ranges.

- Walmart offering GoLocal fulfillment services or expanding into new retail media offerings to brands.

Who is it for?

- This is for companies who face incoming disruption, or want to cause disruption.

- Market leaders looking to challenge their own business model and assumptions.

- Companies with a specific and advanced capability that are looking to leverage that competitive advantage.

- It's unlikely to be suitable for risk-adverse companies or those with limited resources and time.

What are the benefits?

- Offers the chance to open new customer or market segments, or even establish entirely new markets.

- The chance to develop a robust competitive advantage and economic moat.[30]

- The opportunity to focus on more profitable propositions and customer segments.

What are the risks and pitfalls?

- Presents significant uncertainty with future results and performance, in terms of timescales and KPIs.

- There will be significant resistance and fear in the organization and with key stakeholders who struggle to see the disruption or are concerned for future impact.

- There may seem many reasons not to proceed, and it will be easy to slow or stop progress as a result. It may feel too far from the company's comfort zone.

- Setting incorrect assumptions, especially relative to the existing business.

- Innovative ideas may struggle to prove guaranteed value against traditional business cases for less fundamental transformation types.

What skills and capabilities are needed?

- Creativity is essential to see a future that doesn't yet exist.

- Ability to thrive in uncertainty and define a path forward when there is incomplete, incoherent or illogical insight.

- Resilience and determination will be tested throughout.

- Adaptability and a willingness to react to what's working or not. Adopting the mentality and attitudes of a start-up will help enormously.

- Change management is an essential skillset given the scale of change and the newness of the operating model.

- There are many parts to this including understanding customer needs and wants, monitoring industry trends, handling experimentation, communicating and certainly much more.

'You can't just ask customers what they want and then try to give that to them. By the time you get it built, they'll want something new.'

Steve Jobs, Founder of Apple

Selecting the right type for you

This is a very specific decision. Segmenting into the six types we have covered helps to assign patterns and opportunities, but it's not a black and white decision. It's entirely feasible that the challenges and opportunities you face means that it may align to two or more types. If this is the case, I'll share a word of caution around scope and prioritization. Don't try to take on too much or you open a significant risk of delivering nothing.

However, selecting your type (or primary type) of transformation allows you to set expectations and set the vision and destination for the journey of transformation.

Setting the vision or destination

At this stage, we've identified the various challenges and opportunities. After understanding the organization's appetite, the type of transformation suggests a reasonable horizon and allows us to propose the destination.

Consider where you will take the company, and what that journey looks like? Encourage people to feed into this too and they will naturally feel more ownership and support for the idea throughout the transformation. This forms the vision for the transformation.

The transformation vision should outline the status quo and define the challenges, opportunities and sets out what must change. The vision considers forecasts and trends for how the world will continue to evolve. At this stage, the transformation may either be focused on a particular solution already, or could still be solution agnostic and focused on tackling the challenges on hand.

Tip: Creating a short, compelling transformation vision statement

To create a simple vision statement in collaboration with other relevant people, use this simple template:

▸ **Context:** Briefly describe the current situation and why the change is necessary.

▸ **Future State:** Articulate what the 'end goal' looks like. This should be specific, compelling and vivid.

▸ **Timeframe:** Define a realistic but ambitious timeframe for when the vision will be realized.

▸ **Results:** List the main benefits that the transformation will deliver to customers, colleagues and other stakeholders.

Example:

[Context] In the face of rapidly evolving consumer behaviour and increased competition from online disruptors, we must transform to remain a leading player in our category. *[Future state]* We will redesign our stores to encourage customers to experience our most important products in meaningful and realistic ways whilst being supported by empowered and expert colleagues and with more seamless connection to our digital storefronts. *[Timeframe]* Within 3 years, *[Results]* we will be the #1 in our category for customer satisfaction, driving 20% channel-agnostic sales growth, with focused commercial and operational excellence increasing profitability by 14%.

What is your transformation vision statement?

You'll want to continue to illustrate your vision with more detail and specifics for your transformation before sharing it more widely across relevant function of the organization and through different levels of the business, continually refining the vision whilst earning support. The vision allows you to paint an inspiring and aspirational picture of the future as you start to encourage people to come on the journey with you.

Using the word 'imagine' as you explain the vision can be an incredibly useful technique to engage individuals and teams. Empower people and tempt them to use their creativity to also see a viable picture of the future. Early on, we're still thinking expansively and considering the 'art of the possible'. This opportunity is brilliant to start understanding assumptions and expectations from your stakeholders.

The transformation vision must align with the company strategy, and we'll come back to that shortly. But as you define the vision, you should also focus on the customers of the change.

Who is the customer of the change?

When embarking on any transformation, it's important to recognize that there are three distinct customers of that transformation. And these customers of the change are not necessarily your actual end customers or consumers, either.

The first customer is the 'direct customer' who is receiving the transformation. They see and experience the deliverables first hand.

The second customer is the 'indirect customer' who benefits from the output.

Finally, the transformation's 'sponsor' is also a customer. This is the person within the company who want the change to happen for a specific reason. They are ultimately accountable for the benefits. Aim to have only one sponsor for clarity and ownership. Let's consider some examples to clarify (see Table 6.1).

Table 6.1: Identifying the customer of the change

Example transformation	Direct customer	Indirect customer	Sponsor
A new subscription service to make purchasing easier for consumers.	Consumers, who subscribe to make repeat purchases easier.	Sales teams, where orders are automatically placed.	Chief Customer Officer, who is responsible for loyalty and repeat purchases.
A new supplier portal to automate ordering.	Suppliers, who receive the orders from the portal.	Buyers, who are minimizing time spent relaying information and orders to suppliers.	Buying Director/ VP, who is responsible for buyers and supplier relationships.
Improved stock control process to resolve out of stocks.	Stock control team, who run the process daily.	Consumers, who benefit from improved availability.	Chief Operating Officer, who is responsible for availability and sales.

Revamped payroll system to alleviate pressure and delays from old system.	Finance payroll administrators, who operate the system.	Colleagues, who want their salary paid accurately and on time.	Chief HR Officer, who is responsible for colleague salary payments.
	HR managers, who enter and amend employee information and salary details. Colleagues, who can check upcoming payments.		

In your transformation, like in the final example, you may have multiple customers, especially for your direct customers, where many people could be interacting with the product or deliverable of the transformation. Equally, you may also have a customer who is both a direct and indirect customer or could be the sponsor too.

To discover who your various customers are, ask yourself:

- Who is feeling the pain of the status quo?

- What is the deliverable of the transformation and who will interact directly with it?

- What does that deliverable do differently and who benefits from this?

- Who champions this initiative, and where did it originate from?

Consider your different customers at every step of the transformation journey. This will focus your attention and ensure that you are customer centric. In turn, the transformation experience will be more positive for those impacted by or benefiting from the change.

Thinking strategically about your transformation

Your transformation and your business strategy are not the same, but they must align.

The strategy should come first, but, depending on the scale and timelines of the transformation, it could be that the strategy develops and evolves whilst your journey of transformation continues.

The concept of 'alignment' can be woolly and often judged by personal perceptions. It can be easy to talk any transformation into a position where it seems to be consistent with the strategy.

For example, a key theme in your strategy is to offer everyday low prices across the range to more customers. Your transformation is about streamlining. Could you argue that closing unprofitable stores helps to offer lower prices. Sure, you could. But in my view, it's a tenuous link.

If you find that the transformation is not aligned to the strategy, you have an interesting conversation on your hands. This is crucial to discover and confront as early as possible and there are a couple of different outcomes. Does the transformation have the wrong focus for the business and should time, effort and resources be invested into alternative plans? Or is the strategy missing something that represents a genuine challenge and opportunity for the company?

In the *Art of War*,[31] Sun Tzu talks about pre-empting your opponent and being one step ahead. An important strategic concept but one that is often missed in strategic business thinking today. From defining your transformation through to delivery, the world will continue to change. Your customers will have new expectations. Your competitors will evolve. All being well, the company strategy should have moved forward too. So, in this new world, will the transformation still ring true?

In a motor car race, you want to think dynamically and strategically plus try to second-guess your competitors, especially when it comes to the pit stop approach. The strategy here can be the difference between winning and losing, as can reacting quickly if another race team makes an unexpected pit stop.

So, like a pit stop strategy during a race, consider the transformation and broader performance: are you likely to be in the lead or are you chasing the market? What are other companies likely to be planning in their board rooms and war rooms right now? What would competitors do in response to your transformation launching? Equally, what would they do if news of your transformation leaked?

Weather forecasts are another essential input to the pit stop strategy in a race. So, what are the unavoidable and external factors that will play into your transformation journey? How will you forecast and detect these factors and what will you do as a result?

In a race team, there must be clear communication between the pit crew on the frontline and the race strategy team. Equivalently, clear communication creates alignment between the transformation team and operational teams, sharing visibility of the latest perspective on challenges and opportunities.

Additionally, there are plenty of strategic tools which you can use, from SWOT[32] and PESTLE[33] to OKRs[34] and plenty more to aid thinking. If the tool can add value to the thinking, the approach and the collaborative conversation, then use it.

Whilst your transformation is not your strategy, you can still apply strategic thinking to great effect. And one of the most important considerations is what success means.

Defining transformation success

By taking an honest look in the mirror and reading the signals, you know there is a purpose for the transformation. This purpose along with the broader strategy defines what success means.

However, success can only be achieved with three elements.

1. **A clear definition of success factors:** Perhaps it sounds obvious, but your transformation can only be successful if you know beforehand what that success is. Break down the meaning of success into smaller, more defined success factors to help you understand and measure the outcome. These success factors define your target benefits. Additionally, recognize that the resources used, additional on-costs or other investments required are also part of the transformation's success factors too.

2. **The transformation gets delivered:** Again, an obvious one. Without deliverables being completed, nothing changes, and the transformation is not a success.

3. **The benefits are realized:** Does your transformation do what it said on the tin? If the delivery falls short of expectations, it's not going to meet the success factors. And if you miss any of the success factors, there will be questions over the overall success of the transformation.

Technology solutions without a clear business need are dangerous. Suddenly the meaning of success can become about deploying 'cool stuff' and not delivering value. I'm sure you can imagine what happens next when a business is in a fiercely competitive environment and distracted by vanity or hobby projects.

Once you're clear on what the success factors are and the potential benefits of doing so, you'll want to ask if 'the juice is worth the squeeze'. The effort to travel the journey of transformation takes time, money, energy and other resources too. It's critical to understand what's required early on, and as you discover more along the journey, question if those invested resources are worth the outcome?

Defining the meaning of success for your transformation is essential. It defines the reason to go on the journey. And an organization will likely have many journeys which it *could* go on. But this comes down to a choice, a prioritization, and how the teams pursue the best option.

Prioritizing when everything is important

One of the common challenges when it comes to strategy and transformation is becoming overwhelmed. There are so many initiatives and ideas, so many options, and all appear viable and reasonable. Meanwhile, the world doesn't stand still whilst you transform. Day-to-day business and operations continue and require effort and focus to run.

Like the analogies of 'boiling the ocean' or 'stopping world hunger' suggest, doing everything isn't feasible. So, the answer is prioritization. And often, after much debate (you can probably guess what's coming next) everything gets prioritized as important. Back to square one again.

However, we all know the impact of being unable to prioritize. Over-promising and under-delivering, leading to overwhelm, anxiety, confusion and many other negative emotions. And perhaps the biggest risk is that nothing gets delivered, nothing changes and the status quo lives on.

Prioritization is as much about choosing what
not to do, as it is about what you will do.

There are three levels of prioritization to consider:

1. First, transformation must be prioritized against the non-negotiables of the ongoing day-to-day operations. It's not viable to ignore either so time and headspace must be reasonably allocated between transformation and business as usual.

2. Second, prioritizing the transformation against the other initiatives in the company, including other transformation programmes to deliver the broad strategy. It's crucial to clarify the challenge and the opportunity in a way that allows the transformation to be fairly assessed against the alternatives so that the business can make the optimum decision overall.

3. Finally, the third level is prioritization within the transformation which helps drive progress, delivery and results, focusing on the most valuable features, aspects and activities.

Developing roadmaps to divide the transformation into smaller, more agile projects and deliver over multiple years is a good approach that helps focus on the quick wins in the short term but starts to think about the longer term plays concurrently. 'Phase 2' is another valuable approach. Dividing into multiple phases helps the team to prioritize based on dependency and delivering value sooner.

Whilst there is obviously a desire to have everything delivered sooner, it's not possible. Instead, apply a laser-like focus on individual parts. Take the example of two simple projects where you have limited resource to deliver them. Each takes ten weeks of focused effort, or 20 weeks working at 50% capacity. By focusing on each project in turn, you start delivering benefits ten weeks sooner and deliver more overall.

Consider how you could divide the transformation into smaller chunks to start delivering value sooner. What is the DNA or the essence of the transformation? Can you define the constituent parts that build up to deliver value? Which parts are totally independent of others, and where are there strong dependencies? Which order must they be delivered in? What is the effort and timescales on these?

The additional benefit of prioritizing and ordering transformation by breaking down into smaller parts is that you build momentum much faster. And we'll be talking about that later in Chapter 12.

Clear prioritization helps deliver the ideal projects in a faster way and helps your transformation achieve more 'success' sooner. Once the transformation has been prioritized among the company's other initiatives, it is time to define and develop the solution.

What we've covered

> It is essential to find the why and target the right scale of transformation for your business.

> The six types of transformation allow you to define a relevant and viable vision to act as your destination.

> The transformation must align with the strategy and needs prioritizing against other initiatives in the company.

Chapter 7
Defining the
solution

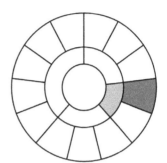

Amazing; you've defined a vision for your transformation to achieve the strategy, overcome challenges and deliver value for your customers. The destination for your transformation is a glorious future, and perhaps you can't wait to finish the journey.

To realize this vision, we must get into the nitty-gritty of defining a solution, and in turn, discovering the journey we must go on. Realistically, we may not know the exact solution at this point and must explore options along the way.

There will undoubtedly be many questions, most of which will not yet have answers. It's easy to unintentionally let confusion, scepticism and resistance take over.

To avoid this, the solution you define will be realistic, fair and detailed. You recognize that there will be both benefits and impacts, or upsides and downsides. These will be both tangible and intangible in nature, and different customers of the change will gravitate towards different outcomes.

The solution will also exist in the real world. That is, integrate within the current organization and the existing operating model. There will be requirements to identify and realize, plus restrictions which exist beyond your scope that the transformation must abide by. Defining your solution clearly will be the first step in making the transformation real.

Writing it down

One of the easiest and most tangible ways to define the solution and the transformation is to write it down. The humble transformation charter or brief is often overlooked. Alternatively, you may want to use a prospective press release to show the future vision and development journey. Perhaps it's a task that never makes it high enough up the to-do list, maybe it's seen as too basic, or just another bureaucratic bit of documentation to slow everything down.

However, the act of documenting the transformation serves two purposes, and neither is a tick box exercise.

> *'It's not the piece of paper that adds the value.'*
>
> Doug Nesbit, Strategy Director, WHSmith, Tesco, Currys, Holland & Barrett

First, capturing the key facts about the transformation is a thinking process for you and those taking on the transformation. It prompts the various elements to consider and encourages well-rounded thinking about challenges, the opportunity, the destination and the journey of transformation. If there are multiple people working on this, this encourages alignment and provokes discussion on areas where there is disagreement or mixed understanding.

Second, it's a tool to enable conversations with stakeholders. A transformation charter says: this is where we are, what we suggest and why, and how we'll get there. This should highlight many discussion topics which can help refine the document (for future conversations) and importantly, the overall approach.

Yes, you could consider the elements and have conversations without a written document. But as with all thinking, it's easy to let those brilliant golden nuggets and ideas slip through your fingers as more and more tasks, problems and ideas get loaded into your brain. And free flowing thinking and conversations are harder to keep on track, especially when a transformation has so many angles.

The skill of the transformation brief is to document the facts but not let it become excessively admin heavy. Get the brief written, but don't spend ages wordsmithing it to within an inch of its life. Keep it factual and helpful, don't let beautiful fluff or buzzwords start to obscure, confuse or distract. Remove any 'sign off' processes, as this is more about engaging and aligning senior stakeholders. The document shouldn't become so long that it becomes unwieldy and detract from useful conversations, so try aiming for a one-page version. But there could be a longer working document as a 'second brain' or for the transformation team to work on as a shared repository of pertinent information.

Example: Amazon's imaginary press release

One of the most famous ways of working at Amazon is dubbed 'working backwards'[35] and based around a future-thinking press release. Before delivering a change or new product, the team must first write a customer-focused draft press release, imagining the future after the change is implemented. This can then be critiqued, debated and improved to maximize the likelihood and impact of the change. Writing the idea down in this way helps people understand the vision.

What could you do to try working backwards from the future state?

Each of the six types of transformation will need different thinking throughout. To access simple one-page templates for each type and a mock press release template, go to DrivingRetailTransformation.com/types or scan the QR code below.

As part of the act of writing it down, you'll also start to understand the different milestones that you will pass on the journey, and these can act as excellent signposts.

Signposts and milestones

With a vision for where you're going, you'll need signposts and milestones to show you the way. Signposts show you're going in the right direction and act as a reminder about the bigger journey. The milestones are clearly defined stages that show the progress and help you keep track of how far you've gone and how far remains.

Signposts show the key stages and critical activities in your transformation. Examples include a customer research study, developing a proof-of-concept solution or running trials. Signposts are not a detailed worklist of activities, but show the big stages which help set expectations, encourage conversations and forward planning. Keep signposts at a high level and let this feed into more detailed project planning. And if your transformation is more exploratory in nature, you might not know all the signposts yet.

Milestones are precise moments in time which demonstrate your progress. Examples could include trial start or completion dates, gaining capital investment approval, sign off at a steering group or regulatory board, and again, these are transformation specific. Milestones help communicate and chart progress plus are an excellent way to build momentum, so we'll return to them in Chapter 12.

Communicating your signposts and milestones early will, like the transformation brief, encourage conversation and elicit wise counsel and advice. They are excellent to show and explain the journey that will get to the destination and the assumptions that this is based upon. And even if you suspect or assume that people already know this, it's always good to clarify.

By continuing to add details, you define the solution. Two of the most important questions to expand on the signposts and milestones are 'how' and 'why'.

How and why: the forgotten questions

There will be many questions raised or in people's heads. 'What exactly is changing?' 'Who knows how to do this?' 'What about this particular use case?' These questions are inspired by uncertainty and fuelled by confusion.

One of the most confusing aspects of defining a solution is to capture all the intricacies that exist. Retail is simple on the face of it, but the complexity comes with real-life variation and scale. This complexity deters us from defining the details, but of course, the devil is in the details. And these details clarify and dispel the unknown.

The best way to develop these details is by simply asking 'how?' and 'why?'. They're brilliant questions and allies of each other but often ignored or forgotten.

People like to stay in their comfort zones based on 'what' and 'who'. I've often found with discussions, people steer the conversation down avenues they feel comfortable and knowledgeable with. We gravitate towards these aspects and forget to look at the broader picture, and this is further amplified by assumptions created by the 'curse of knowledge'. 'How' and 'why' takes us out of these comfort zones.

'How' and 'why' encourage us to think about the whole picture. 'How' challenges us to consider all the important elements that make something work. 'Why' shows us the purpose and meaning behind any given element.

'How' and 'why' are opposites too. If you ask how something works, you'll get details of what's needed. If you then ask why, you'll confirm the value of the details and how they deliver the objective.

Both can be used to multiple levels. Process improvement methodology Lean Six Sigma includes the tool '5 why' where asking 'why?' five times will help you find the root cause. 'How' works in the same way.

Asking 'how' many times over allows us to break down a topic into a deeper and deeper level of understanding. Starting with the details and asking 'why' allows us to bring it up a level to see a broader picture.

Let's look at Figure 7.1, which shows a simplified example of a car and ask how it works, working from left to right.

Now, in that same example, we ask why, and we can work from right to left.

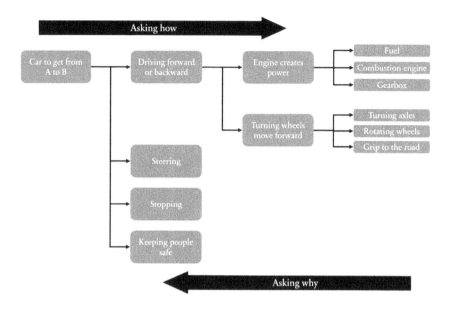

Figure 7.1: Asking how a car works to define the details and why to reveal the bigger picture

'How' and 'why' are incredible at breaking down your solution into smaller parts and defining the details that disperse the uncertainty. They help to uncover and document both the present and/or the future state. They aid understanding and communication. How and why can be used to stratify a topic into layers and show the relevance of small details against the bigger picture.

Stratify with how and why

If a goal or problem is too big or seems too complicated, we feel intimidated. We want to avoid or procrastinate these tasks. But when you're looking to dispel uncertainty and confusion, not clarifying the details will not help. Like the analogy: how do you eat an elephant? One bite at a time. By seeing the various 'bites' available, we have the intentional choice of where to start.

With the power of 'how' and 'why', I've developed the 'stratification' technique to explore complex topics in different layers and capture them in a more manageable and easier-to-understand manner. The stratification technique can be used in many ways throughout your transformation.

Stratify the status quo to capture the 'as is' processes and procedures to discover and document how things work. Identify the loose ends that are not feeding into your objective and where they don't answer 'how' or 'why'. These loose ends may be non-value add tasks which can be removed. It also helps indicates task frequency which can highlight automation opportunities.

Stratify your future state transformation or 'to be' solution, splitting into the constituent parts showing the full extent of the changes and how it integrates to the broader business and operating model. You can outline deliverables, smaller subprojects and even define requirements.

Stratify your transformation signposts and milestones into various activities. This will show dependencies and ensure no task gets forgotten about. This can then be developed into a detailed plan.

Stratify your problems to help understand the root causes and how you can discover solutions to tackle the issues.

Example: Stratifying a new operating model

I've used the stratification technique to explore and clarify the operating model in many transformation initiatives. In one instance, I was helping prepare a company to significantly expand their store estate from only a handful of stores. We needed to create a scalable operating model but the team felt this was an enormous and complex task and they were unsure where to start.

Through a series of interviews, operational observations, workshops and external research, we defined the multiple layers of the stratification, one layer at a time. It clarified the ways of working, how the various propositions were realized on a day-to-day basis, assigned where operational and organizational responsibility and decision authority lay. Plus it defined training demands, new IT requirements and suggested future changes and simplifications.

It suddenly became easy to communicate and explain how the stores and operations would work, and it enabled the successful expansion programme.

What goal or topic could you start to stratify by asking 'how' and 'why'?

The stratification of the transformation can be done in a workshop with sticky notes which can be moved around, or using Microsoft Visio, PowerPoint, Excel or online meeting tools if done through a virtual meeting. Then transfer onto a computer and I'd suggest spreadsheets are the best tool as they enable easy access and allow rows to be added for more details and reordering and making additions , edits or simplification easy. As you get into the deeper levels of detail this can take a reasonable amount of time based on your scope and scale, so I've found it's more productive for an individual to create the first pass and then review as a group. Figure 7.2 shows how I lay out stratifications in a spreadsheet where every column to the right explores 'how' and every column to the left explains 'why'.

Asking how →

Ref	Level 1	Ref	Level 2	Aim	Ref	Level 3	Ref	Level 4
3	Move	3.1	Receive at warehouse	To receive parcels from couriers, other warehouses, or retailers	3.1.1	Welcome courier and instruct where to unload		
					3.1.2	Check number of parcels is correct		
					3.1.3	Check for damaged parcels, photograph and record accordingly		
					3.1.4	Check for non-compliant parcels (e.g., very dirty, leaking, live animals, will damage other parcels, dangerous warning labels) and reject accordingly		
					3.1.5	Check correct addresses for all (e.g., name and customer ID number) or collect more info		
					3.1.6	Sign drivers POD		
					3.1.7	Move parcels safely to start of processing area		
		3.2	Process into system	To accept parcels into the system and identify the customer	3.2.1	Low volume warehouse	3.2.1.1	Move parcel to processing area one at a time
							3.2.1.2	Check and record customer number in system
							3.2.1.3	Check customer name is correct
							3.2.1.4	Measure dimensions
							3.2.1.5	Check parcel is safely on scales and in photo area
							3.2.1.6	Record weight
							3.2.1.7	Take picture
							3.2.1.8	Print and apply label and barcode
							3.2.1.9	Place onto shelving, waiting for packing, split by country according to label initials
							3.2.1.10	Unknown parcels separated to exception area (with error code added)
							3.2.1.11	Parcels needing repacking or additional packaging separated to exception area (with error code added)

← **Asking why**

Figure 7.2: Extract of a stratification expanding a topic into deeper levels of detail

Start with the happy path

When you're defining your solution, some people are happy to understand at a high level where others want the exact detail that will happen in any number of various circumstances.

Defining the solution clearly makes it more likely that you'll realize the success factors identified and therefore the transformation will be a success.

If you try to consider all the numerous details and edge cases which could happen, you'll quickly find yourself being intimidated. So, start with the happy path where the process works in the simplest way possible. Let's say: a customer makes a regular purchase with a common payment method and is satisfied with everything. Nice and simple.

Then you can start adding in the intricacies and even the failure modes. What happens when a customer wants to order something that's not available? What happens when they want to split payment between different payment methods? What happens if the order never arrives? What happens if the customer returns it? What happens if that return never arrives or has another issue?

The number of different use cases will be potentially infinite, so concentrate your efforts based on relative likeliness to occur and severity of occurrence. If a use case could end with loads of customers being aggrieved, concentrate on this. If another throws up a rare chance for an accident which could result in death, concentrate on this, even though it's unlikely to happen. The failure modes will happen, and you'll want a plan to be ready for them. As you layer on more 'what if…?' scenarios, the chance of being caught unprepared becomes more and more unlikely.

As the solution is critiqued by more customers and stakeholders, having clear answers and approaches for the main edge cases and failure modes will build confidence and demonstrate that the transformation is robust. The multi-stacked 'what if…?' edge cases, that realistically never happen, should not derail your transformation. Identify the common scenarios to help close these extreme edge cases and aim for simple solutions that guide towards sensible problem-solving approaches rather than excessively complex policies and multi-tiered rules which never get finalized or understood.

The complications raised during these stages may however uncover genuine restrictions or perceived limitations which will guide us.

Knowing and challenging the limitations

The transformation solution exists within the real world and alongside existing processes, operations, regulations and systems. These provide constraints, restrictions and limitations.

'The system won't allow this…' 'The process stops that…' 'The law states this…' 'We can't do this because…' I'm sure you can think of plenty of your own examples that you've come up against in the past.

These restrictions may impede the transformation and create blockers. They may help reinforce the scope and avoid your transformation from expanding to an unwieldy size.

The key word here is 'may'. Don't make assumptions about what is and is not possible. Many restrictions are more flexible than they first appear.

In some instances, you'll unlock the limitations, whilst others will be genuine restrictions, like national laws or existing contracts. It may be worth a conversation still, but if elements are locked in place, don't dwell on what could have been. It's wasted energy and time, especially if the issue is out of your circle of influence or control.

The unintended consequences

Retail is a complex system with many interlinking elements. When one aspect changes, there can be an implication elsewhere that was not anticipated. These are the unintended consequences, and they happen more often than we realize. Whilst they may be positive or negative, we do tend to notice the latter more.

Finding the unintended consequences is hard; by definition, they're not expected. You'll want to collaborate with diverse expertise and experiences in a workshop setting where ideas inspire more ideas. Seek unexpected consequences before and after the area of change. Consider the situation from a macro level and a micro level. View the situation from different people's perspectives.

Let's take the example of checkout-free grocery stores. On the face of it, these hi-tech stores reduce friction and make it easier to shop. By making customers scan in with an app or account, you have fantastic levels of customer data and shopping behaviour intel. But what are the unintended consequences of this?

▷ Forcing people to use the app means you instantly turn away some customers or add a major barrier of downloading the app and registering. Could you remove the need for an app?

▷ Having fewer staff is likely to present more confusion when customers can't find what they want. How could you help customers find what they want, without people?

▷ Without the personality of store staff, the shopping experience becomes more generic and less differentiated from competitors, meaning less instantly controllable aspects like price or location become more critical. How could you add more personality and service into the shopping experience?

▷ With fewer store colleagues and interaction, the team morale could be lower and encourage staff turnover. How could you build a strong culture in a small team?

▷ After shopping, one error is likely to strongly deter customers from returning and the experience will probably be shared among friends. How will you minimize the number of overcharged items, or perhaps bias toward undercharging? Would this open a new unintended consequence that attracts would-be shoplifters to exploit the opportunity?

There could also be unintended consequences impacting the core performance of the business, especially during deployment and ramp up phases. Consider how you could forecast this and take preventative action. Also communicate this expectation clearly to avoid distracting and disruptive conversations when this consequence is realized.

With a range of potential unintended consequences, consider how to detect if these will occur and consider what actions would mitigate or minimize negative impact.

Proceeding with care when fog creates uncertainty

When fog descends on the road, visibility is reduced. Market uncertainty, shifting customer behaviours and emerging technologies all reduce the visibility on our journey of transformation.

As a result, you may not be ready to stratify the solution into details early on. Exploration activities are required as the path ahead is obscured and hidden with too many unknowns. This is especially true as you take on a disruptive transformation or fundamental shift.

When you can't see the road ahead, you should navigate extra carefully. Obstacles can appear at the last minute, and this will require extra levels of responsiveness, adaptability and creativity.

It's also easy to get lost in the fog. Clear alignment with the strategy and company North Star will help enormously. These guide you in the right direction if you lose the way or get turned around.

In addition, the passengers that are on the journey with you will be more nervous and scared than you will be, due to a lack of visibility. Passengers are not in control, and this can result in negative chatter, concern and regret. Clear communications are essential to share the various potential challenges and options that you have at any moment in time. Additionally, reminding people of what you do know about the destination helps reinforce the reason for the journey.

When you're unsure of the path ahead, test-and-learn approaches will be vital to keep moving forward tentatively. Series of tests and experiments will help uncover the way, providing clarity about the current situation and where to go. And building the plans and approaches as you go ensures you stay aligned and on track.

What we've covered

▸ Documenting your transformation acts as a thinking tool and aids positive conversations, also use signposts and milestones to explain the journey.

▸ Ask how and why to stratify the solution, plan and challenges to develop understanding and build clarity.

▸ You won't always know the answers or the way forward. Collaboration and communication are essential in these situations.

Chapter 8
Aligning thinking
behind the plan

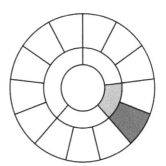

Chaotic transformation is exciting. You don't know what happens next. Every day presents surprises. Every day presents you with an opportunity to feel like you won or lost. You must think on your feet. It's an ongoing test of resilience with a chance to prove worth and value. Firefighting issues attracts support, and you get the hero status when any issue is extinguished. The chaos demonstrates your adaptability as an excellent asset for the volatile world.

Chaotic transformation is exhausting. It's stressful, unproductive and dangerous. A single slip-up and you may become overwhelmed, mentally, physically and emotionally.

Planning, relatively speaking, is not exciting. It gives stability, consistency, predictability and confidence. A plan is a prediction of the future, and this can be used to create alignment, improve teamwork, set expectations and prepare resources accordingly.

The best transformation efforts are arguably boring and uneventful. Someone says what will happen and it happens. These boring transformation efforts do not tend to attract hero status, but they absolutely should do!

Marching or meandering

One of the characteristics I love about retail operations is the ability to jump into a challenge and act quickly. I also see this regularly with transformation programmes. However, after an initial spurt of energy, progress falls away. From the initial sprint, it moves into a casual meander towards whatever might be interesting at that moment in time.

The journey of transformation is best achieved as a '20 Mile March', as popularized by Jim Collins in his book Great By Choice.[36] The concept outlines that a steady and regular pace gets you to your destination far sooner than surging forward unpredictably and then pausing to catch your energy. Collins found that businesses that achieved enormous growth were far more likely to do so when applying the 20 Mile March concept.

Planning is like marching. Planning defines the path forward. Planning implies order despite chaos. Planning asks for discipline in volatility. Planning asks you to consistently step up and deliver. This approach clarifies ownership and assigns responsibility. It sets expectations and aligns assumptions. It gives rhythm and routine to build momentum and motivation.

A clear set of plans also plots your journey. It's highly likely to need adjusting and replanning over time as you discover challenges or as external conditions evolve. With your plans in place, you're empowered to make intentional decisions about what happens next. It maintains focus and minimizes chances of drifting.

Avoiding the drift

As you pursue your destination, many factors may take you off course. You might miss important directions or turns. This might expose unexpected new dangers. Drifting along is perhaps the best way to let a great transformation stall and falter.

The drift is unintentional and usually unobserved until it's too late. I'm sure all drivers have experienced a time when your mind is on something else, you're on auto-pilot and suddenly realize that you've missed your turning. But you'll only know that you've missed the turning if you're clear on the journey and directions.

When our attention is distracted by the external environment, our eye is on other vehicles on the road, and we're dealing with squabbles or engaging, irrelevant discussions in the car, I'll let you imagine how these could affect your transformation.

Your plan allows you to see where you deviated and how to get back on track, or how to adjust to reach the destination. But unlike a simple road-based journey, when we're talking about a transformation, multiple types of plans will help us drive effectively and carefully.

The six plans

A plan is a forecast or prediction based on a set of assumptions about the future. Often when you talk about a plan in transformation, people imagine a Gantt chart or other time-based schedule. This is absolutely an important plan and it's not the only one you need.

A plan is a forecast of the future to create alignment.

Planning is crucial through transformation, whether you're using a more classical waterfall type project management or more Agile methodologies. Plans help communicate our intentions and expectations as much as possible. They also provoke relevant discussions in the best interest of the company, customers and colleagues.

Let's explore these different plans, why they're used and the various tips and pitfalls to watch out for. Different companies tend to use varying terms, so I'm sharing names that they may also be known as (a.k.a.).

Plan 1: The time schedule plan (a.k.a. Gantt chart, project plan)

Let's start with the classic project plan, showing what tasks should happen and when. Often portrayed as a Gantt chart, this plan is used to show the workflow required to deliver the transformation. By arranging the tasks, you can see the relevant dependencies and ultimately determine important delivery dates and deadlines.

The aim of this plan is to communicate what work is required, provoke action to complete that work and calculate accurate deadlines.

Without developing a time plan, it's much more likely that time will uncontrollably and invisibly slip through your fingers. The team will be unclear on activities and wait for instruction. Interdependencies will be invisible and handover work or follow on tasks will consume extra time before getting started. Tasks will be forgotten which will present problems and delays later. Deadlines and delivery timescales will be a complete guess.

Tips and tactics

- Develop two versions of the time plan: a detailed version for project managers and team members for completing tasks, and high-level programme plan (see Plan 2) for communication with stakeholders, highlighting key stages and important deadlines.

- Split the work into phases and stages, assigning owners to ensure clarity over responsibilities, and prevent tasks falling through the cracks.

- Ensure tasks have a clear completion step that triggers the next activity.

- Include approximately ten milestones in the plan, as suggested by research by Bain & Company.[37]

- Clearly indicate tasks dependencies or prerequisites to minimize schedule delays, improve productivity and ensure clean handovers.

- Continuously refine the plan over time, adjusting to the current best forecast of the future.

- Don't over-polish the plan. The purpose is to communicate the work requirements and provoke action, not to invest excessive time in planning.

- Keep the plan as simple as possible and only add as much detail as is needed. Excessive details will be overkill, conversely, omitting too much detail will make it harder to manage. Make a sensible level of plan based on the complexity and total duration of the work.

The critical path is a variation of the time schedule. I often hear people talking about the 'critical path' but what they actually mean is just a regular plan. The critical path is an analysis of the plan and concurrent activities to highlight a subset of tasks that show the order of the most restrictive activities. It shows the minimal list of tasks to preserve the overall schedule or timeline. If a single item on the critical path is delayed, the entire plan is delayed. It's definitely worth understanding what your critical path is, especially in more complex transformation activities with multiple concurrent streams, to ensure that the team's focus is minimizing any delays to these essential tasks.

Plan 2: The programme plan (a.k.a. roadmap)

The programme plan is at a higher level than the time schedule plan. It shows multiple pieces of work which all feed into the ultimate objective.

The goal of the programme plan is to communicate the bigger picture and the various pieces of work involved and their interdependencies. It is also crucial to assess if there is a risk of becoming overwhelmed. Depending on the size of the total transformation portfolio, it may be wise to review change capacity, to highlight pinch points and realign plans.

Without a programme plan, complex pieces of work are harder to understand. Taking stakeholders through more detailed plans will add confusion and focuses on the wrong topics. Remember, this is primarily a communication tool, not a project management tool.

The programme plan can take several formats. It can be displayed as a Gantt chart or a roadmap showing the relative order. The programme plan may also split work into different workstreams depending on the complexity. Figure 8.1 shows various format of programme plan.

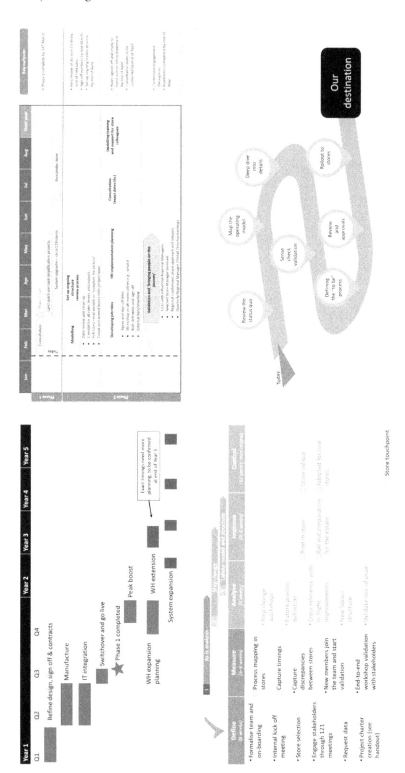

Figure 8.1: Examples of programme plan formats

Tips and tactics

- Find a format that works for you. There may already be a standard format that is used in your organization already. If this works, use it as people already understand the layout and style.

- Remember the programme plan's primary goal is about communication and helping people see the bigger picture, so adjust the format and information to ensure it meets that goal for your specific transformation.

- Consider what you're trying to communicate and how this can be shown on the programme plan. In more complex transformation initiatives, I've found it useful to have different versions of the programme plan for different communication messages or for different audiences.

- Unlike the time schedule plan, the programme plan should not be under constant revision as the bigger picture timescales and main activities should be less volatile.

Plan 3: The financial plan (a.k.a. business case, benefits case, transformation P&L)

This plan predicts the financial impact of the transformation. It should show the financial benefits delivered directly (e.g., labour savings) and indirectly (e.g., improved availability leading to more sales). Additionally, it shows the various costs involved, including the on-costs (e.g., investment in process, additional operating costs), project costs (e.g., project team cost, one-off agency or advisory fees), and capital investments (e.g., new equipment, building development).

The goal of the financial plan is to show business justification for the transformation. It should show that the change is financially viable and should aid decision making, especially around investment.

The format will be highly dependent on your organization's finance team. Hopefully, there will be a business case template or similar which exists. This will show the financial metrics that will be most important for the CFO, CEO and board and will include any relevant terminology that your company uses.

Tips and tactics

- Depending on the complexity of the transformation, it may be useful to have a master or overall financial plan with then more detailed versions that feed into it.

- Include cannibalization of the existing business. If the transformation impacts the current business model, this must be accounted for. This is particularly relevant if you're contemplating new business models, expanding product lines or categories, or introducing new services and propositions. Cannibalization of the existing business is an important factor and can easily be missed through optimism or 'it's too hard to assess.'

- Explore the sensitivity of the financial plan. What happens if benefits are not fully realized? What happens if there is a delay? What happens if costs come in higher than expected? All of these and more have a material impact on the financial viability.

- Include ramp-up times, especially when planning benefits. Depending on the change, it's unlikely to be fully productive on day one. Consider the date of delivering benefits, not only the implementation date. Additionally, look for leading indicators to act as an early signal to give confidence or provoke a proactive response.

- Include all the on-costs and project costs, including any additional preparation or training time and costs.

Plan 4: The resource plan (a.k.a. people plan)

The resource plan captures what will be needed to bring the transformation to fruition. This could include team members, individuals or teams from across the business, partners, suppliers, data, money or other resources.

The goal for this plan is to confirm what the transformation requires to complete the journey and enable discussions to collect these resources or bring the people together.

The easiest format for this plan is a list or table and shows what resources will be needed, where to get them from, when they're required and who is responsible for realizing them.

Tips and tactics

▷ Especially with people, there will be both short and longer-term requirements. For example, the need for a data analyst to support a one-off piece of analysis compared to a need for an additional transformation manager to lead a particular piece of work.

▷ With people, consider what proportion of their availability will be required over time.

▷ Consider when resources will be needed and cross reference against the bigger picture of what's going on in the company. Other transformation initiatives, peak trading, year-end or busy periods can all impact resource availability. Often these clashes are predictable so act now to ease the situation.

▷ Form fallback plans should a particular resource not be available. What alternatives do you have?

▷ In volatile and uncertain situations where you don't know, look ahead as far as possible and review regularly.

Plan 5: The deliverables plan (a.k.a. outputs)

Delivering business value and achieving the transformation's goals will require a series of outcomes. These are behaviours or performance shifts, including improved customer service levels, better availability, increased revenues or superior profitability. These outcomes are only possible due to a meaningful set of deliverables or outputs.

A tangible deliverable should be a defined piece of work, something which can be held (physically or digitally). Examples include a customer research report, training documentation, physical equipment, a custom-built IT application or an investment proposal paper. These deliverables are essential to enable the outcome that you need. For example, training documentation is required to provide training which prepares the team to operate effectively in the future, delivering improved customer service levels. The latter is ultimately what you are looking for, but the documentation is the vehicle to achieve it.

The deliverables plan is a clear list of the tangible deliverables that will be required throughout the transformation to deliver the change.

The purpose of the deliverables plan is to clarify with the team, the suppliers and the customers of the transformation about what will be produced during the transformation. When deliverables are completed, you're ready to add value through the transformation.

The format of the deliverables plan is a list or table. For each item, it should be clear what it is, any specific requirements or specifications, who is producing it (aligned to the people plan), when it will be done (aligned to the time schedule plan). You may also want to confirm the customers of the specific deliverable and any acceptance criteria or approvals. Using a training documentation example, confirm who will be giving and receiving the training, consider if sign off by the Learning and Development team is needed, or if there are relevant tests or certification requirements.

Tips and tactics

- Use a stratification to help define what deliverables will be required. You can also ask why a deliverable is required to explain what it enables.

- Cross reference against your other plans to ensure required deliverables are captured. This should provoke questions both ways. Does the time schedule confirm when the relevant deliverable will be produced? Is there any cost involved in producing a deliverable and is this accounted for? Are there deliverables created for each project cost in the financial plan? Are the best people involved to create each deliverable?

- Deliverables should be delivered throughout the transformation, not just at the end. This keeps up the tempo and builds momentum.

- Also consider what deliverables will be required for various decision points, which could include slide decks, papers or demonstration units.

Plan 6: The hypothesis plan

This final plan is a new type which I've created in response to the uncertainty that exists in the modern world. Remember, a plan is a forecast of the future. The hypothesis plan is the way to capture what we suspect will happen in the future. It defines the world that the transformation will live in once delivered.

The purpose of this plan is to clarify expectations, assumptions, bets and predictions and to encourage positive conversations to align the team and stakeholders.

The format is best done as a list or table showing the various forecasts that are made through the transformation against timescales. These could be around market conditions, customer shopping behaviour, business performance, competitor responses and other relevant and specific topics. In addition to each hypothesis, capture when you should review and identify proactive mitigating actions or planned reactions.

This plan will evoke reactions and disagreements. Provoking discussion and surfacing differing opinions and assumptions helps to create alignment. It's also possible to agree to include conflicting hypotheses, whereby the transformation may need to exist in varying versions of the future. This makes the future less of a surprise and ensures the transformation is more robust.

Tips and tactics

- Start talking to the team and stakeholders about hypotheses and how they impact your transformation.

- Capture an appropriate level of hypotheses for the transformation. Theoretically, there are infinite hypotheses that exist, so discuss and record what seems sensible. Figure 8.2 shows a template for capturing hypotheses in a workshop format.

- Use the hypotheses to capture different potential futures or what if scenarios that you want to formally recognize and work towards. This is especially useful around specific forks in the road. For example, what if the company has physical locations or not.

- Consider the likelihood of each hypothesis coming true. There is no science to this, but it can give different weighting between those dead certs, ongoing trends and wild crystal ball predictions or guesses.

- For each hypothesis, especially those less likely ones, also consider what happens if the future turns out a different way.

- Return to review the hypothesis to assess if the future prediction came true, and learn how to improve future predictions.

- You can link in with risk and issue logs, which we'll be returning to in Chapter 13 and techniques to deal with uncertainty which we discuss in Chapter 14.

Example: Putting the hypothesis plan into action

An executive team were faced with an extraordinarily large change portfolio and were struggling with prioritization. Each member had their own views on priorities with sensible logic, but each was built on very different assumptions for business growth, category expansion and external factors.

In a workshop, we built a hypothesis plan together, capturing the differing views of the future. It was a mechanism to prompt discussions about expectations, not about the individual initiatives. During the workshop, the team agreed several high probability hypotheses alongside more tentative predictions. They also identified a 'research wish list' where more external intel and insight was needed. The team loved using the hypothesis plan as a structured forecast and with an agreed view on the future, enabling productive prioritization.

What differing hypotheses and assumptions exist in your organization and need alignment?

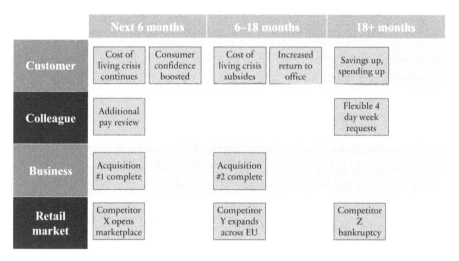

	Next 6 months		6–18 months		18+ months
Customer	Cost of living crisis continues	Consumer confidence boosted	Cost of living crisis subsides	Increased return to office	Savings up, spending up
Colleague	Additional pay review				Flexible 4 day week requests
Business	Acquisition #1 complete		Acquisition #2 complete		
Retail market	Competitor X opens marketplace		Competitor Y expands across EU		Competitor Z bankruptcy

Figure 8.2: Simplified example output from hypothesis workshop

For all these plans, you may have noticed that communication is a regular theme, and the ultimate aim of this communication is to create alignment between everyone involved.

Aligning expectations and predictions

Each plan is a way to capture your prediction of what will happen in the future. In turn, they present you with an awesome opportunity to align understanding across the team and various stakeholders. This alignment will mean that you're all working towards the same version of the vision of the future.

Each communication allows multiple conversation opportunities.

- **Clarity and explanations:** A chance to explain and explore the predictions of the future from the transformation's point of view. Sharing this allows for better understanding and clarity, which in turn allows for more collaboration and prevents future surprises and misunderstandings from pushing you off course. Be sure to state assumptions clearly to provoke discussion and a shared understanding.

- **Alternative views:** Highlighting differences of opinion can lead to conflict, but it's always preferential to bring this out on your own terms rather than leave it festering. If there is an alternative view, the worst case is that the organization is working against itself and pulling in two different directions simultaneously.

- **Changes and adjustments:** Finally, through conversation, you will uncover various changes to your plan. Improving forecasts of the future will allow for a more consistent and predictable transformation. Adjust the plans accordingly and communicate this to keep in alignment.

It's important to continually adjust each plan. There is no point in time when a plan is the 'final' iteration, aim to get the plan to be as good as it can be right now. As you continue along the transformation journey and as time passes, it's natural to learn new intel and this will lead to a better forecast of the future. Plus, as transformation is a bespoke and unique journey, you can also expect that you'll need an element of exploring the route as you go.

Exploring the route when you don't know the way

Throughout the journey of transformation, there will be times where you don't know the exact route. Perhaps there is an element of intentional exploration or maybe the details or scenarios are unclear. These situations require savviness, resilience and adaptability to navigate through successfully. Continuously iterate your plans as you discover the way.

With no clear path ahead, it would be easy to cancel the march and revert to a meander. Whilst this keeps you highly agile to navigate the terrain and challenges, it also can result in moving away from the destination and the transformation vision. Plus, it's easy to lose any momentum that you've built up.

Remember the destination. Remember why you are making the journey. Let the North Star guide you and make good decisions.

> ### Example: Assessing options when there is no right answer
>
> A company was keen to explore the opportunities with upgrading their warehouse capabilities. Among the options, we assessed several semi-automated and fully-automated options. Each option was significantly different, and whilst on the face of it, all appeared positive with varying benefits, there were downsides too. Some options required an extensive technology overhaul to integrate into current systems whilst others needed no changes. Some options were capital intensive upfront whilst other options offered as-a-service and rental options which increased operational on-costs but required minimal up-front investment. And each option presented installation headaches of different varieties.
>
> There was no clear 'best' option and the path ahead was confused, although what was apparent was that each option differed greatly. We decided that the clearest approach was to detail each option with its own set of high-level plans, and reference back against the key aims and success criteria for the initiative. This allowed conversations to have more clarity and helped dismiss options one by one. Slowly but surely, we explored and defined the future route.
>
> *How do you establish the criteria to assess and evaluate options when each path presents unique benefits and concerns?*

It's ok to not know the way at certain stages, but you must keep up the pace and maintain progress. Set short-term goals and milestones. Check in regularly with those involved and continue to communicate. You will find the way and you will continue to learn and adjust your plan towards the goal.

Learning as you adjust

However diligent you and the team are, there will be changes to the original set of plans. In every transformation, there will be unexpected events which will require rerouting. These changes will drive adjustments in the plans as you refine and tweak your predictions of the future.

This presents a learning opportunity and a chance to improve how we make these forecasts.

- Where did the adjustments originate?
- How could these have been foreseen?
- Which plans were most affected?
- Which changes made the biggest impact? Consider both the impact as a measurement (e.g., weeks, £/$/€ etc., or similar) as well as by percentage.

Review and reflect on the changes and consider what could be learnt. Ask yourself, how would these learnings affect the rest of the journey? Should you consider more sensitivities? Does it present more risks? Does it adjust the hypotheses of the transformation?

It's also valuable to consider how these learnings would adjust future transformation journeys. Is there anything that you could share with other transformation leaders in the organization to help them make better predictions of the future?

Planning allows for positive conversation and alignment. Capture the adjustments and valuable learnings from these conversations. Improved plans enhance your forecast accuracy about how the future unfolds. However, shaping the future also relies on winning hearts and minds.

What we've covered

- ▶ Chaotic transformation is exciting but not ideal. The solution is consistent (boring) progress and forecasts that mostly come true.

- ▶ Plans are predictions for the future and there are six types of plan to use in transformation, even when the future is uncertain.

- ▶ Each of these plans is a communication tool to build alignment and ultimately define and adjust to a more accurate prediction of the future.

Chapter 9
Winning hearts and minds starts with you

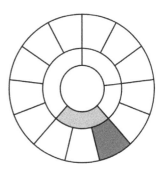

'Winning hearts and minds' is a phrase I've heard in multiple companies. Recognizing the need to focus on winning support based on logic and sense as well as on emotion and instinct, it's a sensible approach.

Aiming to earn stakeholders support, as transformation leaders, we are occasionally open to a crisis of confidence. 'Is this a good solution?' 'Will this work out for the company?' 'Should I put my name to this?' 'Will this work out for me and other people involved?' 'Do we have the capability to do this?' 'Are we good enough?' 'Am I good enough?'

In this time of mental and emotional anguish, the battle for hearts and minds starts much closer to home. It starts with you.

Our primal brain

Our ancestors faced mortal danger on a regular basis. The limbic system or reptilian brain developed to manage our automatic, immediate and primitive actions. It's the part of the brain that takes care so that we stay alive.

When our brain becomes overly active with emotions, we can feel stress. Executive coach and best-selling author Steph Tranter tells us that 'stress' is not an emotion. Stress is not even real. We use terms like 'stress' and 'overwhelm' as a general term for many other emotions that we struggle to name, like worry, fear, frustration, disappointment, anger. We especially feel these when things are out of control. And in transformation, there are many aspects which are out of our direct control. The 'known unknowns' eat us alive and clarity acts as the light to give more definition to those unknowns.

> *'Stop calling everything "stress", and instead start to identify, understand and explore the emotions you are feeling underneath that label. Develop a better understanding of what triggers your emotions, how emotions show up in you and how you can manage those emotions.'*
>
> Steph Tranter, Executive coach

Using the umbrella term of stress has many negative elements. It closes down our thinking, limiting creativity, encourages task switching and plate spinning but not task completion, and it welcomes procrastination. It's different for everyone.

But what effect do the opposite feelings have. Playfulness, focus, drive, energy. These are characteristics that help us progress successfully. Avoiding stress for our primal brain is therefore a crucial strategy.

Adding clarity to the transformation gives us a feeling of control and thus reduces our stress levels. That clarity also allows us to compare expectations with reality or our best forecasts. Although that increases the potential of conflict, a trigger moment for our primal brain to feel the concept of fear.

Our primal brain also excels at managing actions through fear, as we discussed earlier in this book. Fear highlights risks and tries to stop us making horrendous decisions. Fear is an emotion to keep us safe. There are different forms of fear: fear of the unknown, of failure, of rejection, of losing control and even fear of success. Whilst each can be triggered by separate events, each is processed in a similar way by the brain.

Initiated by part of our brain called the amygdala, when we sense fear, our intelligent brain, controlled by the cerebral cortex, shuts down. That's right, the area of the brain that is brilliant at reasoning, judgement and logic is substituted off. Blood is diverted to muscles in your legs and arms instead. Great for that close encounter with a pack of wolves; not so useful when faced with a challenging discussion in the boardroom. But those two scenarios are identical when our primal brain, the amygdala, is making a decision. Your clever, analytical, sensible decision-making brain is postponed in exchange for the instinctive fight, flight, freeze or fawn behaviours.

But understanding the behavioural science of the brain allows us to encourage positive and intentional actions rather than the instinctive ones that kept our ancestors alive.

Resilience for running the gauntlet

Whilst our primal brain may prefer us to avoid danger at all costs, our transformation requires us to confront potential conflict to find the best path forward. There are times where leading transformation can feel like running the gauntlet and intentionally making yourself open for 'attack'. Examples include technical challenges, managing delays, people challenges, difficult conversations, rigorous questioning and critique of ideas.

The reality is that the change you're driving must be challenged and tested to make it as robust as possible. The attacks are not usually aggressive actions towards you, they're honest challenges but may appear more hostile than they are.

Never-the-less, each time we perceive ourselves to run the gauntlet, we spend energy deflecting, defending or dodging 'attacks' and our stamina depletes a little more.

Resilience is not the ability to repel or defend an 'attack' or challenge. It's the ability to resist them over an extended duration. It's the ability to suffer setbacks, find alternative options and keep going. The ability to get knocked down and to get back up again. Optimism and positivity are advantageous attributes to encourage resilience.

But resilience is not limitless and when we finish our allotted stamina, we put ourselves at risk of burnout which can impact others too, further adding that feeling of 'stress'. Developing resilience is about learning from setbacks and moving forward.

Developing resilience in yourself and others

- Encourage open communications and dialogue, explaining perspectives and reasoning. Lead by example.

> Celebrate successes regularly with those involved, recognizing that people may feel like they completed the gauntlet. Also acknowledge and learn from aspects that haven't worked well.

> Develop problem-solving skills to analytically approach a challenge rather than emotionally.

> Provide support, especially for less battle-hardened team members, where people can share their experience and advice on how they have overcome obstacles.

> Learn to recognize the signs of burnout, such as fatigue, irritability or reduced passion, and prioritize time to rest, recharge and seek support when needed.

Determination to persevere

Strongly connected to resilience, determination is the willingness and energy to push through to completion, even when things get tough. This is about staying committed to the transformation goals. This is about recognizing that the journey towards your destination is long and needs energy. It's recognizing that the journey has uphill sections which must be climbed before reaching the downhill section.

This is about both self-confidence and confidence in the transformation. Self-confidence or belief that you could make the journey and overcome obstacles along the way. Confidence in the transformation is about understanding the destination and why you want to go there, whilst recognizing that the energy investments are worthwhile. Determination is required at various points, including during the intense period of launching an initiative, or maintaining regular and relevant communication with difficult stakeholders.

Developing determination in yourself and others

> Set clear goals and take on the 20 Mile March mindset discussed in Chapter 8.

> Remind yourself and others about the destination and the reason for transforming. Continue to take an honest look in the mirror to provide motivation and stay up-to-date.

- ▷ Update on progress regularly to highlight achievements, discuss challenges and provide support. Sharing this creates momentum and reinforces commitment to the goal.

- ▷ Plan and manage resources to complete the transformation.

The humility to be 'not right'

Modern day knowledge workers, including those working on and in retail transformation initiatives, are headstrong. Being right is important and this drives many to prove their knowledge and instinct. In fact, one of Amazon's values[38] is that leaders 'are right, a lot.'

> *'Management is doing things right; leadership is doing the right things.'*
>
> *Anonymous[39]*

It's likely that to get to a senior position, being right has been a key attribute. However, in an ever-evolving and volatile world, situations change and ideas or perspectives that were previously 'right' are no longer necessarily true.

But this also prompts an important question: 'What is "right"?' Especially in a world where there are multiple paths to success, be that transformation success, business success or individual success. Fiona McDonnell is a business leader with experience at Amazon, Nike, Kellogg's and Booking.com and suggests that 'right' will be relevant to our definition of success.

> *'If you are measuring yourself against someone else's definition of success, you will never be satisfied.'*
>
> *Fiona McDonnell[40]*

Humility is about recognizing the limitations in your own thinking or approach. It's about being open to challenging your own meaning of 'right'. And it's about recognizing that other people's perspectives and opinions may be right too, even if they contradict yours.

Developing humility in yourself and others

- ▷ Develop a culture of psychological safety where it's ok to make a mistake or be 'wrong' as you ask for help or advice. Leading by example is a must-have to get the ball rolling.

- Encourage feedback between individuals as well as self-reflection.

- Ask 'what if?' and consider alternative assumptions that differ to what you consider to be 'right'.

Curiosity to question and learn

Curiosity is a desire to learn more, ask questions, investigate, understand and explore new ideas. Some individuals are more naturally curious or have a tendency to be more curious about particular topics.

Strongly connected to humility, this is about seeking alternative ideas and viewpoints. When we are curious and explore new ideas, our brains release dopamine,[41] a chemical that plays a key role in motivation and reward. It makes us feel great and there is increased activity in the memory part of the brain, the hippocampus, allowing us to take on and retain more information. The brain chemistry of curiosity makes us feel good and encourages further learning of new topics and ideas.

Curiosity will be especially important as you take an honest look in the mirror, read the signals and find the ideal transformation. But as the transformation continues, this remains an important skill and attitude to find the best way forward.

Developing curiosity in yourself and others

- Ask 'why?' to gain a bigger picture view and connect how different elements are related.

- Research and learn more about relevant topics through reading, podcasts, videos, attending events and having conversations.

- Encourage people to take on side projects or to explore their ideas further and broaden their knowledge.

- Explore outside the comfort zone to learn and develop further.

The courage to take risks

Courage is an ability or trait that isn't discussed enough. Courage is about working outside the comfort zone and facing fear. It's about being brave and taking calculated risks. It's about following your beliefs and having conviction.

In transformation, courage is expected, almost as if it's taken for granted. Transformation is about moving forward into the unknown, facing fears, dangers and uncertainty. It's closely connected with resilience and determination.

Courage is not being fearless. It's about confronting fear sensibly and confidently. To be courageous, you must trust your heart, your instinct, your mind, your intelligence. Additionally, trust your colleagues that are on the journey with you.

Developing courage in yourself and others

- Learn to assess risks based on both logic and feeling. Explore how you define what is an acceptable level of calculated risk.

- Gradually expose yourself to more fears to build confidence in yourself as well as confidence in how you react to fear.

- Learn from past risks, understanding what has and hasn't worked. Discuss these with others to build a support network.

- Challenge your mindset to name and explain the fear. Then ask if these fears are factual or fictional.

Learning about the industry and subject matter

A deeper understanding of the industry helps develop the logical justification in what you're doing. Winning 'the mind' needs an intellectual argument to inform decision making and direction.

The industry is continually changing, and old knowledge expires. Meanwhile, customer habits are formed by younger generations and what's happening in the external environment (e.g., pandemics, wars, politics, economy, social changes, technologies). New business technologies also are developing and elements like AI, blockchain, data, robotics, xR (extended reality) and others may be far more advanced than you realize, which opens new opportunities. Knowledge of the relevant subject matter is also important and may extend beyond the boundaries of retail, for example, with company culture or the economy.

All this knowledge will give greater confidence in the approach, open new creative thoughts and add broader strategic viewpoint of the industry and marketplace. However, this can only happen once your head has had time to process the information, identifying patterns and trends.

Developing knowledge in yourself and others

- Being curious to explore and understand more.

- Feed your brain with new intel, either by absorbing content of various forms (through books, articles, podcasts, videos), engaging in debate and discussion (through events, roundtable discussions, networking) or by experiencing it yourself (through being a customer or taking an honest look in the mirror).

- Consider how you will record and process knowledge, and avoid it fading and decaying.

- Head over to DrivingRetailTransformation.com/extras or scan the QR code below to discover more resources to help learn knowledge of the industry and your relevant subject matter.

Leading with the right attitude and mindset

The attitudes and mindsets that we've discussed in this chapter will help you drive transformation. There are many other elements which we could discuss: leadership (which is a complex web of many topics), creativity, critical thinking, relationship building, decision making and many more. There are whole books on each of these individual topics and I encourage you to continue exploring and developing yourself on these topics.

It's important to hone your strengths in these areas. Lead by example and demonstrate the approach that you'd like to inspire others with. I believe that the most effective and reliable way to shift a culture is to model the ideal behaviours and act as a consistent role model.

Because winning hearts and minds starts with you. After all, as a leader, why would you expect others to work or act differently to you?

Personal goals and missions are also relevant as they reinforce the attributes and strengths that you show. What are your personal goals? What is your purpose or reason for being? How does this impact how you work and what you do? Is there alignment? If not, this can result in deep dissatisfaction and frustration with life which will spill out into everything you do, impacting both life and work.

Example: Discovering personal alignment

Whilst we might assume alignment between your personal mission, your strengths and your career, yet I can think of several instances where this hasn't been true, and this has led to many negative experiences.

Jo was caught in a company and a career path that she fell into. She was responsible for retail transformation programmes at an international company. Jo's raw talent and ability allowed her to achieve results, but relationships with colleagues were continually strained. She left work each day with a mix of emotions and feelings; anger from the day's interactions, relief from leaving it all behind (for a few hours at least), emptiness from not really caring about what she did and exhaustion from the internal struggles to concentrate and do things she just didn't want to do. This all impacted her personal life significantly and time was passing by, leaving her unfulfilled.

After recognizing that there was personal misalignment present, she decided to swap careers, then Jo excelled. And she excelled despite lower pay and longer hours, usually factors that people want to change about their job. She loved her new life, and this brought success at work and happiness at home. Jo's original path did not have the right alignment, especially between her mission and the job, and she's not looked back since.

How do you ensure that your personal mission and strengths align with your professional path? And how would you resolve any misalignment?

Consider at this very moment, how aligned is your current set up? And if you're on the right path, how will you challenge yourself to be a better leader of transformation? How will you become more equipped to lead the team, better prepared to navigate the route and ready to drive onto your destination? How will you continually improve?

You chose to be the driver,
now choose to be a better driver.

Helping others take this same path

You already know that transformation is not a one-player game. Other people must come on the journey too. And once you've won your own heart and mind, and that you're satisfied that you're on the right life path, it's time to inspire others.

Through coaching and mentoring, you can share your experiences and learnings with those new to the journey of transformation. Explore their expectations and the realities you've discovered. Define what's challenged you and how you overcame these.

Actively collaborate across the organization. It doesn't need to be in an official coaching or mentoring role. But supporting and guiding colleagues who are ultimately on the same team will build strong foundations for effective cross-functional working and will help break down functional silo walls.

Network externally too, either at events or on social media. I'm sure you'll have seen how small the industry tends to be and active connections at other companies could offer plenty of future opportunities.

As the retail industry faces more threats, the need for transformation will only increase. The need for effective and experienced transformation drivers increases.

Consider how you will inspire more people to step up
from being a passenger and take the driver's seat?

What we've covered

- Our primal brain is trying to fight us and tries to disrupt how we approach the journey of transformation.

- There are essential mindsets and attitudes which develop your brain's emotional and logical side.

- Challenge yourself to continually improve and help others to actively choose to develop and drive transformation.

Chapter 10
Getting the best
people involved

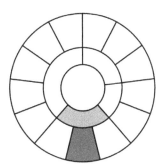

People are essential to transformation. Building the best team to help you drive retail transformation remains a critical success factor. This ideal team blends the right mix of skills, experience and perspectives. However, unlike classic teams, transformation teams may include a mix of expertise and available time, plus people may join or leave the team part way through the journey.

As with all teams, some tension can be helpful to sharpen everyone's game, but too much tension and conflict is destructive so finding compatible individuals is important too. Individuals and the team must overcome challenges and grasp the opportunities along the journey. Bringing diversity ensures there is a mix of talent, experience and perspective.

Creating a cohesive team requires careful orchestration. Everyone must be aligned to the same goals, strategy and vision. The best people tend to be more naturally competitive and can therefore be tempted to compete against each other. Creating an open culture is essential for the collaboration and trust that allows the team to reach maximum potential. And attitudes and strengths are key considerations.

Managing a talented core team is demanding. But first, you'll need to find the best people to drive your initiatives, and that is a tough challenge that many retailers face.

Why it is hard to find the ideal people

To realize the future ambitions of the company, you need exceptional individuals who can actively drive and steer an organization through change, not just wait for it to happen. But finding these people can feel like hunting down a mythical creature. They're hard to describe, rarely spotted and are also likely to be chased by other companies looking to fulfil their ambitions.

There are broadly four options:

1. Using existing in-house skills and capabilities.

2. Developing new transformation talent from existing individuals.

3. Recruit talented individuals from outside the business.

4. Engaging consultants, contractors or interim staff for a short-term 'stop-gap'.

Let's explore each of these.

Using in-house resources

Finding the most suitable in-house person can be a great solution which can be realized quickly. Unfortunately, the rare skills required are probably already otherwise engaged in other important work which means there is a priority call for the organization to make. Additionally, individuals must be backfilled or have their workload reallocated or reduced.

Developing new transformation talent

Developing people with great potential can be a super avenue to pursue. The strategic perspective and ability to get things done will be hugely valuable to the business in the future. Consider how it will be best to train, coach, mentor and support these individuals in the knowledge that nearly everyone's learning journey will be unique. This can be a demanding ask without the right support.

Recruiting externally

As more companies and retailers turn to transformation to rescue or grow their business, the big mismatch between the high demand and the low supply of skilled and adaptable people becomes more apparent. And the trends suggest that we'll probably see an even greater demand for this highly sought-after type of individual. Nevertheless, once recruited, these individuals need time to join and onboard before climbing the effectiveness curve.

Bringing in short-term resources

This option allows for speed, assuming the network exists, relationships have been formed previously and that trust has been earned. Consultants, contractors and interim people can all be valid and are used to working rapidly to drive progress.

Unfortunately, it's likely that your transformation timelines will demand action and progress quickly without the luxury of postponing until you find the best people to run and lead the initiatives. However, the risk of pausing or waiting must also be tempered against the unknown time taken to find that elusive individual. Also consider the opportunity cost for postponing your transformation. Either way, identify the driver of transformation to ignite progress and move it forward.

Maybe this is you and you want to know how to develop further. Or maybe you need to find or develop the ideal driver and want to know what to look for.

The ideal driver of transformation

We recognize that those adept at transformation are hard to find. But what is it about someone that defines them as a potential transformation driver? It's a blend of capabilities, skills and personal characteristics which are interconnected but different.

Capabilities

The broader competencies or abilities to perform a task or function. They allow someone to navigate complex situations, make good decisions and ultimately achieve the desired outcome.

1. **Strategic thinking:** Identifying both long- and short-term goals, assessing risks and developing viable approaches for transformation.

2. **Financial acumen:** Making sensible, realistic and profitable business decisions, considering all opportunities and implications fairly from operational, customer and colleague points of view.

3. **Stakeholder and customer focus:** Identifying, communicating with and influencing key stakeholders and customers to understand their needs and gain support.

4. **Ruthless prioritization:** Recognizing when decisions are needed and assessing the various initiatives and actions to clarify priorities and allocate resources accordingly.

5. **Cross-functional collaboration:** Working effectively with various teams and departments both internal and external to the business, naturally considerate and thoughtful for other people's aims.

6. **Cultural adaptability:** Recognizing and comprehending the existing organization and culture, able to identify and lead the required shifts in behaviour to evolve the broader culture as part of the transformation.

Skills

The learnable techniques which are gained and developed through training or practice over time.

1. **Programme and project management:** Organizing, planning and executing transformation initiatives to achieve desired outcomes.

2. **Change leadership:** Inspiring, motivating, educating and guiding individuals, teams or whole companies through change and the emotional rollercoaster this brings, creating a positive, supportive and collaborative environment to usher in new ways of working.

3. **Business analysis:** Analysing processes, performance and data to understand situations and identify areas for improvement and innovation, recognizing the pertinent questions to ask about a situation or dataset.

4. **Communication and influencing:** Sharing complex information, guidance or reasoning clearly and persuasively, in written and verbal forms, which can be performed over any channel.

5. **Adaptability:** Adjusting to volatile and ever-changing circumstances, willing to learn and be wrong, embracing new ideas, and learning from failures or setbacks.

6. **Critical thinking:** Evaluating available information objectively and fairly, identifying your own biases and those of others, making logical and well-informed decisions.

7. **Problem solving:** Understanding how to approach challenges and find a solution, without being caught in or starting a blame game, identifying and assessing all potential options.

Personal characteristics

The personal traits, attributes or attitudes that form a distinctive individual. These factors have a major impact on how any given person approaches a challenge and affects their mindset and behaviour. These are more natural traits but can be developed through rigorous coaching and experience.

1. **Common sense:** Having sound judgment based on a simple perception of the situation or available information.

2. **Resilience:** Possessing the grit and determination to continue in the face of adversity, or responding positively to setbacks, remaining calm under pressure.

3. **Courage:** Progressing bravely into the unknown and into potentially hostile environments, with trust in their own resilience.

4. **Curiosity:** Questioning the status quo and considering other potential truths, exploring new ideas willingly, open to learning from other people or intel.

5. **Initiative:** Recognizing the best path forward proactively, taking opportunities to improve, innovate or progress, demonstrating a strong sense of ownership and accountability.

6. **Empathy:** Understanding and appreciating how stakeholders, customers or other people could be feeling at an individual level, appreciating the challenges and opportunities that people may face.

7. **Optimism:** Keeping a positive outlook on challenges and opportunities with a mindset that thinks that anything is possible, and inspiring this hope and confidence in others.

8. **Integrity:** Complying with strong moral and ethical principles, always ensuring that actions and decisions are guided by honesty,

transparency, and both personal and corporate accountability, plus remaining aligned with the company's goals and values.

I must stress, however, that the likelihood of finding all 21 of these traits in one person is remote. So, it's important to prioritize these traits for your specific transformation and company, there may be more focus on some areas than others.

Try rating which traits will be most relevant for your transformation, and which will be less important. You can then focus on these traits through recruitment and people-development activities.

Transformation is after all a team effort and team members will play different roles.

Analogy: The driver is only a part of the race team

Consider a professional racing team, in Formula 1 or other motorsports. The driver is undoubtedly an important part of achieving results, but by no means the exclusive factor of success. There are many important topics that the driver is not an expert in: aerodynamic car design, weather-dependent race strategies or pit stop wheel changes to name a few. All of these and many more are not the remit of the driver. Instead, the entire team of around 1,000 people must work together, combing their capabilities, skills and characteristics to take the lead and finish in first place.

The transformation team

'Those who build great companies understand that the ultimate throttle on growth for any great company is not markets, or technology, or competition, or products. It is one thing above all others: the ability to get and keep enough of the right people.'

Jim Collins[42]

The transformation team will be formed alongside the driver or drivers of transformation. This team will be specific to your plans and may include project managers, workstream leads, analysts, subject matter experts and others.

There may be certain aspects which will be more biased or relevant in your transformation. For example, in an optimization transformation, there may be a need for more data analysis and modelling, and the team will want to be resourced accordingly. Whereas, other transformations may need more commercial expertise, process reengineering capabilities or other skills.

Additionally, specific technical skills or domain knowledge will be required in the team too, again, bespoke to the transformation and your organization. These may include elements such as familiarity with relevant and local HR policies or procedures, technical knowledge of particular systems or interfaces, working relationships with key suppliers, or category experience based on your retail focus and transformation effort.

It's likely that the team are not going to be working full-time on the transformation. Whilst it's brilliant if this is the case, usually, there is an ongoing requirement for continuing with the 'day job' or being part of other initiatives. Clarify the ask and roles for these situations.

I imagine, with high certainty, that your transformation will impact different parts of the organization. And therefore, your transformation team must be cross-functional too. This brings balance and extends an excellent network across the business. But also brings challenges too, which we'll come back to shortly.

Once you've identified the team, consider how to get people assigned and on board. Whilst there may be the opportunity to operate internal application and recruitment processes, often the urgency and the need to get cracking sooner remains. Commandeering the team from across the business may be essential to ensure the right individuals get on board. The right people are likely to be in demand and probably already head-down and engaged in other work. Knowing if this is the right decision for the company is, in itself, a question of integrity and collaboration. Does it make sense for the overall company prioritization and are there the right relationships to deliver this? Also factor in the company culture and working practices to minimize the scale of upset and conflict caused.

As you form this new team, new connections will be forged, and new working relationships must be fostered. Differing experiences and perspectives will result in differing opinions, and create the potential for tension and conflict, so consider how to make this cross-functional team tick.

Making the cross-functional team tick

When you bring your transformation team together, as with any other team, it's essential to get the team to work effectively. Individuals will have different levels of awareness of the transformation and may be arriving with different agendas. An effective onboarding meeting is a great chance to surge ahead at the start, and regular transformation meetings continue to offer opportunities to make the team effective over time. Additionally, consider how the team working behaviours mature and evolve over the course of the transformation. Looking ahead, in Chapter 11, we'll explore more about stakeholders, silos and the broader transformation ecosystem.

Onboarding meetings to formally kick off a transformation are a great way to communicate and align the team. Whilst they are unlikely to be the very first conversation, they should be among the first official meetings. On the agenda should be:

- **Team introductions:** A chance to find out who's who, their role and background.

- **Transformation overview and goals:** Discussing the challenges and opportunities, clearly stating what the transformation is and why we're doing it.

- **What we know so far:** This section allows you to bring everyone up to speed with the latest intel, research or historical progress. Whilst some transformations may be clearly defined, others will not be.

- **Ways of working:** Including check-ins, regular meetings, guiding principles, problem-solving approaches, communication, responsibilities and other expectations.

- **Open discussion:** Allowing time for questions, concerns or conversations.

- **What's next:** The onboarding meeting should clearly specify what happens next and what individuals should do.

Regular transformation meetings allow time to communicate and align. It's likely that there will be various frequently occurring and ad hoc meetings and workshops, which may be focused on particular challenges or sub-topics. However, a regular meeting is a great place to drive the transformation. Confirm these elements:

- **The purpose of the meeting:** Clarify what the point of this meeting should be, and ensure it's written down prominently to be referred to in the future to maintain meeting efficiency and effectiveness.

- **What will be discussed:** What will the meeting cover, and it's equally important to determine what will not be included. Technical subjects across any function are essential to the transformation but the details may not be right for this meeting or audience.

- **How the meeting will operate:** Include expectations for individuals and transformation updates, agenda planning, ways of working for discussions and decisions.

- **When and where:** The logistics of the meeting should be clear and consistent, and if it's an in-person, online or hybrid meeting.

- **Who is expected to attend and why:** Larger meetings get increasingly inefficient and expensive for the company so focus on the right but minimal attendance. Also clarify expectations for sharing planned or unplanned absence.

- **Meeting hierarchy:** What other relevant meetings occur around this one, including working groups or steering groups, to give visibility to interested parties.

- **Documentation:** Consider how to document the meeting and share a digest more widely, bearing in mind confidentiality. This helps minimize attendees that attend only to listen in and improves productivity.

The onboarding meeting and regular meetings help to foster teamwork and ensure alignment. Additional communication channels, including chat or messaging systems, can help remote or dispersed teams to collaborate, share updates and foster a team culture. Decision making is a key aspect, and we'll return to this topic in Chapter 15.

The effectiveness of this team develops over time. Initially, the team is a collection of individuals, all who will have a mix of emotions, similar to Fisher's Change Curve as discussed in Chapter 2. Tuckman's stages of group development model[43] (also known as Forming, Storming, Norming, Performing) is essential to understand as it shows how to mature a newly created transformation team (see Table 10.1). Starting at Forming, the new team will progress through the stages, ultimately learning to be effective based on the completely unique combination of individuals and topics.

Table 10.1: Using the stages of group development model

Stage	What you'll see	Watchouts	How to move onto the next stage
Forming (new teams start here)	Politeness, anxiety, tentativeness, excitement, unsure of the roles across the team, looking for approval from leaders on direction.	The team may be hesitant to share ideas or opinions, limiting effectiveness for creativity or solving problems.	Clearly stating the goals and objectives. Defining roles and responsibilities, which may include a RACI[44] matrix. Allowing opportunities for the team to get to know each other.
Storming	Differences of opinions, arguments and conflict. There will be power struggles and some team members may seem to disengage from the team to avoid conflict.	Conflicts and power struggles may or may not be visible or public, but must be resolved or will lead to disengagement and prevent moving on to the next stage.	Recognize the conflicts and address them to find a suitable resolution. Encourage respectful communication, always. Allow opportunities for collaborating or solving problems.

Norming	Establishing ways of working as an effective team, more effective collaboration, supporting each other, more naturally occurring communication and intel being shared proactively.	Reluctance to formally define ways of working. The existing team may feel that newer members should adopt the previous ways of working.	Celebrating wins, achievements and positive behaviours. Encourage people to learn from the other team members. Reinforce and role-model open communication and sharing.
Performing	Independent and effective team working together, open communication, helping each other and solving problems together.	Any small changes (new or changing team members, change of working practices even long periods of annual leave) can cause upset at this stage and regress to earlier points in Tuckman's model.	(Or rather: How to stay in this stage) Challenge the team to continue to improve. Maintaining good communication. Celebrating examples of great teamwork.

Whenever team changes occur, including new joiners or leavers, it upsets team dynamics and progress reverts to the Forming stage again. Tuckman also added a final stage of Adjourning[45] which is about the team's termination. We'll return to the end of the transformation in Chapter 16.

Looking after your team

We've already discussed the challenges of change and transformation. Your team will be susceptible to these challenges too. Stress, fatigue and burnout are all very real risks for those working on transformation initiatives as well as those leading them.

Watch for signs of exhaustion, frustration, reduced productivity, disengagement, and other indications that someone may be struggling.

For more junior team members, this may be the first time they are privy to more strategic or sensitive information, which can empower people to rise to their 'A game', but is also at risk of weighing on someone's conscience, especially if job losses or other negative impacts are part of the transformation. However, that said, these negative impacts pose mental health risks to all involved.

If you're working with a cross functional team in a matrix organization, you must collaborate with an individual's line manager or with HR. Clear communication on workload, progress, behaviours and potential conflict of priorities are essential to find the best path forwards for all involved.

Example: Uncovering conflicting priorities

Jay was involved in a transformation that I was driving. He started to forget tasks, was not completing work and was being uncharacteristically curt in meetings. He was showing signs that he was struggling. In conversation, he revealed that he was being pulled in multiple different directions, from both his 'day job' but also other transformation initiatives that he'd been assigned to.

All stakeholders were unaware of the other demands, meaning any conflicting priorities were invisible to all except Jay. By working with him and his manager, we agreed on a range of solutions to simplify the workload and coach him on managing task lists, stakeholders and competing priorities.

How do you proactively identify and resolve conflicting priorities within your team, especially for non-direct reports or in matrix organizations?

Regular touchpoints with the team members will help identify issues and offer opportunities for open conversations about struggles or behaviours. The solution will be bespoke to the individual and may include training, coaching, flexibility or reassessing their workload or priorities.

Recognizing the efforts and accomplishments of team members is often easy to bypass, but presents a massively missed opportunity. Individuals often invest huge effort and headspace in the transformation in response to the responsibility given to them by the company. Acknowledging and celebrating these efforts is highly valued and enormously motivating, even if only a simple 'thank you' and recognition in a meeting.

Depending on the size of your organization and transformation, there is also likely to be an extended ecosystem of people who support the transformation. If you lead by example, encourage your team to care for those in the wider ecosystem too to maintain the transformation's effectiveness and the organization's wellbeing.

What we've covered

- ▷ Transformation initiatives can be extremely hard to resource against due to the complex combination of six capabilities, seven skills and eight characteristics.

- ▷ Your transformation must be driven by someone, and it is ultimately a team game.

- ▷ Developing a group of cross-functional individuals into a high performing team takes time and intentional effort.

Chapter 11
Creating and
fostering your
transformation ecosystem

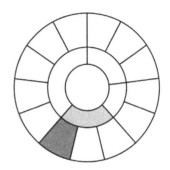

The transformation will extend across the organization and perhaps externally too. The type and scale may extend the reach and complexity.

The transformation does not exist in a bubble. This journey exists in a dynamic environment of ongoing operations, external factors and additional initiatives to pursue the corporate strategy.

Whilst sole individuals can help drive transformation, it is ultimately a team game, as discussed. One person can't deliver the complete change. Instead, this effort will require huge input and expertise from an extended team to develop and deliver. This extended team will undoubtedly require cross-functional support from the organization where this may be just one of many projects or pieces of work they're focused on.

The success relies on this broad transformation ecosystem and a multitude of interconnected factors.

What is a transformation ecosystem

Your transformation exists within a complex system of many interacting elements. Deep-down, I'm sure you know this already, but when you see the complexity of these linkages, you begin to understand how to best influence the system.

Meanwhile, we all experience frustration at certain points along the journey of transformation, whoever we are and whatever role we play in the initiative. This frustration is born from when the ecosystem is not flowing.

There are eight elements of the ecosystem:

1. **Strategy:** The company strategy for the future, guided by a North Star, targets business improvement for future performance, considering the competitive market, industry trends and forecasts.

2. **Transformation:** Recognize that your transformation exists in the ecosystem alongside many other transformation initiatives. Like in nature-based ecosystems, these may compete for resources, cooperate to support each other or coexist relatively independently.

3. **People:** People from across the organization and external parties such as suppliers, are the dynamic part and ultimately influence the entire ecosystem to work effectively. Or not. Additionally, the different people involved have individual interests based on each specific transformation. These interests are an invisible and immeasurable force that inspire individuals into action, positively or negatively.

4. **Priorities:** The business priorities focus the attention of the organization, setting a relative importance to help unlock resources, focus and support.

5. **Resources:** The varying factors that enable a transformation, including capital investment, budget, equipment, tools, data, time and skills. People are inherently linked as a human resource.

6. **Business and operating model:** How the business functions, including the commercial, financial and customer proposition, the ways of working for all business units and overall rules of engagement for the organization. This also includes the processes that enable transformation, including governance, various approvals, methodologies and terminology.

7. **Consumers and performance:** The lifeblood of the business. Converting consumers into customers and keeping the tills ringing is what allows the business to trade effectively and profitably. Many factors are involved in this deeply complex section. For the purposes

of simplicity, we will consider this is best represented by the metrics that matter most to the business as a proxy.

8. **External environment:** The ecosystem exists within a wider environment, consisting of local and global situations, competitors, politics, regulations and other industries impacting the world (e.g., technology, media).

These elements exist together, and a series of interactions is ever-present.

The ecosystem is intrinsically interlinked together

Figure 11.1 shows a simplified representation of how these different elements are interacting. There are complex forces at play. Some may be clearly defined which allows them to be managed or controlled (e.g., resources). Others are complex, ever-changing and relatively uncontrollable (e.g., the external environment). And some can be defined but not all companies are at this place yet (e.g., clear business and operating model, priorities).

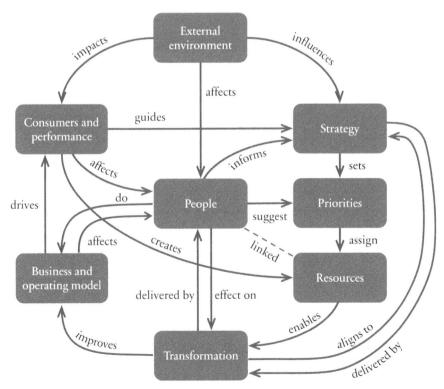

Figure 11.1: System diagram of the transformation ecosystem

Other interactions exist but for *relative* simplicity, let's leave them off for now.

The ecosystem naturally has uncontrollable elements which can have huge impacts, so you want to ensure that you appreciate the complex network. In turn, you can begin to find levers to unblock your transformation or stop it from getting blocked in the first place.

It's also clear when you map out the ecosystem, that people sit at the heart, both literally and metaphorically, and they represent the most complex and dynamic element.

People are the complex and dynamic element

People play a crucial role in making the transformation ecosystem function. To help understand how to best leverage this critical factor, we must first break this group into smaller elements (as shown in Figure 11.2).

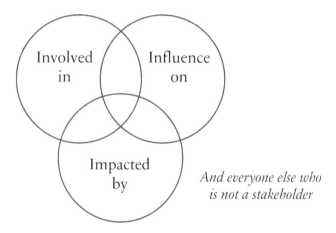

Figure 11.2: The people in your transformation ecosystem

▷ **Involved in:** These people are directly part of the transformation effort. Perhaps they're an active and regular member of the work team (e.g., a subject matter expert representing their functional area). Or maybe they play a part for a relatively short time only (e.g., the Learning and Development team who will create a short training guide).

- **Influence on:** Are connected to the transformation and will be a key decision maker or able to provide significant sway to the direction and future of the transformation (e.g., CFO who is accountable for capital expenditure allowances).

- **Impacted by:** These individuals are on the receiving end of the transformation and will include the customers of the change. The type of impact felt by these stakeholders will vary. It could be an impact to ways of working, perhaps it means a significant change of role, or even being displaced altogether. Shareholders may also be impacted financially by the transformation.

- And finally, there are those people who are not part of the transformation. Whilst these individuals may have opinions, they aren't relevant to the transformation or how it will affect the future.

As the Venn diagram suggests, individuals may sit across multiple groups. Stakeholders could be internal or external to the organization, including suppliers, regulatory bodies, advisors, agencies and the end consumer too.

It's critical to discuss and identify the different stakeholders of the change. They're probably more far reaching that you might initially imagine.

Additionally, and I'm sure you can imagine this, not all stakeholders carry the same level of importance. Although it's crucial to recognize by importance, we don't mean hierarchy-based importance. It's about relevance to the transformation. Perhaps that's based on their role, their relationships, or the influence, respect and sway they command in the organization.

The challenge is to connect with all these relevant stakeholders, listen to their experiences, challenges and ideas and continue to engage and communicate through the journey of change. These individuals may be your greatest advocate or present an enormous challenge.

Engaging stakeholders

The greatest myth of stakeholder management is that stakeholders are ready to be or can be 'managed'.
Instead, it's about earning their engagement.

Having identified the stakeholders, decide on a realistic and manageable approach to engage and communicate these individuals. The size of the transformation, the number of relevant stakeholders or stakeholder groups and your team size will ultimately determine what's feasible. Whilst having one-on-one interviews with 10,000 store colleagues might sound like a nice idea, it's not going to be feasible without significant investment and delegation.

Example: The hard work to engage stakeholders at a relevant level

In one major change project, which impacted approximately 40,000 individuals across 2,000 stores, it was critical to turn to the regional and area management hierarchy to support with rollout and deployment. However, even then, there were still over 100 people and group teams to involve.

Given the importance of the change, the impact to the operation and other constraints, I decided that detailed and personalized plans would be the best route forwards, tailoring the approach for different types and formats of store. I was questioned if this was really necessary. I felt it was the best way to ensure effective execution. For each group, briefing packs with personalized details of stores, dates, local points of contact and more factors were created and distributed. These were supported with conference calls, team meeting updates and various other forms of communication. Briefings also went out to the senior management teams to help provide complete clarity.

The change was exceptionally smooth, and every group had the personalized information they needed. The hard work that went into creating these engagement plans paid off significantly and would have been far more successful than adopting a simple one size fits all plan.

How could you improve personalization as you engage stakeholders whilst considering the resource and time constraints?

Ultimately, each individual stakeholder is busy with their own interests, goals, priorities and perspectives. The transformation may be a distraction for them. It may represent a positive or negative impact, but either way, it disrupts the status quo.

As such, the approach may need to be personalized and relevant to the part that they play in the transformation, or the part that the transformation plays for them. You'll need to discuss, listen, inform and ultimately inspire these individuals into action.

Inspiring others to get on board

Throughout the transformation, there will be different stakeholders or people to get 'on board'. Fortunately, we tend to recognize the importance of 'taking people with you' but it's not always clear how to get this 'buy-in'. In Chapter 9, we discussed winning your own heart and mind. This is now about inspiring others to follow suit. Adopting the attitudes, mindsets and behaviours that will transform the organization for the better.

Briefly looking ahead, in Chapter 16, we'll return to think about inspiring and preparing people during deployment and execution.

Let's be honest, there are always times where we or those around us might feel that people should 'get with the programme' or 'tow the company line'. Yes, there are times where compliance must be met at all costs, including safety, ethics, regulation, privacy and other highly regulated or life and death situations. But a forced hand isn't going to be motivated to do or be the best.

If you don't share or explain your vision, it's harder for people to genuinely get on board. And if you can't enthuse people, they won't work hard for the goal, they won't prioritize the transformation and they won't be excited by it or for it.

With buy-in across the different stakeholders and stakeholder groups, there will be more organizational motivation to get things done and more grit and determination to help overcome the challenges along the way. Inspiring different stakeholders will also have different impacts to the transformation. For example, gaining positive buy-in from the board will enable resources throughout the transformation and will prevent surprise blockers before final delivery. Equally, earning buy-in from frontline colleagues will streamline the deployment and encourage utilization and therefore benefit realization.

The road to inspiring people is challenging. Different people respond and react to different aspects. The FACES framework (Frame, Attain, Conversations, Explain, Sustain, see Figure 11.3) helps to engage and motivate stakeholders and should be employed for listening and sharing aims, aspirations and details about the transformation. Tailor the approach to be relevant to individual stakeholders.

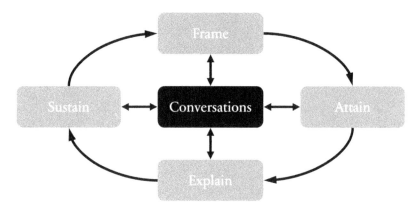

Figure 11.3: The FACES framework to engage and inspire stakeholders

- **Frame:** Define the business challenge and illustrate with insight and feedback to create a compelling vision for the transformation journey, setting a clear direction for all stakeholders to follow.

- **Attain:** Make the vision of the future state more realistic by outlining the roadmap and approach to achieve and attain it, ensuring that everyone understands their role and the broader expectations in the process.

- **Conversations:** Foster a culture of open and honest two-way dialogue between stakeholders which is present in all stages and should encourage a positive exchange of ideas, concerns and feedback to improve the transformation and the relationship.

- **Explain:** Openly share the rationale behind the transformation and the approach, recognizing the potential risks and roadblocks, plus emphasizing the collaborative effort needed to help drive success. When possible and relevant, use prototypes, mock-ups, models or engaging documents to help people understand the vision and future state as early as possible. Make requests or 'asks' and ensure their outcomes are clear.

▷ **Sustain:** Consistently reinforce the vision and approach to continually act as a reminder about the importance of the transformation and maintain focus without the initiative being side-tracked. The consistent, sustained nature over time builds confidence and clarity.

Whilst going through the FACES framework, there are different factors to include, as shown in Table 11.1.

Table 11.1: Elements of the FACES framework

Stage	Factor	With it	Without it
Frame	Painting a clear picture of the vision.	Understanding and appreciation of the goal and intent.	Confusion, lack of motivation, making assumptions about the true reasoning.
	Including data-based and people-based insight.	Engages people's hearts and minds.	Different people may be confused or disillusioned by the change without this background and evidence.
	Highlighting what's in it for them.	Individual motivation to see the transformation deliver.	Uncertain about why they should invest time, energy or resource for no reason.
Attain	Sharing confidence in the approach and goal.	Engaged and excited, full of optimism and hope.	Delays through waiting to see what happens.

	Clarifying expectations and assumptions.	Clarity and calmness about what happens next.	Inconsistent understanding of what will happen or what is needed. Unreasonable and invisible expectations and assumptions.
Conversations	Holding two-way communication.	Everyone feels heard about overcoming future challenges. Plus, lots of good ideas will come out of conversations.	Disengaged or a feeling of being 'done to' by people that don't understand or haven't experienced reality recently.
	Listening and feeding back.	People feel like part of the process and have the opportunity to add value.	Feeling like a helpless victim with no ability to change for the better.
Explain	Making a clear ask.	Clarity and agreement on who will do what, and open conversations if this is unreasonable.	People not being clear on what role they play, likely leading to missed expectations.
	Including specific details.	Confidence that effective planning and thinking has built up the transformation.	Internal questions and uncertainty about the change. Gives the illusion that it's all 'smoke and mirrors'.

	Demonstrating prototypes, models and mock-ups.	People understand the future state and it encourages people to foresee and experience future risks and opportunities.	Assumptions are made about the future state which may not be true. Missed opportunity to win support and get helpful suggestions.
	Referencing challenges and roadblocks.	Boosts integrity and openness that it will be a challenging journey. Encourages people to play a part and make a difference.	Feeling of over-optimism or that something is being covered up.
Sustain	Consistent between people.	Shared understanding across teams and individuals where everyone is on the same page.	Misalignment as different parts of the organization head off in different directions.
	Consistent over time.	Reinforces the transformation and builds energy to overcome the challenge or realize the opportunity.	Confusion that the strategy is flip-flopping, and that the transformation is just the flavour of the month.
	Continuing to reference and act on people's thoughts.	Builds trust and shows integrity and humility.	Creates an ignorant appearance with engagement as a 'tick box' exercise only.

However, despite your best efforts to inspire people, there will always be a mix of views when it comes to your transformation. It's change and change always divides people.

The promoters and detractors of transformation

Many retailers track NPS (Net Promoter Score) to measure customer experience and the likelihood of positive recommendations. However, customers who receive or perceive to have experienced bad service will still make recommendations to friends and family… only that the recommendation is to avoid a specific business or product!

The same is true when it comes to transformation. Your stakeholders will divide into promoters and detractors.

The promoters buy into the transformation and feel it's a brilliant direction for the organization. They will actively support and champion the initiative throughout. They're excellent allies and their infectious enthusiasm can convert others to become promoters too.

However, your detractors will criticize and reject the transformation. At the most extreme, they may actively try to derail the initiative but more often, they will create a negative vibe, highlighting problem after problem, failing to do relevant tasks and encouraging others to rebel against the transformation.

Then you have those in the middle, the neutral people, who are still sitting on the fence. Either this is because they've not yet decided if the transformation is for them, or that they feel the transformation is less relevant for them but are not against it. Generally, these individuals can play a positive part but will not be proactive in their actions or thoughts. They'll do what is asked of them.

However, the interesting battle here is whether the neutral people will be turned into promoters or detractors. Will they become positive supporters to move the transformation forwards or will they slip into a negative viewpoint, swayed by the dark side.

Like with customer experience, it is possible to convert a detractor into a promoter through regular engagement, active listening, genuinely acting on feedback and excellent service. Equally, someone can slip the other way through being ignored or not engaged.

> **Example: Converting the nay-sayer into a champion**
>
> I was working with Scott, a retail store director, to organize a trial. I hadn't realized at the time but Scott was a detractor of the transformation. He identified a series of stores for the trial and my team got to work on engaging the teams and running the trial. The trial presented a series of issues and feedback which we quickly responded to and acted on, looking to continually improve the solution. The trial feedback became more and more positive, and the solution was ultimately rolled out.
>
> After the initiative had successfully deployed and the transformation was over, Scott revealed that he was not a fan of the change. He'd selected the hardest and most challenging stores and store managers. The reaction of continually listening had formed a better solution and had won him over to become a promoter, and perhaps the most vociferous champion of the change in the entire company.
>
> *Who are the promoters and detractors of your transformation and how are you winning them over?*

Your mission, like NPS, is to ensure that the actions and behaviours taken help drive a swell of promoters. When promoters overwhelm the detractors, your ecosystem becomes a positive force for driving transformation forwards and through any barriers.

Breaking down the silo walls

The functional silo is perhaps the greatest barrier to effective companies. They prevent clear and timely communication, block collaboration and prevent help. They lead to disagreement and conflict. And in turn, silos result in infighting across the organization, rather than the company working together as a cohesive unit that is focused on the competitive environment and delivering for customers and shareholders.

Silos are created as an organization grows and functional or topical specialities are divided across teams and divisions, each with their own goals, vision and work. Sitting within one of these silos, it's easy to focus on your own work, goals and priorities. In turn, you see positive performance, although only within the silo.

Whilst the silo walls are invisible and exist only as a proverb, they're felt throughout the business. And, most importantly, they're felt by the end customer. The organizational divisions and disputes block seamless integrations and make the shopping experience clunky.

Without overcoming these silos, the transformation will suffer a similar fate. The solution will seem unusually difficult for customers and frontline colleagues.

Fortunately, your transformation is an excellent vehicle for bursting through silo walls to encourage a more collaborative approach and working environment. Suddenly, you can initiate cross-functional working. You can start the conversation to connect the business and work as one. And you allow the company to have a joined-up perspective. But you must initiate this. It's hard and people will resist, at first. Persevere. Encourage others to persist, too. Listen and consider the different viewpoints. Look at the bigger picture. Consider benefits and impacts more widely than you might at first imagine.

Ask yourself: What will be the single action that will
allow your transformation to break down the
silo walls that exist in your organization?

Not only will the transformation be stronger after connecting the silos, but the organization will be too. New relationships will open new ways of working. And you may have just started an invisible revolution of collaborative working to propel the organization forward.

Generating genuine collaboration opportunities

Cross-functional collaboration is a crucial enabler for driving successful transformation. By tapping into the wealth of skills and experience available across the organization, you create an aligned team atmosphere to unleash creativity, enhance critical thinking, build resilience, earn trust, maximize value and deliver coherent experiences for both customers and colleagues.

There are numerous collaboration opportunities in your transformation, and you begin by establishing connections with stakeholders from across the organization, including those that are involved in, impacted by or an influence on the transformation. Identifying and engaging people early on paves the way for a collaborative and inclusive atmosphere.

It's then critical to identify and take on the specific collaboration opportunities, including cross-functional workshops to:

- Define the transformation and strategy.
- Define existing or new processes.
- Identify cross-functional handover points.
- Benchmark or research the market.
- Review customer feedback and insight.
- Prioritise tasks or features on the development backlog.
- Generate ideas and solve problems.
- Identify and manage risks.
- Create communication, trial or deployment strategies.
- Review lessons learned from past initiatives.

There are also many non-workshop or non-meeting collaboration opportunities, including:

- Gemba walk or experiencing the day-to-day operations.
- Cross-functional rotations or temporary job swaps.
- Knowledge sharing sessions.
- Store visits.
- Hack-a-thons and innovation events.

Collaboration is both the act of working together
and recognizing that we can achieve more
together than we can apart.

Celebrating success is a great way to recognize the collaborative efforts, highlight excellent teamwork and offer a chance to let the hair down and build personal connections. Remember this opportunity for recognition exists throughout the transformation, not just at the end.

As you create a more collaborative atmosphere, for the transformation and more broadly for the organization, you'll also want to think about the collaborative activity plus demonstrating the act of collaboration and the behaviours that you'd like to be adopted by others too. But even without silos, conflict will still exist.

Conflict is guaranteed and must be addressed

It would be naïve to think that everyone gets on well and is happy at all times. Conflict is guaranteed in transformation. As we reach out and converse with stakeholders and encourage a diverse group of people to work together on a strategically important initiative, it's natural to uncover differences of opinion as well as functional differences. However, it's crucial to address these conflicts in a constructive manner.

Unfortunately, unresolved conflicts don't wither over time. Worse, they fester and become more obscure and deep-rooted, leading to future bias, pre-conceived ideas about others, avoidance and mistrust. Different people react to conflict differently. Additionally, the conflict approach is connected to corporate culture too. So, as much as some people might prefer sticking their head in the sand, it's not a viable way out.

Instead, maintaining open communication throughout the conflict is essential as it's the vehicle for encouraging transparent and honest discussions. Allowing all parties the time and space to express their thoughts and rationale is valuable and is the first step to reaching a shared understanding. A neutral mediator can be useful here as it maintains a professional edge and allows someone to ask sensible questions.

Managing the emotions involved in these conversations can be challenging, especially if one or more parties feels a personal attachment to the conflict. Excessive negative emotions can spiral out of control, entrench positions, lead to regrettable comments or actions and ultimately, they make it increasingly challenging to find a suitable resolution. Developing your emotional intelligence and empathy are critical skills to navigate these situations.

Highlighting points of similarity and points of difference is a smart way to name the actual conflict. Often, naming the areas of disagreement and recognizing the common ground can significantly deescalate the conflict and allows a more positive and progressive discussion to take place.

Finding solutions that accommodate all concerns from all parties is ideal, but not always possible. Elements of compromise are reasonable and allow the conflict to move forwards. However, if one party feels 'short-changed' or that they have 'lost' then there is a risk of the conflict living on. Embarrassment, frustration or reluctance to collaborate or cooperate are all signs of a lingering conflict.

Unchecked conflict can be a major blocker to transformation, creating barriers and setting up future additional points of conflicts too. But by addressing disagreements proactively and collaboratively, you can strengthen and improve the transformation and the various people relationships that exist as part of that.

Steering group playbook

Steering groups are a useful forum for transformation initiatives. They have varying names, including governance groups, steering committees or could be hidden within senior executive-level meetings. For clarity, I'll call them steering groups. They allow time and space for senior stakeholders to be updated, to discuss challenges and most importantly, to make decisions. Decisions are an important part of transformation, and we'll continue this topic in Chapter 15.

With people as the central role in making the ecosystem work, steering and governance processes are a way of facilitating and overseeing the different interactions, for example, setting priorities or understanding the impact of the external environment.

The steering group might be specific to a transformation, a functional area or responsible for a broader scope. Either way, it's a structured and senior group to guide and govern the change, ensuring it's the sensible path for the company. Steering groups should be attended by senior leaders from the various cross-functional elements involved and possibly more widely too.

One of the dangers with these groups is getting sucked into the detail. A potentially large gathering of people who may only have partial knowledge of the specific detail can quickly get bogged down. Discussions will undoubtedly be vibrant and long-lasting, but this is not the purpose and they're unlikely to come to a useful conclusion. Therefore, it's crucial to define the rules through a 'terms of reference' to clarify the purpose, people, process, approach and logistics for the steering group. However, I have found this term can confuse and gives an air of bureaucracy, so I prefer to simply call it a 'steering group playbook'. This is a written document which helps confirm the purpose, membership, scope and approach of the group for those in the group or people who interact with it.

The group should be discussing:

- Strategic alignment for the transformation.

- Priorities and prioritization relative to other initiatives.

- Decision making and approvals, including for resources (larger organizations may also have separate governance processes for these, such as capital investment boards).

- Resolving escalated issues and problems.

- Reviewing change plans and monitoring change capacity across the organization.

- Ensuring the transformation is being managed and driven carefully at the right pace, including updates on progress, stakeholders, plans and risks.

But unless explicitly defined otherwise, transformation steering groups should not be discussing aspects like day-to-day operational details, micromanaging tasks, or discussing an individual's performance.

Creating the steering group playbook may identify interesting and specific topics which are not suitable for this group. Ensure there is an alternative forum or meeting with the relevant people where this can be included in the scope.

Another watchout or danger is that steering group degrades into a non-value-adding tick box exercise. Having such senior attendees in this room will be hugely expensive and therefore if it's not adding value, it's very wasteful, but it also adds more admin work and bureaucracy to the process and company. To avoid this, clearly explain how senior leaders can help drive the change which encourages active involvement, rather than passively overseeing or managing, and will help build organizational momentum behind the transformation. Another approach to help avoid bureaucracy is to adopt the mindset of a new and energetic start-up for steering and the transformation as a whole.

Developing the ecosystem like a start-up

Your transformation ecosystem exists within the organization. Depending on the size of the company there may be other transformation ecosystems which also exist. With people at the heart, these ecosystems are naturally open to the company culture. You may have heard of the phrase: 'culture eats strategy for breakfast', but through many of the challenges discussed in Chapter 2, culture resists change, so I'll add to the popular quote.

Culture eats strategy for breakfast,
but it detests the taste of change.

Culture wants to enforce the status quo where it's safe. So, developing your ecosystem may present culture-shifting changes to ways of working, especially if you'll be bursting through those silo walls.

To help create a change-tolerant culture, we can learn from an entrepreneurial or start-up mentality. By applying this to our ecosystem, it will help the transformation and the broader culture become more innovative, agile, customer-focused and competitive. Start-up cultures are incredibly adaptable and open to change. Consider how you can adopt the mentality of a start-up in your organization:

- **Listening:** To customers, colleagues and stakeholders. Collate and prioritize this feedback to help deliver relevant value in a meaningful way.

- **Lean thinking:** Focusing on delivering value with minimal resources and bureaucracy. Seeking and realizing efficiency opportunities in all areas.

- **Continuously improving:** Refining and tweaking everything that you do for a better outcome. The Japanese concept of kaizen looks for enhancements in everything you do. Sports teams also seek that 1% improvement to build up marginal gains.

> **Experimenting and adapting:** Embracing a culture of trying things out, encouraging risks and potential failure to discover the valuable lessons in both the wins and losses. Adjusting the transformation based on these learnings and pivoting (or even stopping) when needed.

> **Collaborating:** Working across the business as start-ups have much weaker (or no) functional silos. This creates a culture where everyone contributes and can play a part.

> **Sense of urgency:** Proactively solving problems and making decisions with the essence of speed and getting things done.

Ask yourself: How could you develop a
start-up mentality in your organization?

As the entrepreneurial or start-up mindset embeds and as the company culture is exposed to more positive change and transformation, it will become more tolerant of future change. In turn, the organization becomes more dynamic and the transformation ecosystems functions more smoothly.

What we've covered

> The eight elements of the transformation ecosystem which interact with each other.

> Engage and inspire your stakeholders, with the aim of converting them to become transformation promoters.

> Bust through silo walls by encouraging cross-functional collaboration and resolving conflicts along the journey.

Chapter 12
Accelerating meaningful progress

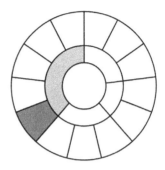

'Pushing water uphill.' This was how one retail leader described their experience of transformation. 'Wading through treacle' is another I've heard. And even images of 'herding cats.'

Analogies aside, the point is that progress is hard. Once you have identified a destination and a clear route to get there, each mile takes huge effort and needs to overcome numerous barriers and obstacles. Technical and cultural challenges will arise and demand the best of you and your team.

At times, when you're leading or working on a transformation initiative, it can feel like everything is against you. Each task is tough, however simple and small, there seems to be something to slow you down or set you back.

And as you slow down a little, it feels harder with more challenges impacting you. In turn, you slow down more. To get through, put the pedal to the metal, build momentum and achieve meaningful progress which all starts with action.

Transformation requires action

How many times have you sat in a meeting, debating a great topic and agreeing a feasible outcome, only to return to the conversation in the future and find that nothing has happened?

To deliver transformation, work must be done. Action must be taken to move forward and build progress. It seems simple.

Taking the right intentional action is harder than it sounds with multiple barriers in the way, including the following:

> **Lack of clarity, ownership, urgency or meaning:** About what to do, who's meant to do it, when it should be done by, and why it's important.

> **Alternative priorities:** Especially true when the transformation isn't the only thing that an individual is focused on. Business priorities clash and something must give.

> **Personal disagreement:** Whilst this shouldn't happen, it does. If an individual doesn't agree with the task or even the transformation, it's likely to mean nothing happens and other activities take priority.

> **Running into obstacles:** Unexpected issues may crop up, either slowing progress or presenting a complete blocker.

> **Resource constraint:** When the action is waiting on other people or other resources.

> **Incomplete or unavailable prerequisites:** If there are inputs required, especially from other teams, this can present blockages, especially if that dependency or requirement is not clear or hasn't been understood.

> **Technical challenge:** A technically tougher action than expected, requiring more effort, time or resource than originally anticipated.

> **Forgotten tasks:** It's simple to make mistakes when there is a lot going on. Sometimes, lack of progress is born from simply missing the action.

Other transformation-specific issues can block action and progress. Some blockers will be predictable, but most won't be. Individuals have good intentions and issues still arise. So, consider how to enable progress by simply getting work done.

Getting work done

The secret to making progress in your transformation isn't particularly special. It's about getting work done and leaders can enable this in several ways.

First, getting work done is easier said than done. Especially if the transformation is across a matrix organization where there are competing and conflicting priorities. Take a bespoke approach based on the scenario and what is relevant for each individual involved. Here are ten ways to get more work done:

1. **Set clear goals and expectations:** To help accelerate getting work done, be clear on what that work is. Be specific in confirming the goal and what is expected of the team. This clarifies the individual roles as well as aligning the overall team effort. Double check this understanding to avoid future missed expectations. Also be clear to set expectations about communicating challenges and when work has been completed. Communication of completion is part of each task or activity.

2. **Clarify why the work delivers a meaningful shift:** Increasingly, it is important for colleagues to understand the bigger picture about why the work is required and why it's meaningful. Explain how the individual pieces of work build up towards the broader transformation, and in turn, how the transformation builds toward the corporate strategy and performance. Use the stratification to help clarify the why.

3. **Stratify the work into more manageable chunks:** It's easy for larger pieces of work to feel overwhelming, especially for people with less experience or with limited time. Tiny advances in progress feel like nothing which can be demoralizing for everyone. Stratify the work, as discussed in Chapter 7, into smaller tasks which can be taken one step at a time.

4. **Focus on the customer of the change:** Stay focused on the direct and indirect customers of the change, as discussed in Chapter 6. This will help make the work more relevant and meaningful.

Plus, it helps ensure that you remain customer centric for the individual task and the whole transformation. Ensure the team recognize these customers too.

5. **Create a collaborative effort:** Transformation takes a team and collaboration helps foster that teamwork. Lead the way and encourage collaboration, especially cross-functional working, whenever possible, as discussed in Chapter 11. This breaks down functional silo walls and builds trusting relationships.

6. **Give clear communication and check-ins:** Clear and ongoing communication is critical, and this should be a two-way dialogue. Regular check-ins help create alignment and project meetings can be a useful mechanism for this dialogue. Chat and messaging tools can be a quick and convenient way to stay informed. Whichever way works best, ensure there is a safe forum to update on progress, ask questions and highlight issues. And this will aid further collaboration.

7. **Celebrate successes and progress along the way:** It's easy to keep the head down and save any celebrations until the end of the programme. However, with transient team members, large cross-functional teams and complex, lengthy transformation initiatives, this isn't always optimal. With milestones and deliverables along the journey, ensure that you take time to acknowledge the team's inputs and outputs. This builds morale and reinforces the positive effect of getting work done.

8. **Give feedback and support:** It's also easy to avoid difficult situations, especially in the heat of the moment or if there is a matrix organization in place. Feedback is your tool to adjust future behaviour so use it to reinforce and encourage more of the right behaviours and highlight opportunities to adjust and improve. Peer-to-peer or 360° feedback across the transformation team can also be a great way to build trusted working relationships and foster more teamwork. Ensure the transformation team are equipped and empowered to be giving feedback. Help and support people, especially as you highlight opportunities through negative feedback which boosts confidence and morale.

9. **Knock down barriers:** Problems will crop up and prevent work from being done. Have clear escalation routes and encourage

people to solve their own issues, or at least prepare a series of recommendations rather than just presenting the problem and expecting you to deal with it. Remember who owns the monkey. Don't let problems fester through neglect, be caught in an avoidable bottleneck or by letting someone stick their head in the sand. React quickly to issues and risks to avoid excessive impact, firefighting or delays. Empower people to tackle challenges themselves and also be ready to steer or guide, especially if panic increases. More on this in Chapter 13.

10. **Empower and encourage others to think on their feet:** Trust people, encourage their active involvement and give as many opportunities as you can for people to take responsibility, from problem-solving, to engaging stakeholders or making decisions. Give people the opportunity to prove themselves.

These ten ways are important to help you get more done. In addition, you'll want to inject pace and energy into the transformation.

Injecting pace and energy

Transformation initiatives require pace and energy. Often in retail, there is a brilliant and strong mentality of getting things done as soon as possible. Usually, the faster a transformation can deliver value, the better.

To inject pace and energy, start by leading by example. Drive the transformation with a high level of energy in behaviours and action. Don't let meetings dwindle and drag on. Inspire the team with the pace and enthusiasm that you hope they'll adopt.

Pace and energy are infectious. Demonstrate
these behaviours to inspire faster velocity
and energetic enthusiasm.

When everything is required 'ASAP', it can diminish the effect of urgency. It's the equivalent to prioritizing everything as important. I've made this mistake before and it's always disappointing when ASAP isn't met with furious effort to do literally 'as soon as possible', as was intended. 'Immediate' is better. A specific deadline is better still to foster the sense of urgency.

To help create a genuine sense of urgency, try calculating your transformation benefits down to a daily or even hourly rate. Knowing that a £1m benefit equates to a daily burn rate of £3,846 (£1,000,000 / 260 working days a year = £3,846 per day), helps sharpen the attention significantly towards getting work done, especially as the size and scale of your transformation goes up. When I highlighted this for a £100m project, I'm sure you can imagine how that focused the discussion and encouraged positive and urgent action.

Adding in opportunity for innovation and creative thinking energizes the team. Whether it's idea generation sessions, collaborative workshops or taking risks, this energy can be harnessed to get things done. And when things do get done, be sure to recognize and congratulate the team. Reinforce those energetic, collaborative and productive behaviours with positive feedback.

However, whilst I'm sure you want to keep that accelerator pedal pressed firmly down, beware of burnout. Pace and energy can achieve huge amounts, but they're not everlasting. An individual can't be continually 'on'. Effective teamwork can help alleviate or support people working at peak. And after an intense, gruelling part of the transformation journey, consider giving time back to rest, recharge and reflect.

Finally, share what's working with your transformation team and across the rest of the organization. Knowledge share sessions demonstrate what can be achieved and give opportunities to reflect as well as inform and inspire others.

These approaches must be tailored, and I'll challenge you to experiment with these ideas to help accelerate progress in your transformation.

Challenging for more

Challenging the transformation team (including yourself) for more is an essential part of accelerating progress. As humans, when we challenge ourselves and take ourselves outside our comfort zone, amazing things happen. We expand our limits and show our true potential. Your transformation needs you to enable this across the team.

Example: The first answer is always wrong

Innovative retailers can move at a fast pace, especially given their size. Early on at one forward thinking retailer, I learnt a key lesson from a great transformation leader: 'The first answer is always wrong.'

They always demanded more; more research, more speed, more action. At first, this could be seen as demoralizing or frustrating, and I recall seeing team members feeling negative emotions. However, being keen to make the exacting standards and make sure the first answer was *not* wrong, I learnt to challenge myself to deliver more. And the more you ask, especially of yourself, the more you tend to achieve. By always demanding more, it allowed me to push on the relentless pace and inject energy into the various transformation initiatives I have led since.

How could you adopt the mindset of 'the first answer is always wrong' to be more rigorous and creative?

Setting ambitious goals and tasks helps challenge for more, although will feel uncomfortable at times. Jim Collins and Jerry Porras[46] introduced the concept of BHAGs (Big, Hairy, Audacious Goals) and this can be a great mentality to motivate the team and add in the level of challenge.

Ask yourself and your team: What would be
next-level for us? What would be game-changing
for the transformation?

A stretch goal or task should be inspiring and hard. It's there to take you out of the comfort zone, encourage you to think differently and ultimately expand your capability. There should be a real likelihood of not achieving it.

Don't just think about these stretch goals at the once-a-year annual review. Consider this mentality of challenging for more, week in, week out, to achieve greater results and avoid the risk of procrastination sneaking in.

Overcoming procrastination

One of the banes to great progress is procrastination. Procrastination can occur at company and individual levels.

At a company level, the usual suspects that prevent progress come out to play again. Lack of clarity, ownership and poor communication are ongoing challenges. A lack of clear and timely decision making inspires delays throughout the organization. It removes the element of urgency and is often frustrating to those involved in preparing options or supporting the decision.

For individuals, there are many aspects which lead to procrastination. Whilst time management has a role to play, there are many emotions and feelings which drive this challenge. Confusion, fear, anxiety, overwhelm and burnout are negative states which kill productivity. Lack of motivation or commitment to the cause introduce another reason not to get started. Perfectionism and distractions add in an extra encouragement to procrastinate.

This is agitated further when you add in the high-distraction level of notifications and task-switching that we all live with now. With ongoing research[47] into procrastination along with increasing awareness and consideration of mental health issues and conditions like ADHD (Attention Deficit Hyperactivity Disorder), the ability to concentrate and focus is an important topic to conquer.

Procrastination is rarely caused by a single element and there are no hard and fast rules. Additionally, the conditions are highly dynamic too. To accelerate progress, support the team and organization to battle procrastination with practical approaches and by building momentum. Use stratification to find easy, clear and meaningful tasks to start with.

Building momentum

In physics, momentum is the impetus gained by a moving object. The more energy or momentum that it has, the further it will travel and the more power it will take to stop it. The Amazon Flywheel Concept[48] is the best example of momentum in a business setting, where a loop of traffic, sellers, range, customer experience and price investment continually contribute to growth.

> Jim Collins's Flywheel Concept[49] explains the
> compound effect of smaller, consistent actions which
> build cumulative energy and momentum.

Perhaps you've developed a flywheel concept for your business, and if not, that's an excellent strategic conversation to have.

But with our mind on driving retail transformation, what would the transformation flywheel be? Figure 12.1 shows the key elements.

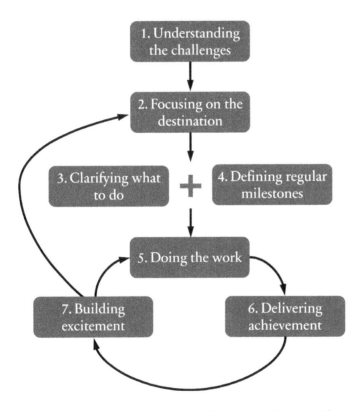

Figure 12.1: Building momentum through the flywheel effect

1. **Understanding the challenges:** The process starts with understanding the challenges facing the company and where the company is headed.

2. **Focusing on the destination:** The flywheel of momentum can start as the transformation goals and objectives are clearly defined, and by stratifying the overall transformation into more detail to define the deliverables.

3. **Clarifying what to do:** By stratifying the goals and deliverables, you'll clarify what work needs to be done.

4. **Defining regular milestones:** Review the work and deliverables and identify goals to aim for throughout the transformation journey to encourage the 20 Mile March mentality discussed in Chapter 8, so there is always a nearby goal to aim for.

5. **Doing the work:** The inevitable activity of getting the task done. Without this, momentum grinds to a halt quickly.

6. **Delivering achievement:** With clarity over the near-term work required, and how that fits into the regular milestones, delivery is an event that happens regularly, not just at the end.

7. **Building excitement:** Regular delivery means the transformation attracts positive attention and energy. People want to be involved in positive shifts and want to do the work, consequently building the snowball effect that gets the flywheel moving.

As a former engineer, I will also add in a scientific consideration. The greater the transformation, the greater the effort required to get the flywheel moving. To start, assess smaller and simpler changes to spin a smaller flywheel. This momentum can then power up the larger transformation. Use the stratification to find suitably manageable and bite sized activities and deliverables to get started with.

From there, the focus is on continuing to spin the flywheel. Maintaining focus on the bigger picture and destination keeps you on the right track whilst work completed energizes itself and builds positive reputation. This positive energy accumulates and helps overcome challenges and engages people. It builds focus and allows you to flexibly steer around obstacles, roadblocks or external influences.

Updating and reporting on progress

Many people get frustrated with reporting or updating on progress on a consistent or regular basis. It can feel like an administrative task; a report which no one reads or a blocker to actually doing the work.

However, the first valuable portion of work is in the thinking and reflection that goes into the progress update. It encourages a moment to stand back and take a broader and more strategic view of progress and direction.

Many progress reports may feel like they never get read unless there is a critical issue. However, it's likely that progress updates are consumed but do not evoke an intervention unless there is a critical issue. The business is empowering the transformation to continue. And only when there is a critical issue or problem, does it need additional attention from leadership.

Make the progress reporting as simple as it can be. A commentary on the transformation, a summary of progress and achievements, the challenges and concerns, where help or focus is needed and an overall status rating. Many businesses use a traffic light system or 'RAG' rating (red, amber or green) to set a high-level overview of progress. RAG definitions are critical and should be best aligned with the wider organization. If no definition exists, use this:

- **Red:** The transformation is experiencing a critical issue, risk, or delay that requires immediate attention and action. The initiative is off track and corrective measures must be taken to bring it back on course. These significant issues will impact the overall value delivered.

- **Amber:** The transformation is under threat from notable risks which need monitoring and might require corrective action in the near future. An amber status suggests challenges are not severe enough to endanger the whole initiative, yet.

- **Green:** The transformation is in control and on track to deliver value as expected. Everything is running smoothly, and no attention is required.

The RAG rating allows a very quick review of the initiative and if consistently used, RAG ratings for each initiative in the portfolio helps focus the attention from leadership.

Focused and flexible

Delivering progress in the transformation is a delicate balance between being determined and driven to go forward whilst also being agile to divert at the right time. If the transformation grinds to a halt for every barrier and query, it will never get finished. But if a transformation is so ruthlessly focused on a goal, then there is a risk that you miss the warning signs and drive into trouble or even off a cliff.

With the bespoke nature of transformation, there is no rock-solid rule. I have experienced times where too much caution is exhibited although challenges have time to be resolved. However, it's crucial that you diligently investigate these properly and not just ignore them.

'Ask for forgiveness, not permission.'

Empowering adage, unknown origin

With momentum to press ahead, and confidence that you're on the right path, you can apply the focus throttle to surge forward. And use the ultimate destination as a balancing element to slow progress slightly if needing to be more flexible and proactive, especially if there are roadblocks ahead.

What we've covered

- Encourage action and get work done which are essential for accelerating meaningful progress.

- Inject pace and energy into the transformation and lead by example.

- Building momentum will help you progress through your journey, and being intentional about the flywheel will help accumulate positive energy.

Chapter 13
Avoiding the
inevitable
roadblocks

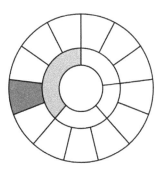

Here's the thing. Your transformation will run into problems. Just like every other transformation. And if it doesn't then either the transformation is not bold or brave enough, or people are merrily sitting around unaware that the world is on fire around them.

When it comes to solving problems in a transformation, firefighting can be a great role. It's exciting, it feels dangerous and meaningful. Everyone is in awe and there is a tonne of gratitude and respect from across the organization.

Yet, the best transformation professionals aren't firefighters. The best transformations are those which are smooth and steady. No surprises. No alarms. No urgent escalations and no 'all hands to the pump' moments. Or at least, minimizing these unexpected moments.

Because people don't like surprises. Not the board, nor your colleagues, not your customers and certainly not your shareholders. Not your team and not even those that appreciate a great firefighter.

Instead, people strive for certainty. Predictability. They want to quench that fear of the unknown with a clear view of the future, or as much as is possible.

Given this and given the inevitable problems that you will run into on the transformation journey, consider how to best predict and then avoid, mitigate or overcome the roadblocks along the way. These roadblocks cause delays and erode value. Risk and issue management is therefore a crucial skill for successfully and calmly navigating the way.

The thing about risks and issues

Risks and issues are often misunderstood, confused or combined but there is a subtle but important difference.

Issues are your current problems, challenges and obstacles. They have occurred and are already affecting the progress or performance of a transformation. Unless they are resolved, there will be further negative consequences.

Risks are your potential problems which may turn into your future issues. There are levels of uncertainty with risks in terms of the impact they have and if they will even occur. Risks can be avoided or mitigated through effective risk management. Alternatively, you may decide to ignore them, focus on other items and accept any potential impact further down the road.

When driving, a risk is brought to your attention when your navigation system highlights a blocked road and suggests a diversion, or when a warning light starts to flash up on your car dashboard. An issue is when you're caught in a five-mile traffic jam and just missed the exit, or when you have smoke pouring out of the bonnet and you come to an unglamourous, spluttering stop.

In transformation, these may present in different forms:

- ▷ Technical restriction means you can't integrate systems as planned (issue).

- ▷ Capital investment budgets are significantly reduced (issue).

- ▷ Steering group cannot make decisions in time (issue).

- ▷ Low volumes of data are captured from a trial (risk).

- ▷ Stakeholders are not engaging in workshops (risk).

- ▷ Supply chain may be strained over peak period (risk).

When faced with issues, you must decide your plan immediately. Issues are happening right now so you must either act quickly or be willing to accept further consequences.

But given that risks have an element of chance in them, this is your opportunity to remove the element of surprise and take intentional, preventative action ahead of time.

Intentional, preventative action

Effectively managing risks allows you to decide what action to take to maximize business, customer and colleague value from the transformation.

The first stage is to identify risks. This can be done through group discussions, interviews with subject-matter experts as well as more logical analysis of the plan, solution or data. In many ways, everything presents a risk, but you'll want to find a level that is practical and reasonable based on your transformation. It's also important to note the differences between existing company or market risks and new risks presented by the transformation. Ultimately, it's about being sensible and practical to avoid future issues.

Different functional or technical areas of a transformation may find it useful to identify their own risks which can feed into a broader programme-level risk analysis. Again, it's about being sensible with how you approach this.

To assess your risks, there are three aspects of chance to consider:

1. **Severity:** If the risk were to come true, how bad would the impact be?

2. **Likelihood:** What are the chances of the risk coming true?

3. **Velocity:** If the risk were to come true, how long would it take for the impact to materialize?

Now for each risk, score these three factors from a scale of 0–10 (severity: 10 is very bad; likelihood: 10 is almost guaranteed; velocity: 10 is a near immediate impact).

Then multiply the three scores together to give a prioritization and the ability to rank them, where the highest score is the most in need of attention. See an example in Figure 13.1.

Issue or risk	Category	It is a risk/issue that…	Likelihood (chances of occurring)	Severity (size of impact)	Velocity (speed of impact)	Priority (likelihood × severity × velocity)	Owner	Agreed next steps	Next step due date
Risk	Business case	Perceived high value projects do not deliver the right benefit	4	6	8	192	Kamil	Detail benefits model to be continually reviewed throughout project	Ongoing, next review January
Risk	Change management	Stores to not adopt changes in the long term	6	7	3	126	Ruth	Use new change management framework and tools	10-Jan
Risk	Project	In flight projects remain undelivered	6	3	6	108	Kamil	Follow up with in-flight owners to ensure alignment	02-Feb
Issue	Management	Managers feel the need to spend a lot of time in the office	6	3	5	90	Ruth	Re-assess following launch of Phase 1	05-Ap
Risk	Management	Management do not continue to commit to the new structure over time	2	5	4	40	Dave	Set up a 3 monthly review of payroll management FTE and compare to plan	01-Jul

Figure 13.1: Example of a risk matrix

Now it's time to decide how to react to each individual risk, from five different approaches:

1. **Avoid:** Deciding to intentionally change the transformation or the approach to take a diversion and avoid the risk. This is the ideal approach assuming there are no major downsides to diverting (e.g., moving the location of a new store due to high crime forecast in the area).

2. **Mitigate:** Taking action to reduce the likelihood or severity of the risk (e.g., providing additional training so a checkout error is less likely to happen).

3. **Share:** This is partnering with another team or third party to protect against the risk (e.g., taking out insurance to protect or cover the consequences of a customer accident in-store).

4. **Defer:** Taking action to push out the risk or reduce the velocity (e.g., delaying a trial or launch to gather more data or intel).

5. **Accept:** When the cost or implications of the risk happening is more acceptable than the cost or effort to take alternative action (e.g., expanding to a new market despite the chance that customer returns rates could be more costly).

By the time you work your way down through the priorities, there will come a point where you decide to ignore or accept remaining risks, deemed insignificant. There is no guideline about when that point is, as it depends on your transformation, the organization's appetite for risk and the resources available. It should be an intentional decision to ignore these risks, not just 'forgetting to look at them' or running out of time; that's when surprises sneak up on you!

It may also be prudent to consider a series of actions to exist as a plan B. In this instance, we're essentially hedging our bets that a risk is unlikely to occur and therefore we want to continue with plan A as the primary route. But we're also ready if this risk does come true as the alternative approach is in place already as a fall-back plan.

By tackling risks with a logical approach like this, you help to dispel opinion and emotion from the process, and you allow all risks to be considered fairly, rather than attention being drawn to a single risk.

It also encourages people to be more forward-thinking. Whilst we can't predict the future, we can consider potential futures and what is likely to happen, with a view of helping be more prepared and hopefully avoiding roadblocks.

The avoidable roadblocks

Through effective risk management, there are several roadblocks which we'll want to avoid and the aim here is to plan a diversion earlier on. These are some of the most common avoidable mistakes that transformation initiatives can succumb to:

- **Focusing on the wrong challenge:** This diversion must be taken as soon as possible to focus on a meaningful problem. However, the complication is that this mistake may not become apparent until much later. The best prevention is to research and focus on understanding the status quo early on, not just assuming that you know it already.

- **Not the Goldilocks solution:** By either working on a transformation that is too simple or too complex, we miss the real opportunity. A solution that's too simple will probably not achieve or realize the benefits whilst a solution that's too complex may take ages to (or may never) deliver or could be too complicated to deploy effectively. The Goldilocks solution is *just right*.

- **Lack of alignment:** I'm sure you've come across the 'herding cats' analogy, and without good alignment through the organization, this is where you'll find yourself. A clear vision and goals with consistent, coherent messaging will help avoid this roadblock. There should also be alignment with organizational structure, goals, bonus and reward mechanics and relevant people policies.

- **Lack of engagement:** People are at the centre of the transformation ecosystem and without engagement, this ecosystem won't function effectively. Engagement from your stakeholders can be earned through clear and relevant communication, clarity and education on the future state, regular and meaningful involvement, showing prototypes and mock-ups, and exhibiting trust and transparency.

- **Lack of progress:** This challenge creeps up and will eventually cause the transformation to stall completely. There are many potential root causes, but the outcome is the same: frustration, missed opportunity and a feeling of what could have been.

▷ **Predictable technical issues:** More technical solutions will usually present more challenges, so it's key to avoid as many of these as possible. Thorough scoping and specification requirements can prevent these, and an Agile approach can allow you to quickly resolve them. Recognize that Agile practices work beyond only software or IT use cases.

▷ **Striving for perfection:** High standards are important, but seeking the perfect solution can lead to frequent delays and postponements. Instead seek a 'good enough' solution that delivers the bulk of the benefit in the shortest possible time and then continuously improve over time.

▷ **Ineffective decision making:** Poor governance and planning can lead to rushed or delayed decisions which are more likely to result in a non-optimal endpoint. Consider how decisions can be planned and prepared for and how to improve your decision-making capability as an individual and a team.

▷ **Trying to boil the ocean:** Taking on too much work causes overwhelm, confusion and spreads resources too thinly. It's better to spend more time and effort on prioritization so that the organization can focus on delivering fewer but more impactful transformation initiatives.

By identifying and being aware of the risks and the avoidable roadblocks in your transformation, you can take intentional action to increase the likelihood of a successful conclusion. However, there will also be roadblocks that are unpredictable and unavoidable.

The unavoidable roadblocks

Some challenges will always crop up. There is little that you can do to avoid them, so instead, the transformation must be ready to react accordingly. Examples of these are:

▷ **External market shifts and fluctuations:** As the wider world evolves, we can expect volatility. Economic conditions, changing consumer trends, competitor actions, new regulations and more are out of our circle of control and influence. What we can do is foresee the potential ways they could change and monitor closely.

▷ **Crisis events:** Disasters at a global, local or personal level are unforeseen and can be hugely disruptive. Like we saw with the Covid-19 pandemic, the only viable way to manage this is to remain adaptable, flexible and be prepared for anything.

▷ **People changes:** There will always be a dynamic element of people involved as individuals retire, change jobs, leave the company or as new talent emerges or is recruited. This change of perspective can lead to a broader change of direction or new priorities which can disrupt transformation.

▷ **Resistance:** Despite the best engagement and communication strategy in the world, you'll still encounter resistance and the emotional cycle of change. This resistance can be within the wider stakeholder group, the transformation team or even in yourself. What will be your plan to counter and react to this?

▷ **Unpredictable technical issues:** Whilst some challenges can be resolved through effective planning, in my experience, there always seem to be additional technical roadblocks caused by complexity, competing priorities or lack of knowledge. Alternatively, when diving into the detail, you find that the solution is technically impossible for a number of reasons. Being able to work a new problem through to solution is crucial in these instances.

▷ **Business case that doesn't add up:** When you get into the details of the solution, sometimes it's hard to make the numbers work. The costs outweigh the benefits and that's ok. Continue to challenge all areas of the business case, the problem and the solution. But if there is no justification to continue then that's an informed and interesting discussion to present to the business and steering group.

▷ **Mistakes:** Despite the careful, hard and smart work, we're still human and still make mistakes. Important aspects get forgotten, crucial points are overseen, important calculations include an error, the requirements are misstated, and another infinitely long list of 'whoops' moments exist. The solution is to react effectively and learn from our mistakes, as individuals and as organizations.

With some of these unavoidable roadblocks, you may get some advanced warning, but others will appear from nowhere. When avoidable or unavoidable roadblocks do suddenly appear, it's important to tackle problems quickly.

Tackling problems quickly

Despite your best efforts to avoid or mitigate potential issues, there will still be problems that crop up. Either you knew about them before and despite your best efforts, they still occurred. Or they're a genuine surprise and must be dealt with.

Tackling problems is crucial and can stop challenges spiralling out of control. Depending on the issue and scenario, it may be prudent to consider raising a specific crisis team to resolve the problem. When I was a mechanical and systems engineer, solving problems was a key skill and I regularly used a standard process (shown in Figure 13.2) to approach any problem.

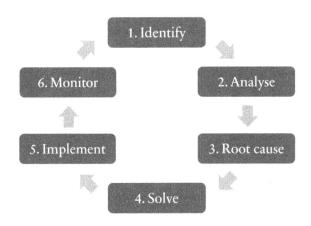

Figure 13.2: Six-step problem solving process

1. **Identify:** First, understand what is going on. Reports of 'a problem' could come from several sources and will likely be surrounded by confusing factors. As part of this stage, assess how big the problem is and therefore the urgency and support needed. It's critical to be responsive and take urgent action, especially if there are safety risks or another material impacts such as a data breach. This urgent action is likely to be a band-aid only whilst further analysis continues.

2. **Analyse:** Gather relevant data and intel to gain a deeper understanding of the issue. This includes understanding the scale, scope, frequency and impact of the problem. For example, does it occur in all stores, or is there a particular set of circumstances which must be present?

3. **Root cause:** Based on the intel gathered so far, you can analyse the causes of the problem. As with medical issues, it's likely that the root cause is not the same as the symptom. Using tools like Ishikawa/fishbone diagrams or 5-Why, it's critical to understand what is causing this problem.

4. **Solve:** Now it's time to tackle the root cause of the problem rather than just apply a band-aid to the symptoms. Develop and create solutions to solve the issue and then evaluate and decide on the best option(s) to move forward with.

5. **Implement:** Now it's time to start applying the fix or solution. Depending on the problem and root cause, it may be suitable to trial the solution first or run a short test before fully adopting and implementing the solution.

6. **Monitor:** The final stage is to monitor that the problem is truly and effectively resolved and that it doesn't come undone. This stage may run concurrently with implementation if you're running trials or tests. If the problem persists, revisit the process starting from the first step again.

Problems will move through this process at different speeds based on urgency and complexity. A standardized process allows the team to share a common understanding of progress and next steps, as well as setting stakeholder expectations. This can help identify the top challenge that exist.

The top challenge list

With different risks and issues impacting the transformation, it can be prudent to keep a top challenge list to monitor the highest-priority risks and the most pressing issues. Seeing all challenges at once allows a more considered approach than the classic 'whack-a-mole' manner of tackling whichever is the newest problem to pop up.

Too often in corporate settings, the top problem is defined by whoever is shouting loudest. Perhaps the most senior person, the most influential or the most vocal. But despite the vocal volume, it doesn't necessarily mean this is the biggest problem. Perhaps there is an invisible (or quiet) elephant in the room.

Consider the most severe and urgent problems or issues you face. These are probably obvious when you're in the moment, but if not, prioritize them on the findings in the Identify and Analyse stages of the problem-solving process. Also consider the progress or what stage they're at; a newly identified problem probably needs more focus than one that is in the Monitoring stage.

The risks are prioritized based on severity, likelihood and velocity, so should be easy to assess the top priority.

The top challenge list is then made of both risks and issues, trying to limit to three items only for focus and simplicity. They warrant the attention of the whole transformation team and may need escalating through steering groups to help share the situation, warn of negative consequences or request additional support and resources.

To effectively manage these top challenges, it is advisable to set a regular review cycle. Whilst this is dependent on many factors, I'd suggest that a weekly review is generally recommended as it maintains pace and progress. However, for more urgent challenges that are critical to the transformation or business' success, it may be prudent to review specific challenges daily, or even more frequently, depending on the evolving situation.

Show full visibility of this process, especially if problem prioritization is traditionally done by whoever shouts loudest. Often, the 'loudest shouter' needs to be heard and have the opportunity to recognize that the problems are being actively and fairly prioritized, else it risks that individual becoming a serious detractor of the transformation.

As you're navigating challenges and roadblocks along the journey, it may be essential to take a diversion, or even an emergency stop, to avoid a larger accident and consider your next move.

Making a diversion

Having spotted a block on the road ahead, there should be an informed, non-emotional decision about the future of the transformation. Perhaps the plans must shift, maybe a major pivot is needed or possibly the transformation is no longer viable. There are multiple factors that will feed into this decision so gathering the intel and the expertise is the first part of this.

Once you've decided on the best diversion or approach, there are several crucial actions to take. First, a clear communication to stakeholders to explain what's happening, the reasons why and what it means for them as individuals or groups. An earlier communication may also be required to those involved in the transformation to alert them to the emergency. This is especially important if there are critical actions such as major communications, contract signing or making cost commitments which are imminent.

There need to be clear action plans to make the diversion and always be careful about assuming that people understand the implications or what they must do differently. In turn, the six plans or forecasts outlined in Chapter 8 will need updating and sharing with relevant stakeholders.

Perhaps there was an indication of the challenge and that you had a plan B (or C, D…) in place already. This will be fantastic news and will give that clear action plan a head start.

Consider the implication to the wider ecosystem and other transformation efforts. Changes to schedules, priorities, resources and more can have wide-reaching implications, either positive or negative.

However, considering the challenges faced, intentionally stopping the transformation altogether is far better than continuing to plod on regardless of what's happened. Essentially, if things have changed, there is no point mindlessly throwing good money after bad.

Ultimately, making an emergency stop or a diversion will be a test of resilience. As with any journey, it's easy to see a complication on the road, a traffic jam or roadworks for example, and decide to turn around and go home. If you're clear on your destination and are being guided in the right direction, you can and will find an alternative way through. And you'll want to do that as an aligned team, determined to reach your goal.

In Appendix 2, discover how to react if the transformation 'breaks down' and needs rescuing and reinvigorating.

What we've covered

- It's critical to approach both risks and issues in the transformation.

- Taking intentional mitigating action will prevent future problems from spiralling out of control and descending into firefighting mode.

- The transformation will experience both avoidable and unavoidable challenges and you must be ready to make diversions to reach the end goal.

Chapter 14
Overcoming the uncertainty and unknowns

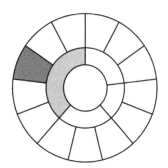

We must navigate the uncertainty that the retail industry is experiencing, from pandemics to politics, along with shifts to the economic and natural environments. We've also seen the pace of change accelerating. Changing consumer habits and evolving technology create uncertainty like a dense fog obscuring the way.

We are increasingly recognizing the VUCA (Volatile, Uncertain, Complex, Ambiguous) nature of the world, as discussed previously. But whilst the changing world has been the catalyst for the transformation, the transformation itself must also be adaptable and resilient to further uncertainty.

Uncertainty is the only certainty.

Uncertainty fuels our fear of the unknown and leaves more questions than answers. These questions mount up and we've all been in countless conversations where we've discussed 'what if...?' or 'If this happens...?' in an attempt to find a way through the unknown. And with so many questions, it's easy to submit or succumb to uncertainty until everything clears up a little.

The danger of succumbing to uncertainty

When faced with a hugely unknown future, it's easy to decide to wait. It's easy to decide to do nothing. To stay where we are until it's obvious what to do. And in some instances, this can be valuable, especially in fast-moving situations, where pausing for just a moment to gather information helps enable a considered decision.

When you wait to see what happens, recognize that the status quo lives on. That may be for minutes or years depending on the circumstances and only you can determine how acceptable this delay will be. And we must also remember that transformation doesn't instantly happen by itself. We can't just click our fingers for rapid change, so the delay is felt for much longer than the waiting time.

And I'm sure we can all think of those companies who left it too late before acting and experienced market share decline, missed the boat on new channels or suffered other consequences.

But in the face of uncertainty, it's important to identify burning questions. Ask yourself: What would we need to know to be more certain, and know what to do?

By naming the unknowns and writing out the various questions or uncertainties, we can begin to challenge them. Are they real unknowns? What are the possible answers or outcomes? How could we research to find the answer? What are other businesses doing about this? Does it actually matter or make a difference, or could we proceed anyway? Who could help us, either from within the company or external experts?

It's also useful to engage in conversation about uncertainties across the organization. Are other divisions or individuals hung up on the same challenges or have they found an alternative route? Is there alignment about which questions are in the way of progress?

Then, with this list of unknown elements, we can free up headspace from speculation, conjecture and unhelpful thoughts to move forward.

Recognizing the unknowns and moving forward

With a list of questions that are preventing progress, our challenge with uncertainty becomes not about guessing into the void, but about making intelligent forecasts.

> *'There are known knowns; there are things we know we know. We also know there are known unknowns; that is to say we know there are some things we do not know. But there are also unknown unknowns – the ones we don't know we don't know.'*
>
> *Donald Rumsfeld, former USA Defense Secretary*[50]

The first essential approach is to make assumptions. An assumption is an educated, informed and intentional forecast about what will happen at a specific point. You should use assumptions to create a 'holding answer' for some of those questions. This 'holding answer' is a way that allows you to move forward based on this forecast being true.

Consider these questions and we can make assumptions about them:

▷ What marketing approach will appeal most to younger consumers?

▷ Which is the next technology to become wildly successful?

▷ How will consumer spending change in the next three years?

▷ Who will be the most influential player in the next World Cup?

It's drilled into many of us that assumptions are bad. Perhaps you've come across the phrase 'to assume is to make and "ass" of "u" and "me"'. Therefore, we shy away from using assumptions in a professional manner.

The reality is that we're probably using assumptions already, despite all the reports, data and insight that we consume. Consider these questions:

1. What will be the greatest cause of colleague turnover this year?

2. Which social media platforms are most influential for your customers?

3. What would your colleagues say about you?

Chances are, you could attempt to answer these questions, but you don't *know*, so it's an assumption. And that's all right. Because *using* an assumption is not the mistake, it's *how* we use them.

There are four common mistakes of using assumptions:

1. **Not recognizing assumptions:** The first mistake is of making assumptions is not even realizing when we do. This confuses speculation with fact.

2. **Keeping assumptions to ourselves:** When we make an assumption and don't share this, then others are making isolated assumptions on the same topic, probably with a different conclusion.

3. **Not recording assumptions:** Given the scale of uncertainty, we are actually making many assumptions across many topics. When we try to remember them all, especially the big ones, we're at risk of forgetting them. Instead, build these assumptions into the hypothesis plan.

4. **Never checking them:** If an assumption is a forecast of what will happen, then we should check back in. Has the assumption come true? Is there more information to include and revise the assumption?

Analogy: Filling in the blanks

Figure 14.1: The incomplete image

Look at the image in Figure 14.1. As you've seen, part of it is missing. Our brains are intelligent and curious and naturally want to complete the missing part. We fill in the blank. Now, if someone else studies the same image, they also fill in the blank. It's probable that between you, there are two entirely different images that now exist. It's fair to imagine that they are envisaging something similar to you. But perhaps not. Is it a bug? A chocolate? A phone? Something else? Without communicating what you think, you'd never know what was in their version and vice versa.

Now, imagine for a moment that your strategy is dependent on this image. I'm sure you'd agree, it's pretty important that you're aligned with each other until you can determine the actual truth of what's missing from the picture.

Assumptions, if used sensibly, can be an excellent way to move forward amidst the uncertainty. The next essential approach is through experimentation.

Exploring the way through experimentation

If we don't know the answers and we can't come to a sensible assumption, then we must carefully explore the way. Experiments are an excellent approach to learning through action.

An experiment's objective is to learn and discover
new patterns or behaviours. It is not about proving
if or how well a solution works; that's a trial.

If you have a high degree of certainty about the topic, it's not true experimentation. Experiments are a way of trying out new thinking and new ideas. If the success rate of your experiments is very high, then it's likely that you're not being bold or brave enough to learn anything new. It's therefore critical to set expectations and communicate clearly about why you're experimenting, how experiments work and what your approach is.

Given the objective of experiments is about learning, the next consideration is the topic. As with a science experiment, you should have a hypothesis or objective clearly laid out. A good hypothesis[51] should:

- Be as brief as possible.

- Be stated with clear and unambiguous terminology.

- State an expected relationship or pattern.

- Be testable.

- Be grounded in past knowledge, research or theory.

- Be based on simple variable changes, so not to combine outputs.

Tip: Creating a strong hypothesis

Consider this hypothesis:

Older people are always more likely to go shopping and are happy to buy more on screens but only when they receive a good experience.

This hypothesis is:

- Complicated and long.

- Not specific (e.g., who is an 'older person'?).

- Unambiguous terminology (e.g., what do we mean by 'go shopping', 'buy more' or 'good experience'?).

- Difficult to test (e.g., what is 'happy'?).

- Testing multiple items which may be disconnected (e.g., 'go shopping' and 'buy more' could be unrelated).

Or alternatively:

People aged 70+ spend 25% more money on digital kiosks in physical stores when a trained sales assistant is available.

The second version tackles many of the issues and is acceptable. It could be that you need multiple hypotheses as part of the same experiment, which is fine.

Then it's about planning and executing the experiment fairly to collect valuable evidence. A sufficient volume of data should be collected, and everyone involved should keep an open mind about the results. It's important not to jump to conclusions, especially in the early stages of an experiment as there can be more volatility before normalizing.

Unfortunately, in many retail settings, it's not possible to control the environment and collect perfectly clean data. So, it's important to be aware that there will be aspects of noise or variability in the data gathered during the experiment. There could be numerous other factors at play, such as time of day, day of week, what part of the month or year, weather, competitive forces, promotions and many other aspects which are relevant and specific to your transformation. This noise is hidden in the data, and you'll need to identify this impact to help get a clear reading.

Finally, draw conclusions from the evidence and review against the hypotheses. Without this final step, you cannot learn, and the experiment will not have met the original objectives. There will be no clarity if it was a success or failure.

Overcoming the stigma of failure

For a long time, failure was an embarrassment. An outcome to avoid at all costs. And in many instances, it still is. Nobody enjoys a poor set of results and there aren't many sports teams who celebrate a loss.

But in the uncertain and ambiguous world, and when we're exploring through experimentation, failure is a learning opportunity. But we want to fail on a small stage rather than gambling the entire company on it.

Simply saying 'failure is acceptable' is a progression but is unlikely to shift the culture. Instead, it relies on repeatable, intentional actions and behaviours which are consistently role-modelled by senior leaders to show it's safe. Changing the stigma attached to failure is a slow shift but you can choose to start that now by identifying and demonstrating which behaviours will best work in your organization's culture to show failure is an option.

Example: Funerals for failures

The bio-tech health and nutrition company, DSM,[52] have embraced failure. They created a hall of failure to showcase their failed experiments and open healthy discussions around failure. Intriguingly, they introduced funerals for failed innovation projects. Leaders and teams come together to celebrate, and say goodbye to these dead projects, helping to encourage reflection, eliminate embarrassment, celebrate the learning and encourage teams to mourn and move on.

How could your organization create a culture to safely celebrate and learn from failure?

Embracing uncertainty by considering likelihood

Technically, recognizing uncertainty is essentially saying that an event, trend or behaviour is not 100% likely (or guaranteed) to happen. Realistically, we're seeing that percentage dive way down whilst more options switch from impossible to plausible to possible.

Chance occurs everywhere in your transformation and it's important to recognize this. The measure of chance is likelihood and although it sounds like a statistic, it's more commonly used to express how confident we feel about a particular forecast or event happening. However, ignoring likelihood is essentially over-confidence; a dangerous mistake to make.

Likelihood can and should build into many different areas of your transformation, for example:

> **Assumptions:** How likely is it that an assumption will come true?

> **Insight and data:** How likely is it that a specific behaviour is representative of the broader customer population?

> **Technical feasibility:** How likely is it that a technology will work?

> **Schedules:** How likely is it that work will be delivered on time?

▶ **Business cases:** How likely is it that sales growth forecasts will be achieved?

▶ **Stakeholders:** How likely is it that a stakeholder group adopts the change?

Likelihood is a factor in risk management too, as discussed in Chapter 13.

Example: Introducing likelihood into a business case

When developing a new proposition with a client, the business case had many estimates and assumptions. There were many unknowns and factors which needed to be explored in more detail. This created ambiguity and regular 'what if?' and 'it depends' conversations where there was no clear answer or outcome. Additionally, the operation included a significant level of variability too, around sales performance, customer behaviour and costs involved, which all impacted the financial forecasts.

By introducing likelihood into the business case, we could see and understand the most sensitive elements where variation had the largest impact to the bottom line. It also highlighted where to focus the attention in terms of getting better quality forecasts and segmenting customer types to get more clarity and predictability in the model.

Where could you start applying the concept of likelihood to improve your transformation?

Once you recognize the aspects of likelihood across your transformation, you are ready to seek ways to improve your chances and encourage those around you to consider likelihood too. This is about improving predictability.

Predictability should be a key aim for a transformation
leader. What you say happens. Otherwise, are
forecasts anything other than wild guesses?
And why then should someone trust you?

Effective use of likelihood will help you and your organization to make better decisions and improve the chance of success in the face of uncertainty. You'll be clear on how to prioritize the best route forward. You'll know where to invest time, effort, resources and money. And you'll be clear on the fragile assumptions and where to challenge and improve the plans. Unfortunately, you'll never get to 100% likely and that will induce some nervous moments.

The nerve-wracking moments

When there is so much to play for, there are likely (see what I did there?) to be some nerve-wracking, edge-of-the-seat moments. More usually, these are in the build-up to major milestones or events, but could equally be in response to a roadblock where the stakes are high, and the pressure is on. There is an element of danger.

In our brains, the amygdala senses this danger and the fear involved, and our primal brain starts to take over. Stress hormones like adrenaline and cortisol race through our blood and our body readies for physical action.

However, it's also important to manage yourself to encourage the intelligent part of our brain to stay active. Deep breathing, mindfulness and relaxation exercises, taking a break and positive self-talk can be ways to regain control. Those anxious moments will pass, and you can focus on driving the transformation forwards in a positive way.

These moments can feel awful and sometimes weirdly wonderful. It's a real mix of emotions that ultimately shows the level of care and passion for a particular initiative, the company and your colleagues. It's also a feeling that you can ease in time, both from experience and by playing with uncertainty.

Playing with uncertainty

Exposing ourselves to uncertainty is one way to become more comfortable with the unknown. However, as the pace of change continues, we'll probably be sitting here in five years thinking that everything was so predictable 'back then'!

So, we need more than just exposure to the 'standard' levels of uncertainty. We need to learn to play with it. Young children may feel nervous when first engaging with a new toy, person or location. There is a feeling of danger and fear. But in time, they learn the rules, conquer the overwhelm and become more confident. As they explore and succeed, recognizing that nothing bad has happened, they form new neural connections which allows the brain to better cope with the situation and similar future situations. In time, human brains develop to assess risk and possibility at a hugely complex scale, naturally filtering out the irrelevant possibilities and focusing on the most likely and most impactful outcomes. As children face new uncertain experiences, practice and persistence leads to confidence and progress.

Dealing with uncertainty is similar for adults. So how can we learn to play with uncertainty? Here are three ways to engage with uncertainty in a safe way, either as individuals or in a group setting:

1. **Challenge your certainties:** Identify elements that we know will happen about the future, perhaps what we know will be true in one to five years. Now, flip that on its head and explore how the opposite could be true. What would need to occur for this to come true. Suddenly, those certainties don't seem quite so secure, and we familiarize with the discomfort.

2. **Extreme scenario planning:** Consider two unrelated but relevant factors related to the future and identify the extremes. For example, if one of these factors was ecommerce as a percentage of total retail sales, the extremes would be 0% and 100%. Plot both factors on a two-by-two matrix to form four potential scenarios. Now explore how these could come true and what you would do in response.

3. **The three-question future:** Take three of your biggest outstanding questions based on your uncertainties and list a range of potential and reasonable answers for each. Now take a coin or dice and assign to the answers. Randomly select the outcomes and consider what happens in a future when the answers to these burning questions materializes.

In many ways, these exercises teach us an important lesson. It's not the uncertainty that we're necessarily nervous about. It's the discomfort of a future that we just don't like. And if we don't like it, we don't want to engage in it. But persist in playing with uncertainty and discomfort and you'll build confidence.

'The problem we have in our brains is we're fixed in a certain mindset, and we are fixed in a certain way of doing things. You have to engage with alternative perspectives. You have to imagine that what you're saying is wrong.'

Dr Jackie Mulligan[53]

The fallout from a leadership change

As stakeholders continue to switch roles and companies, many transformation initiatives will experience a mid-flight change of CEO, senior leader or other key role. This can provide major uncertainty for transformations and those involved in them.

A stereotype suggests that new leaders immediately dispose of what the 'old guard' or management had previously prioritized, favoured and championed, especially if the new individual has been externally recruited rather than developed inside the organization.

Realistically, people expect a new leader to come in and make changes and improvements. The concept of the new job 90-day plan is widely recognized and in the mind of new recruits looking to make an early, positive impact by bringing their experience, expertise and perspective to bear.

With strategically important transformations on the table, it's only natural that these are closely scrutinized. The original challenge, vision, approach, solution, business justification and many other factors will all be investigated.

If there is genuine widespread support for the initiative, with clear and reasonable assumptions, positive, consistent progress and a series of plans about how the future will unfold, the transformation will be ready to stand its ground. And those that believe that the transformation is the right thing for the organization should state this and the reasoning behind it. This will bide well in the inevitable reprioritization that the new leader instigates.

However, if cracks in the thinking show through and previously supportive stakeholders flee like rats from a sinking ship, then the transformation will be in trouble (with or without the new leader in place for that matter) and may be deprioritized, paused, rescoped or cancelled altogether.

The ultimate questions to consider and ask is 'why are we doing this, how are we approaching it and what has changed?'.

Balancing flexibility and perseverance

With all the uncertainty around transformation, often the generic guidance is to be flexible and adaptable. However, blindly following this advice will see have you pivoting at every little bump in the road. A regularly changing strategy is hugely unproductive and reduces trust in the vision and leadership.

There remains a fine line between being adaptable and being determined. There is no simple answer other than 'it depends' when deciding whether to adjust the approach or power up and keep pushing on.

If an unexpected or unavoidable roadblock impacts the transformation, you must consider the impact. Understand the situation and context to confirm elements like: if it is a short-term blip or longer-term trend; what the root cause is; the implications of taking a diversion or alternative approach relative to pushing through. Consulting with stakeholders across the business and taking an informed decision is best advised instead of always flexing or always persevering. Additionally, it's always valuable to remember the challenges that the transformation is tackling and the destination.

Ask yourself: What's the right thing to do?
This will help guide you to the best approach.

Overcoming uncertainty with Agile ways of working

The advent of the Agile methodology and ways of working in software or IT functions came due to uncertainty in the requirements and the difficulty of changing part way through the process.

Understanding what customers value most is of critical importance and an excellent approach in any situation. Additionally, there is a focus on delivering this value as soon as possible, which is also brilliant for transformation initiatives. Agile's use of short, daily stand-up meetings to share latest progress and highlight blockers to future progress is another great opportunity for many transformation initiatives which will build and maintain momentum whilst also helping to miss the avoidable roadblocks. The Agile Manifesto[54] can also be applied to transformation relatively easily too.

One of the common misconceptions and mistakes about Agile working is that there is no plan, no outlook and no commitment beyond the duration of a sprint due to the ever-changing requirements and unknowns in the process and environment. Whilst there should be high-level timescales plan and a roadmap, this isn't always the case. For shareholders and for many stakeholders, this level of uncertainty when it comes to a strategically important transformation is simply not acceptable. Finding a careful balance about predictability and flexibility is essential and maintaining up-to-date versions of the six plans as discussed in Chapter 8 and other techniques discussed here will help navigate the uncertainty and unknowns. Clarity over the approach you take helps enormously.

Agile approaches can work in transformation, and especially when there is a significant technology or software portion to the solution, due to Agile's origins in IT. It would be prudent to onboard and train the transformation team and relevant stakeholders on Agile methodologies to create a shared understanding. This shared understanding ensures a consistent language about sprints, backlogs and stand-ups will help cross-functional working. A shared rhythm around timelines will also aid progress. If you face unprecedented levels of uncertainty with your transformation, adopting more Agile principles could definitely be a way forward.

What we've covered

- Unchecked uncertainty will derail your transformation, so clarify the burning questions blocking progress.

- Assumptions, experiments and the concept of likelihood are approaches to navigate safely into the unknown.

- Learning to 'play' with uncertainty builds confidence and encourages us to consider the uncomfortable options.

Chapter 15
Making bold
decisions

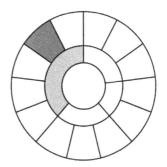

Decisions are a critical aspect of transformation and exist throughout the entire journey. From formally recognizing the reasons to transform, through to investment and implementation decisions. Good decision making enables progress whilst poor decision making leads to delays, financial impacts and missed opportunities.

However, given their importance, we tend to receive very little training or coaching about preparing for or making decisions. It's something we learn through experience. We find a way.

Are we a good decision maker? Usually, it's hard to know. You probably know when you get it very wrong. But that's about it. So, the ultimate truth is that that we never *know* if we have made a good decision. We can *suspect*. We can ask for other people's *opinions*. But we never know.

In the fast paced and volatile world we exist in, making bold decisions becomes an important skill and specific decisions should be made at appropriate levels of the organization. So, let's consider how to approach these and how to avoid the common mistakes.

The common decision-making mistakes and challenges

Perhaps the most common challenge is when there is no obvious answer. You weight up the options, consider the pros and cons, and it's just not clear which is best. This can lead to delays or no decision. And when no decision is made, the status quo lives on for longer, perhaps gaining more sticking power too.

Another common but invisible challenge is making decisions without realizing or without appreciation. When leaders are busy and randomly meandering through time based on what's most urgent in the moment, decisions are made without consideration of the situation, examining the evidence or thought. This will significantly impact decision effectiveness.

There may be a lack of clarity about who is the decision maker, and when, where and how decisions are made. A lack of visibility or awareness of internal decision processes creates confusion, whilst a lack of empowerment through the organization sends minute decisions up the hierarchy.

Many leaders overestimate the clarity of their decision process and fail to explain the decision to those involved or impacted. The Harvard Business Review[55] reported that there is a perception mismatch between CEOs' view of decision process clarity and the understanding of their exec team. On a scale of 1–7, CEOs self-assessed themselves at an average of 5.62 whilst their executive teams scored their own CEO at 3.86. This lack of clarity may exist throughout the organization and destroys motivation whilst failing to prepare future talent to take on the complex nature of decision making.

Our familiar foe, the fear of failure, continues to add anxiety and stress, encouraging procrastination through always wanting more data, insight, options or confidence.

Following our bias or natural tendencies is a mistake. We all succumb to several biases based on our background, past experiences, attitudes, values and outlook. The phenomenon of confirmation bias,[56] causes us to ignore valid evidence that doesn't align to our pre-conceived viewpoint. Groupthink[57] is another bias which guides our preference to the most popular opinions. Optimism bias[58] encourages us to think that things will work themselves out and 'all will be ok in the end'. The book *Noise*[59] by Kahneman, Sibony and Sunstein is an excellent resource to learn more about internal biases.

'Good decision making must be based on objective and accurate predictive judgments that are completely unaffected by hopes and fears, or by preferences and values.'

Daniel Kahneman, Olivier Sibony, Cass R. Sunstein

We also focus our attention on trivial topics and decisions. Parkinson's Law of Triviality[60] suggests that organizations focus disproportionally more time making decisions on topics that are not important. So, when it comes to business-critical decisions about the future of the company, relatively insufficient time is spent coming to the conclusion.

And finally, not committing to decisions can be deadly, either by reversing past decisions or intentionally ignoring the official decision and continuing with an alternative option. This destroys trust and tears teams apart. If there is disagreement about the decision, this must be swallowed at the point of decision.

What is the bold decision?

We're making decisions all day, every day. What to wear, which strategy to pursue, where to invest, what to eat, what to prioritize, who to trust, how to react to that problem. A whole muddle of decisions, so it's crucial to recognize which the important decisions are and when a bold decision is required.

But what makes a decision a *bold* one? A bold decision is one that demands courage and confidence to make. There remains an element of risk but waiting for all risks to be eliminated results in procrastination and delay. Bold decisions require us to step out of the comfort zone despite these risks and step away from the familiar status quo. They need people to believe in the direction and to be willing to continue this unfamiliar but essential journey.

There is likely to be opposition or counter arguments. There may be uncertainty and unanswered questions. But a bold decision is not a rash one. It's not about being reckless. It should be considered, calculated and careful. It recognizes the potential opportunity and that rewards outweigh the risks involved.

Bold decisions require strong leadership, conviction, determination and resilience. To maximize the impact, your transformation needs bold decisions, and this needs you to be a bold decision maker.

Becoming a bold decision maker

Making bold decisions required practice and diligence. It's easy to succumb to the Law of Triviality or rely on confirmation bias when you're not intentionally in decision-making mode.

So, when you're at a crossroads and need a bold decision, here's what to consider to become more intentional and considered with your decision process, whether you're making or prompting the decision:

- What is the ask? Can it be framed as a question? Is it just one decision or a series of decisions?

- What are the options or potential answers on the table? Are there other reasonable options? Has the default option of 'do nothing' been considered and included?

- Why is this decision needed? What does it block or enable?

- What evidence feeds into the decision? Does this evidence support or counter each option or is it one-sided? Is the evidence trustworthy, statistically significant, fair and complete?

- What recommendations are being made? And why was this suggestion reached?

- What will happen next if each option is selected? What are the good and bad implications?

- Who is impacted and how?

- What are the risks in making this decision? And what are the risks or impacts of not making any decision?

- What uncertainties exist? What are the unanswered questions?

- What assumptions are being made and are these consistent across the team?

- When must the decision be made by?

- Who makes the decision and how?

These aspects will move towards a considered decision. Additionally, a bold decision is created by not only what builds up to the point of decision, but also what follows.

Making a good, solid, bold decision

A large part of successful decision making is in recognizing, preparing for and considering the outcome. The moment of deciding is clearly critical and often, the success of a decision is defined by what happens afterwards.

When you're not sure on the outcome, aim to eliminate options. TV talent shows take this approach by eliminating contestants each week and therefore simplifying the decision one step at a time.

To overcome confirmation bias, involve more people in the decision-making process, and especially a diverse set of people with different backgrounds, experiences and expertise. This dilutes the confirmation bias and encourages a fair debate.

Debate and review time is beneficial, and often the law of diminishing returns suggests that there will be less revolutionary, new evidence or discussion over time. Instead, the same pertinent points tend to be revisited and restated. So, at some point, the moment of decision must be actively and intentionally pushed. Without a specific prompt for the decision, it's easy to let debates continue in circles. Therefore, this moment is best prompted by a specific question, the ask, either to an individual decision maker, or to whole a group or committee if relevant.

The final decision must be clearly stated, along with any conditions. If there is a lack of clarity, now is the time to nail that down. Eliminating confusion here helps ensure ongoing alignment. The reasoning behind the decision also provides clarity and guidance for future direction.

Great decision making doesn't stop there, however. Bold decisions need communication, along with relevant reasoning. Who should know? Who will inform people and how? What actions does the decision require? These questions ensure that the transformation continues at maximum speed and can surge ahead without confusion.

After the debate and a bold decision, it's also likely that an element of alignment may need to be re-established. This is where the approach of 'disagree and commit' comes into play. If the evidence and debate has been fair, all voices have been heard, and assuming an ethically-sound decision then any disagreements should be parked. Easier said than done, especially if someone is emotionally invested into one of the undecided options. But, as discussed earlier, not doing this can initiate ongoing conflict, misalignment and reversing decisions.

Example: The danger of reversing decisions

I once worked with a company where decisions were being clearly made in a governance meeting. Then at the next session, the same topic was raised again, and the debate continued, as if no decision had been reached. Decisions were reversed and needed more debate before continuing. This could happen multiple times on a single topic.

Whilst wasting time and money, it was also hugely frustrating for the team who then distrusted the leaders and strategy. Teams felt it was acceptable to wait for a period after any decision in case it was reversed.

How can you establish a clear and definitive decision process and encourage a 'disagree and commit' mentality?

Advisors and valid opinions

Leaders and other decision makers have a lot to consider when making bold decisions. Much is riding on finding the best possible outcome. Additionally, decisions are likely to include functional intricacies and evidence may present contradictions which must be understood.

To help cover all of this, having a suite of trusted advisors can be massively beneficial. These advisors may be relevant to specific functions or topics or can be more general in nature with a broad understanding of the strategy and direction. They can help understand the complexity and nuances of the situation whilst also providing diversity of thought. Having a group of proverbial 'yes-people' will do no good for anyone!

As you drive bold decisions for your transformation, consider who could consult as a trusted advisor. If you are presenting a decision, engaging these individuals whilst understanding perspectives and sticking points can be enormously helpful. Or if you're a decision maker, consider how you can identify relevant individuals and direct them to understand and advise on the decision in front of you.

Some advisors will be optimistic or pessimistic by nature and are subject to their own bias. When presented with the evidence of the decision, especially numbers, different people will have a different understanding and conclusion based on the same number. For example, for any given metric, some may think 90% is good, whilst others think 90% is bad. In many ways, this difference forms the rich tapestry of a diverse perspective, although it also adds an element of confusion.

With many transformation initiatives and relevant decisions, there are often many more opinions than are needed. Whilst everyone is entitled to an opinion, not all opinions are necessarily valid. Some individuals may be observing the transformation but are not a stakeholder who is involved in, impacted by or an influence on the initiative. It's likely that their intentions are honest, and they want the best outcome for the company, yet they may not be informed with all the details and intricacies. Given the complex nature of making bold decisions and the careful balance of risk and reward based on evidence, any uninformed opinions may cloud the decision in ambiguity. And in turn, it's easy to make the wrong decision, or even no decision at all.

Making decision-making forums useful

We're surrounded by distractions, even in meetings, which deteriorate decision making. Scientists can see distractions in our brains and recognize two forms of focus: voluntary and involuntary attention.[61] First, voluntary attention is when we choose what to focus on. Perhaps we're researching specific topics, processing an idea or listening intently to what someone is saying. The intelligent part of our brain is in control. Then involuntary attention distracts us; a sudden noise, movement, or even an unexpected colour or formatting of a document. Control swiftly shifts to the primal side of the brain which developed about 2.5 million years ago[62] and is tasked with keeping us alive. Distractions and distracting topics snatch us away from the voluntary attention essential for important decision making and we must protect attention spans.

Ask yourself: How are distractions stopping meaningful discussions and confusing decision making?

We discussed effective steering groups back in Chapter 11. The playbook for this group should reference the type of decisions made and expectations for making good, bold decisions, including prep and pre-read as well as an expectation of committing to decisions.

A decision-making forum or meeting should be an enabler, not a barrier. So, consider what would encourage these important conversations and avoid them being tied up in more trivial debates.

It's likely that these sessions will be expensive, based on the people sitting around the table. Build an agenda with a reasonable and proportionate amount of time for each decision. Tackle the biggest and most urgent decisions first to avoid being delayed or distracted by smaller discussions. Each item should be crystal clear on the specific decision, ideally framing them as questions. This question then acts as the prompt when it's time to make the call.

Additionally, consider the flow of the session, allowing time for the decision maker(s) and advisors to reset between sessions. Complex decisions demand brain power and it's also important to stop people's primal brains from being summoned and taking over.

Clearly documenting each decision, any related conditions and the reasoning behind it will help align the team and support the onward communication cascade and initiate the ensuing action.

Finally, effective moderation is important to help guide the process and stay removed from the detail and passionate debate. A moderator plays a key role in guiding the group through the process and towards the best possible decision and can challenge when faced with the prospect of reversing decisions or in response to inconsistent or poor decision-making behaviours.

Reversing decisions

As a decision is made and moved into execution, it is possible that new information comes to light, especially with a fast-moving external environment that continually affects business performance and the people involved. In this instance, it may be prudent to revisit a decision. Just getting 'cold feet' or suffering from a form of 'buyer's remorse' is however not a valid reason for revisiting a decision.

Often, many decisions can be 'unmade' although it's likely that there could be consequences; and usually, the bigger the decision, the bigger the consequences. Additionally, the longer the decision has been 'made' for, the more complicated and costly it will be to undo.

Aside from wasting time, money and resources, it will diminish motivation and commitment through the organization, creating confusion and uncertainty. People lose faith and trust in the leadership, and it puts the brakes on any momentum that's been built up.

Reversing out of a decision is made of two decisions: first, to revert a previous decision, and second, to decide on the replacement option. And like any decision, these must be communicated clearly, along with the reasoning and direction of what happens next. It's especially easy for reversed decisions to be misunderstood or even mistrusted, where people decide to carry on anyway on the presumption that things will work out in the end.

Making bold decisions may come with a crisis of conscious at some point. Yet, in the face of adversity and the VUCA world we live in, effective and meaningful transformation favours bold decisions.

What we've covered

▷ Decision making is a learned skill and there are many pitfalls to avoid.

▷ Making bold decisions enables transformation velocity and needs intentional action.

▷ Consulting a diverse group of trusted advisors helps reach a clear and well-rounded decision.

Chapter 16
Executing and realizing the transformation

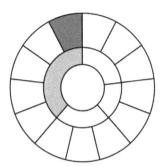

The transformation has been clearly defined and developed from the twinkle of an eye through to a tangible solution that's ready to deliver meaningful value to the business, customers and colleagues. But it all comes down to these final stages. The moment of delivery and execution.

In reality, the delivery and execution is not a single moment as activities extend to include communication, training, and familiarizing with the change through to monitoring the transformation's effectiveness and ultimately closing the initiative and handing over to business-as-usual operational teams.

I'm also including trial phases in this section as they represent a mini deployment.

The easy trap to fall into at this moment is to assume it will all go to plan. With the destination clearly in sight, there are still plenty of roadblocks that could cause challenges and can cause the execution to fail.

Why does execution fail?

There are three types of failure at this stage of a transformation:

- **Catastrophic failure:** Something goes hugely wrong, and the solution must be pulled out for major rework or even to stop the whole transformation. Given the high profile of the retail industry, these can make the industry and even mainstream news. However, whilst severe, these are fortunately quite rare. Causes include technical challenges or major upset by customers or colleagues.

- **Slow-burn failure:** Otherwise known as 'death by a thousand cuts', where many small niggles, bugs or complaints mount up over time. The transformation partially does what it's meant to, but it's a struggle and needs rapid and continuous improvement. Causes include technical challenges, poor training or communication, poor usability and where the solution does not cover all possibilities.

- **Passive failure:** The transformation never lands properly and new ways of working or the changes never embed. The status quo slowly re-emerges, and life continues as if the transformation never happened. Causes include focusing on the wrong problem, poor communication or an excessively complicated solution.

In summary, failure is caused by any number of change management related issues at the deployment or from deep-rooted challenges which have existed and persisted throughout the transformation journey. Therefore, the aim should be to critique the plans and reach a moment of certainty ahead of delivery.

The moment of certainty for delivery

The delivery phase should theoretically be the most predictable; with huge focus and weeks, months or years of hard, smart and careful work building toward this crescendo. And we still want to double check everything is ready and we're not setting ourselves up for failure. Therefore, it's wise to hold 'Go/No Go' decision points to confirm a moment of certainty at relevant and specific points on the transformation journey.

This Go/No Go decision point should include relevant stakeholders, ideally including a sample of the customers of the change. The aim is to critically assess and highlight improvement opportunities for the planned deployment, and should cover several items:

> **The challenge:** Briefly revisit the original business problem or opportunity as context.

> **Transformation solution:** Detailing what is being deployed, how it will tangibly appear in the 'real world' and what impacts (positive and negative) will be seen. Any known limitations should be clearly stated.

> **Deployment strategy:** The approach for introducing the change and ramping up utilization or adoption. This is especially important if deploying to many remote sites, such as stores or warehouses.

> **Communication plans:** Detailing what communications are planned for the customers of the change. This should also include specific details of channels, purpose as well as how queries will be handled. This includes relevant marketing messages to consumers too.

> **Training plans and materials:** What training, upskilling or guidance will be given to relevant parties, and how will future colleagues or consumers be inducted to the change.

> **Support plans:** How the transformation will be monitored, what metrics will be used as 'temperature checks' and how problems will be recognized, triaged and resolved. It should also include the expected duration and effort for support and the known issues that will come up.

> **Handover plans:** How the transformation will be managed in the long term, and how the handover or transition period to business-as-usual will work.

> **Transformation specific items:** Depending on the topic, there will be other specific items to review, including corporate policies or procedures, investor or shareholder updates, partnership agreements, detailed modelling, store layout plans, prototypes, etc.

If there is an issue raised whilst reviewing all of this, you'll want a rapid response to resolve it as a problem fixed pre-deployment will be significantly easier than a problem in the field.

Trials boost confidence

Trials represent a useful opportunity to learn on a manageable scale and build confidence with stakeholders. Throughout the development of the transformation solution, there may be several opportunities for experiments, tests, simulations, prototypes, proof of concepts, alpha and beta trials, pilots and many more. These are similar but have subtly different objectives.

Before a full deployment, series of trials can be immensely useful to learn and build trust and confidence about the process of execution. However, a trial cannot be considered a success if there is no clear objective or way of measuring and assessing that objective.

The final stage of a trial should be a full 'dress-rehearsal' including communications, training, deployment-level support with a minimal level of handholding at all points. The danger of excessive monitoring and protective support is that the trial will not mimic the deployment and will not be viable when rolling out at a larger scale.

Four approaches to deployment

Selecting the right deployment strategy makes a huge difference. There are four main approaches to choose from:

1. **Big bang:** This approach implements the change to the entire scope at one time. This approach can be useful for simpler changes or where there is a solid reason that it must happen at once. For example, a new HR policy must be introduced to all colleagues at one time, across multiple sites. This is a fast route to deployment but with an extreme peak of activity and support requirements.

2. **Waves:** The solution is introduced to segmented groups over an extended period of time. This makes the change more manageable from a support perspective and lowers the risk to the business, but at the cost of extending the time to reap the benefit. For example, a new piece of equipment is introduced to 1,000 stores in groups of 50 stores per week over multiple months.

3. **Phased:** This deploys functionality in phases and gradually builds up to the ultimate solution. Each phase can be deployed as a big bang or using waves. This can be useful to build capability and utilization over time, plus it may mirror a multi-phased approach for developing the transformation too. For example, a new checkout system with the most basic transaction features is deployed to stores in a wave deployment, then once fully introduced and embedded, advanced features are deployed using a big bang approach.

4. **Organic:** The customers of the change can opt-in to the new solution and adoption builds over time. This can be a slow and steady approach that encourages people to want the change, rather than have it 'done to them'. For example, a new livestreaming proposition is added to the operating model and area managers work with stores on finding the ideal and relevant time to introduce this to each specific operation. This is best for non-business critical changes and can be effective with non-urgent disruptive innovations.

Ask yourself: Which deployment approach will be most suitable for your transformation, and why?

There are merits and downsides for each approach, and you must find the best and most feasible fit for your transformation, your organizational culture and the external environment. Additionally, check if technical restrictions or legal requirements that guide you down one path or another. Findings from any trials that you've run may also be a useful guide to selecting the deployment approach.

Whichever approach you select, also factor in the ramp up time. It's likely that when the change deploys, it will not instantly work or operate at full speed or maximum capacity. Depending on your transformation, this ramp up may be in colleague productivity, customer participation, sales uplift or other factors. In my experience, it almost always takes longer than initially expected or hoped. In turn, the benefits and the business case must recognize this reality and should be modelled with a ramp up stage. Plus, there may in fact be an initial blip that brings additional cost, effort or degradation to KPIs whilst the change is adopted. Ideally, this is anticipated and expectations set across the business accordingly.

Relevant, omnichannel, two-way communications

The communication strategy is perhaps the most fragile aspect of managing and deploying change. For many customers of the change, their first impression will be hugely defining and will dictate the confirmation bias that they take into future encounters with the transformation. Whilst we're nearing the end of this book and the transformation, it's valuable to build communication up over time rather than saving it for the moment of deployment.

You must communicate with multiple parties, each with their own particular interests. Internally, this could include a large frontline workforce, distributed area management, regional teams or head-office teams. Each will be impacted differently, and individuals will respond in a variety of ways. Externally, consumers, shareholders, potential investors, the media and suppliers or partners may be affected by the transformation for different reasons.

People are not interested by the change or the communication; they want to understand 'what's in it for me?' and if it represents any threat to their status quo.

Clear and relevant communication sounds like an obvious tip but remains a challenge for many transformation efforts. When the transformation team have been living and breathing a topic, they're often too close to make it simple and relevant to the target audience. It's the 'curse of knowledge' haunting us again. The base-level knowledge is overestimated, important information is assumed to be standard knowledge and not everyone is interested in everything. Seeking independent and unknowledgeable viewpoints is critical to help position the communication in the right way.

The reasons why this change is happening is hugely important. It justifies effort to transform and can help people through the emotional cycle of change. However, this is often omitted by mistake or to avoid conflict. Cost saving and efficiency changes are part of the modern business world but many changes initiatives hope that no-one will notice this benefit.

In the retail industry, it's likely that the communications, of any format, will be to a large and hugely diverse audience. Language, education, culture, time zone, shift patterns and geography are among the variables and create barriers to a one-size-fits-all communication. Knowing your audience and what will work will be critically important.

Additionally, different individuals respond to different formats of communication. Whilst some enjoy written comms, others prefer meetings. Video, pictures, infographics, posters, audio, emails, instant messaging, letters and plenty of other mediums exist. Don't rely on just one medium of communication. Think omnichannel. Consider how consumers have different channel preferences and that you want to offer a seamless shopping experience. Now consider how you can introduce a seamless communications experience across relevant channels for the change.

It's important to be in control of that first impression which usually means communicating clearly and early. If gossip about the transformation leaks before any formal communication, then you will have lost control and it's likely that the rumours will involve negative viewpoints, conjecture or myths. In the media, the concept of 'bad news sells more' also applies to how gossip actively spreads. And if you then start to communicate the facts, it's significantly harder to overcome the 'truth' that already exists.

In addition to communicating early, don't just communicate one time. I'm sure we've all been subject to changes where you've missed the one email that was sent and found its way into the junk folder. Don't let your transformation fall into the same trap. Consider the 'Rule of 7' used by marketers:

> *'The marketing "Rule of 7" states that a potential customer is likely to see a message at least 7 times before they'll be provoked to take an action.'*
>
> *Movie industry, 1930s*

The reality is that in our modern-day multi-channel, information-overload, task-switching, hyper-connected and regularly distracted lifestyle, the classic 'Rule of 7' needs many more than seven touchpoints. Use this concept and apply to your communications approach. Consider beyond the standard written communication and how you could integrate short or long videos, roadshows, live demonstrations, interactive webinars, expert conference calls, group visits, gamified quizzes, infographics, local centres of excellence and other ideas.

And finally, it's critical that communication is not a one-way broadcast. There should be two-way interaction between parties. Consider how you can encourage this interaction which will in turn help the communication to be understood and taken onboard. Educate people about the future state and ask questions to provoke thinking and meaningful discussion. This will increase awareness and understanding whilst also highlighting risks and opportunities at an early stage. Ultimately, the communication is there to inform both parties and drive the shift in capability and behaviour to embed the change.

Personalizing capabilities and behaviours to drive change

Training the change is essential to drive adoption. Training is not about downloading loads of information onto people. It's not a compliance tick-box exercise. It's about developing familiarity of the future state, building relevant capabilities and embedding the behaviours that will drive change. Training exists to help people embrace the 'what', the 'how' and the 'why' for the transformation.

Training frontline colleagues has been transformed in recent times, enabled by technology and digital devices. Ensure your change training makes the most of this. Also consider how a blend of coaches, managers and colleagues can help hold conversations and bring the transformation to life.

Ask yourself: What is the most important behaviour
that will drive the success of your transformation?
And how will you encourage this behaviour?

Personalizing the training experience is increasingly possible based on an individual's existing knowledge and experience. What will be incredibly useful for one person will be the equivalent of teaching another to 'suck eggs'. The one-size-fits-all training approach isn't ideal in any format. You might still have to revert to it in certain instances as required by law or regulation. Just like you'd want to personalize the shopping experience for customers, consider how you can personalize the training experience for colleagues wherever possible.

Example: Making training matter

One retailer set up regional in-person training events for all store colleagues to reinvigorate the teams and launch a major refocus, including new service propositions and store metrics. The day's agenda was full of both education and fun elements, including technical training and focused on values and attitudes. Inspirational talks, training demos, role-specific workshops and team games made the event extremely memorable, relevant and created a highly energized workforce that were excited for the transformation.

For the weeks and months after the event, the key takeaways from the day continued to be revisited to cement in the learning and desired behaviours. These events were the primary catalyst for an ongoing culture change.

How could you blend education, inspiration, engagement and excitement to prepare teams and the organization to adopt change?

Depending on the transformation, frontline colleagues, management, suppliers or even customers might need training. Each will take a different approach and mix of messaging, technical guidance and support.

Finally, to encourage the capabilities and behaviours to embed, it's also important to celebrate successes. Recognizing improvements, gamification rewards and a simple 'thank you' can all be used effectively.

Responsive support

As your communications engage and training develops the required capabilities, the team should be actively ready to support with speed. By the stage of main deployment, this may include a broader team, including various support centre or contact centre colleagues, as well as subject matter coaches to help overcome challenges and embed the change.

Listen to the customers of the change and what they're saying. Collate the feedback and recognize the key messages. Equally, ensure someone has their 'ear to the ground' to listen to the unspoken opinion about your transformation.

Many dissatisfied customers will never raise a formal complaint, but they remain disappointed and less engaged. The same is true with the customer of your change.

Get into the details and day-to-day operations to see how it's going, just like at the start of the transformation. Quick surveys and polls offer a brilliant way to check the pulse of the change and open a two-way conversation.

Answer questions clearly and promptly, and consider including regularly updated FAQs in training materials and further communications. If one person has a question, it's likely to be a common query.

When problems crop up, jump on them. Mistakes, bugs or other niggles can quickly cause a transformation promoter to switch to a detractor. However, recognizing the issue, sharing workarounds and applying fixes or repairs can quickly turn those on the fence or even those against the change into the strongest advocates.

Also consider how to monitor the utilization, progress or performance and share tips and suggestions based on this insight. These are exceptionally powerful when they originate from peers rather than from the transformation team. This demonstrates ownership and adoption, and is an important step to encourage more people to get onboard. Plus, it can help develop tweaks, enhancements or changes to the transformation and elements like the training. In time, you'll see the transformation becoming more valuable and you'll start to realize the change.

Realizing the change

With the transformation solution in place, you'll need many eyes monitoring the change, closely watching specific diagnostics and KPIs. And whilst there will probably be great excitement (and nervousness!) when the performance needle first moves, the real benefit of the transformation comes in the long run. The change must fully embed and become second nature before you can realize the evolution of the business.

Hopefully you already have a high confidence level by this stage but do check that the original problem or opportunity has been resolved. The customer of the change alongside supporting data and evidence should confirm this.

Review utilization or uptake to see if it's been in line with the expected ramp up. Monitor these trends over time to assess if there has been any unusual behaviour or pattern. This could highlight opportunities and threats to the transformation, which in turn could suggest new actions to take.

The benefits and costs outlined in the financial plan should be reviewed and assessed. Depending on the type of transformation, this may involve adjusting budgets or targets that should be done in agreement with relevant stakeholders. It may also be relevant to assess any potential cannibalization or uplift to the existing or core business, expected or not.

Revisit assumptions and check if they have come true or not. Some assumptions will remain unconfirmed and may begin to form the assumptions that the broader businesses uses. Consider the risks too, to identify which risks came true and which preventative actions worked well.

Through the feedback and observations from the first days, weeks and months, it's likely that you'll identify opportunities for improvement and issues to fix. Small tweaks will be quick to resolve or put into place. Others may form longer-term plans that could feed into follow-on phases or even new transformation initiatives.

Finally, we work our way to the point of handover, where the business-as-usual team or operation takes full responsibility. At this stage, the transformation becomes commonplace, and the new standard operating practice creates the next status quo.

After the transformation

As the transformation slowly becomes the status quo, the transformation team will breathe a sigh of relief. A hugely stressful and rewarding journey is approaching the conclusion.

Take time to reflect on the transformation. There will be many learnings, elements that went well, aspects that could have been better; things you'd do again or differently. These lessons are hugely valuable for you and for the organization, but only if they're captured and acted upon. The act of 'lessons learned' is widely practiced and often forgotten. Consider who else can share experiences or learn from your journey. Ensure learnings are collected and easy to access. Consider setting future calendar reminders, prompting you about what you'll do differently.

If lessons learned sessions don't change the future,
then they're not serving their purpose.

Please do celebrate the transformation and, importantly, the individuals that made it happen. The journey is a huge team effort with numerous moments of combined and individual Herculean efforts. This celebration is a way to say thank you, from both the organizations and from yourself. It's a recognition of the whole achievement as well as the process and journey of transformation. Creating a culture to celebrate change and highlight both successes and learnings will develop a positive workforce and pave the way for more successful initiatives in the future.

I'll be honest, I'm often guilty of moving on too quickly, downplaying the achievement, focusing on the next big thing, and I know others are too. Don't make this mistake! It's one I actively try to avoid. Celebrate in a manner that feels right and reasonable. And however you choose to do this, do this as a team, together, as one.

As the celebrations subside and the team disbands, there may be mourning from and for the team. This can present itself as a feeling of loss for the camaraderie, an anxiety about what's next, and questions about how they can add more value. Consider how you will support individuals at this moment as it can be an unexpected response to an otherwise positive transformation.

But as you draw the transformation to a close, it's not fully over yet.

Revisiting the transformation

In the weeks and months after the transformation deploys, it's likely that the transformation team's workload will decline, and individuals will return to their day-jobs or be drafted onto the next big priority.

The best organizations always revisit the transformation after the event. 'When' depends on the transformation, but usually 3–12 months later is effective.

In many ways, the end of the transformation should mimic the start. Take an honest look in the mirror and consider what all the data and insight is telling you. Has the business challenge or opportunity been overcome?

As you investigate, there may be more changes to help optimize performance or grasp new opportunities. These should be fed into the broader strategy and must be prioritized against other work.

There is the occasional requirement to raise a task force to revisit or refresh parts of the transformation. This is especially important if you sense that the change is at risk of becoming a slow-burn failure, brought down by many little challenges. Catastrophic failures would usually raise an urgent action by themselves. And passive failures should be picked up by supporting the change in the initial period after deployment.

However, the key question to ask is: Has the transformation worked? The whole journey started with a catalyst to change and a destination to reach. The appropriate transformation was identified and there was clear business justification to invest resources. Assumptions were made to combat the unknowns and uncertainties. Bold decisions were made based on evidence and forecasts of the future. Were all these correct and fair?

Ask yourself: Should the transformation be
judged a success for the business, for
colleagues and for your customers?

What we've covered

- Everything rests on the execution and final deployment, remain vigilant through this stage.

- Let 'retail thinking' inspire how you execute the transformation, including communication, personalization and service levels.

- The transformation isn't complete until it's embedded and working by itself for an extended time.

Chapter 17
Bringing it
all together

Driving retail transformation is a complex, challenging and hugely rewarding journey. As the retail market continues to evolve, retailers and brands must transform and shift in extraordinary ways to meet customer demand, deliver shareholder value and win in the fiercely competitive arena of shopping.

In Part 1 of this book, I asked if you will be the driver or a passenger? Like the driver of a car, becoming a transformation driver has many aspects to it and is more complicated than it appears. With intentional action and experience, it becomes a learned skill that will help you be more effective in future transformations and in retail.

By using the Retail Transformation Steering Wheel, and all the topics we've covered in Part 2, I want you to be confident and capable of driving transformation initiatives yourself, and inspiring others to do so.

Revisiting the Retail Transformation Steering Wheel

The Retail Transformation Steering Wheel is a way to assess, monitor and improve the health of your transformation. It guides you to resolve potential problems and grasp opportunities to reach your destination.

Having read the book, you're ready to score each section with one point per 'yes' answer to the self-assessment prompts in Appendix 1.

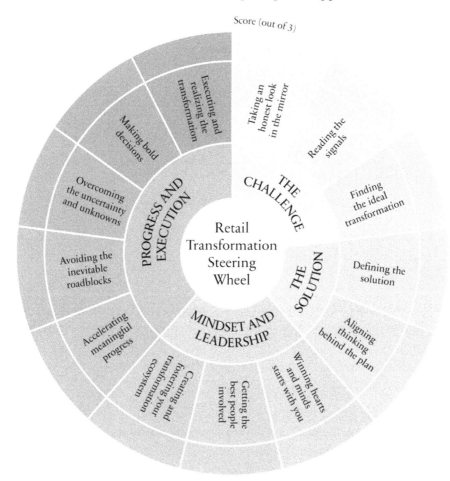

Figure 17.1: The Retail Transformation Steering Wheel

All aspects of the Steering Wheel will need your focus and attention. Demands shift through the journey, and you'll need to concentrate on different aspects at different times. Check the health of your transformation regularly and challenge yourself. It's not a repetitive and time-consuming admin task, but a valuable tool to help you drive.

The Steering Wheel is a self-assessment tool for you and the team to encourage debate and realize opportunities to improve your transformation and how you're approaching it. Focus on areas with low scores and look to maintain focus where you're performing well. After scoring, define and communicate your action plan to collaborate and progress forwards.

Go to DrivingRetailTransformation.com/wheel or scan the QR code below to access your own downloadable template to complete, keep and update.

The end…?

Having achieved the original transformation goals and arrived at your destination, have you reached the end? Is there an end to transformation?

When you reach your original destination, the world has changed and moved on too. Customers, competitors, technology, other aspects of the external environment and your own organization all continue to shift. And this causes you to look to the horizon once again. It tempts you into your next journey. Your next transformation.

The retail industry is still vibrant and there are significant growth opportunities for retailers and consumer-facing brands. The success factors of profitability, customer experience, colleague experience and sustainable business are still relevant. It's how we achieve those success factors that's evolving. The aspects covered in Chapter 1 present threats or opportunities to transform.

And so, it continues. You'll identify more opportunities to develop and will have more business challenges to overcome. It could be connected to your last transformation or alternatively on a completely different topic or area of the business. Maybe it will require a different type of transformation for a new and unique journey.

Every transformation is bespoke

As new threats, opportunities, trends and pressures ignite the next transformation into being, recognize again that each initiative is bespoke.

The precise tools or approaches that work in one project may not work in the next. A new subject matter, fresh objectives, a different group of people and an evolving ecosystem will mean that the journey of transformation will look and feel different.

Adaptability is a key capability for businesses, and so too for transformation. The skills we've learnt, and the Retail Transformation Steering Wheel allow you to focus on the key themes that improve the likelihood of success. With real world practice and application, you'll continue to build confidence and enhance your skills. As you traverse this ever-changing landscape, remember that you don't need to go it alone.

If you're ready to shift your transformation into top gear, whether you're looking to map out a new and viable approach, accelerate a crucial initiative or seek a seasoned navigator to guide you to success, I'm here to help. Let's drive forward together. Connect with me for hands-on consulting and advisory services at DrivingRetailTransformation.com/go or simply scan the QR code below.

Continuous improvement

One of my aims with this book was to help you transform how you approach transformation. You, as the customer of that change, will be the one to determine if that has happened. As we look to the future, I hope you can commit to continuously improving how you approach change.

Change and transformation does not appear to be retreating in our modern world. So, as we shift into a state of continual transformation, or evolution, I hope you are feeling future-proofed to take on that change. In fact, right now, I'd like you to identify and capture a commitment.

Ask yourself: What is the most important behaviour that
you will adopt to help drive transformation better?

What's next?

- Go to DrivingRetailTransformation.com/extras to start using the Steering Wheel and discover more content.

- Make a commitment to continually improve how you're approaching transformation to maximize your chances of success.

- Get into the driver's seat and choose to drive your retail transformation.

APPENDICES

Appendix 1

Self-assessment for the Retail Transformation Steering Wheel

Take the Retail Transformation Steering Wheel self-assessment now by following these steps:

1. Answer each question and add a check for 'yes'.

2. Sum up the checks for each section.

3. Identify the sections with the lowest number of checks and review the relevant chapters of this book.

4. Create an action plan for how to rectify these areas.

5. Decide when you'll next take this self-assessment to monitor progress.

The challenge

Taking an honest look in the mirror

☐ Have you recently experienced operations from a customer or colleague's standpoint?

☐ Have you consulted a diverse range of perspectives in assessing the status quo?

- ☐ Have you tried to identify any elephants in the room which are not being actively addressed?

Reading the signals

- ☐ Is your organization consistently using data to inform the transformation?

- ☐ Are you intentionally balancing data-based insights with experience and instinct?

- ☐ Are you consistently monitoring the right metrics that reflect the past, present and future performance?

Finding the ideal transformation

- ☐ Have you recently considered your company's readiness and appetite for change?

- ☐ Is the transformation clearly aligned with the overarching company strategy?

- ☐ Is there a clear vision statement and definition of success for the transformation?

The solution

Defining the solution

- ☐ Is the business problem and transformation solution written down, both as a thinking and a communication tool?

- ☐ Have you recently stratified the transformation to ensure clarity and stay on track?

- ☐ Have you considered and planned for unintended consequences in the transformation?

Aligning thinking behind the plan

- ☐ Are plans being used to track progress and drive actions?

- ☐ Are the six plans showing an up-to-date forecast of the future?

- ☐ Are you using the plans to align expectations across the business?

Mindset and leadership

Winning hearts and minds starts with you

- ☐ Are you consistently demonstrating the essential attitudes (resilience, determination, humility, adaptability, curiosity, focus, courage)?

- ☐ Have you recently prioritized learning about the industry and subject matter relevant to your transformation?

- ☐ Have you recently emphasized personal and team development with your transformation team?

Getting the best people involved

- ☐ Have you recently evaluated your transformation team to ensure a positive mix of talent, experience and perspective?

- ☐ Do you have clear actions to develop team dynamics and move to the next stage of the Forming, Storming, Norming, Performing model?

- ☐ Are you consistently protecting your team from stress and burnout throughout the transformation?

Creating and fostering your transformation ecosystem

- ☐ Have you identified and recently engaged the different stakeholders?

- ☐ Have you recently created new cross-functional collaboration opportunities to break down silo walls?

- ☐ Does the transformation report into a relevant and functioning steering group?

Progress and execution

Accelerating meaningful progress

- ☐ Are you actively employing techniques to encourage action and get work done?

- Are you leading by example to inject pace and energy?

- Are you intentionally building momentum with bitesize activities and regular milestones?

Avoiding the inevitable roadblocks

- Is the transformation clear of avoidable or unavoidable roadblocks?

- Is a 'top challenge list' kept regularly up-to-date and visible to the team?

- Is preventative action being taken against the transformation risks?

Overcoming the uncertainty and unknowns

- Have you recently identified the burning questions that are influencing your approach to transformation?

- Are there documented assumptions which are visible and understood by stakeholders?

- Is likelihood being regularly considered and openly discussed by the transformation team?

Making bold decisions

- Is it clear to the transformation team and decision makers what decisions are approaching?

- Have you recently involved diverse, trusted advisors when making decisions related to your transformation?

- Are decision-making forums focused on topics relevant to the business prioritization and scale of the decision?

Executing and realizing the transformation

- Have you recently used Go/No Go decisions and trials to aid your transformation's execution?

- Have you recently considered deploying 'retail thinking' and different approaches to your transformation?

- Are the customers of the change aware of the most important behaviour to drive your transformation to success?

Appendix 2
Rescuing and reinvigorating after a breakdown

It would be easy to write or read a book where transformation just works. Everything goes to plan. Everything is amazing.

However, as I'm sure you recognize, it's not all plain sailing. My experience of working in retail has taught me that transformation initiatives regularly get stuck or grind to a halt.

The reasons for transformation breaking down along the journey can be plentiful, and most likely will be a complex web of interacting factors. Some of these factors will be based on the organization or culture. Others will have been created at the start of the transformation or during the process. Some are generated through people and others from external factors. Some of these factors will appear as visible root causes whilst others remain obscured or invisible altogether.

When faced with a faltering transformation, it's unlikely to automatically resolve itself. It may be possible to have a reset, an equivalent of turn it off and on again, which may get a few extra miles out. However, the underlying challenges remain and at some stage, assuming that there is still inherent value in the initiative despite the challenges, the transformation will need rescuing.

The rescue operation

Rescuing a transformation project or programme requires a fully bespoke action plan based on the scenario and people involved. It's important to understand the symptoms and root causes of the breakdown, as well as how the transformation exists within the ecosystem. However, there are common themes of transformation breakdown which require different actions to reinvigorate.

Investigating and understanding the root cause is essential for each type of breakdown. This root cause will undoubtedly inspire specific rescue actions for your transformation.

Loss of energy and burnout

The energy behind the transformation begins to wane, potentially due to insufficient resources, excessive scope, burnout of individuals involved, loss of motivation or lack of plan or incomplete work. Overwhelm sets in and the team is not capable of blending hard work, smart work and careful work.

Possible symptoms and signs	Rescue actions
▸ Individuals seem consistently tired or disengaged. ▸ Missed deadlines or incomplete work without proactive communication. ▸ Increased absenteeism and changes to team members. ▸ Declining quality of work.	▸ Investigate root causes, including balance of transformation and existing 'day job' roles. ▸ Review the six plans to ensure they're realistic and reasonable. ▸ Ensure adequate focus, priority and communication with the team to motivate and energize. ▸ Review delegation and support opportunities. ▸ Consider breaking the scope and work into multiple phases. ▸ Consider adding to or changing team members.

Lost direction

The transformation started well but has since lost its way due to challenges, diversions, conflicting priorities or changing goals and scope. The original aims have been forgotten or obscured, causing unpredictable progress and results.

Possible symptoms and signs	Rescue actions
▷ Frequent changes in forecasted benefits. ▷ Confusion about objectives and priorities within the team. ▷ Inconsistency between actions and stated goals.	▷ Investigate root causes, including previous changes to goals and scope. ▷ Review alignment between the strategy and transformation. ▷ Take an honest look in the mirror and reassess the primary challenge to confirm the most pressing business issues. ▷ Review the transformation stratification to refresh why different elements exist and how they fit together.

Slow speed and no progress

The transformation seems to be a never-ending journey with slow or non-existent progress and the transformation feels increasingly unlikely to deliver value to the business.

Possible symptoms and signs	Rescue actions
▷ Lack of recent achievements or milestones. ▷ Regularly postponed deadlines. ▷ Low urgency and responsiveness among team members.	▷ Review if team members understand the challenges and expectations. ▷ Investigate root causes and empower transformation team to review too. ▷ Critically review progress against expectations to consider the actual challenge and how reasonable the expectations are.

	▷ Add more short-term milestones and checkpoints to motivate and demonstrate progress. ▷ Consider if there is the right blend of attitudes, skills and characteristics involved. ▷ Create urgency by raising awareness of the total opportunity or cost per day of the transformation.

Poor quality of work or key tasks not done

Critical factors are overlooked, and mistakes are frequently made. Key tasks, such as business cases or steering group preparation, are not completed adequately.

Possible symptoms and signs	Rescue actions
▷ Frequent errors in output, often spotted by those outside the transformation team. ▷ Incomplete or missing critical deliverables. ▷ Reluctance or avoidance in discussing project status.	▷ Review questionable work with relevant individuals to align expectations and define specific actions. ▷ Create rapid action plans for reworking low-quality output, mistakes or missing deliverables. ▷ Investigate deeper root causes. ▷ Consider if there is the right blend of attitudes, skills and characteristics involved. ▷ Consider support options to train, mentor or coach relevant people.

Lack of stakeholder commitment

The transformation is not a top priority for senior or cross-functional stakeholders. The transformation appears lower down the priority list than expected and there is a chance that there are misaligned expectations or understanding of the transformation.

Possible symptoms and signs	Rescue actions
‣ Transformation rarely discussed in senior meetings, or discussions are often postponed in favour of other topics. ‣ Resistance or lack of cooperation from various departments. ‣ Perceived disruptive behaviour. ‣ Other business problems are blamed on the transformation or are added to the scope. ‣ Priority given to other projects over the transformation. ‣ Requested or agreed resources are not available or are assigned to other work.	‣ Investigate root causes for each specific stakeholder and in general. ‣ Review the business case and justification to check if the value it creates is compelling. ‣ Consider prioritization against different business initiatives and focus areas. ‣ Excite and earn stakeholder engagement by demonstrating tangible experiments and proofs of concept. ‣ Review FACES framework and engagement. ‣ Introduce more genuine collaboration opportunities.

Stopped too early

As soon as the transformation reaches the point of deployment, the focus and team disperse and it is left to freewheel and risks running into issues at a critical point. It's likely to result in one of the execution failures as discussed in Chapter 16.

Possible symptoms and signs	Rescue actions
‣ Disbanding of project team immediately after a major milestone, including the moment of deployment. ‣ No plans or vague plans for monitoring after deployment.	‣ Investigate root causes of why the team moved on. ‣ Ensure the initiative remains an official priority with allocated resources. Reiterate that the journey continues beyond the point of deployment.

▷ Ignoring or minimizing issues that arise after deployment with ownership pushed to business-as-usual teams.	▷ Closely monitor the deployment for potential issues. ▷ Review outstanding tasks and activities to agree ownership.

The unmovable roadblock

A technical or legal restriction suggests there is no way to achieve the goals.

Possible symptoms and signs	Rescue actions
▷ Inability to progress due to a specific legal or technical issue. ▷ Discussions of who or what is to blame. ▷ The top challenge(s) remain unchanged.	▷ Critically review the reality and impact of the roadblock. ▷ Investigate root causes of the issue and the approach. ▷ Revisit the transformation stratification to help generate alternative routes to achieve the same business outcome. ▷ Consider intermediate steps that can achieve some of the business benefits as an alternative destination.

No driver

Key people have moved roles, left the company or have lost focus and control. The transformation is beginning to drift, and challenges may overwhelm the initiative.

Possible symptoms and signs	Rescue actions
▷ Unclear who is taking the lead for the transformation initiative. ▷ Lack of updates or communication from the transformation team.	▷ Review who should currently be driving the transformation. ▷ Review roles and responsibilities for the transformation.

▶ General lack of organization and momentum in project activities.	▶ Investigate and understand the root causes of why the driver has lost focus.

It's feasible that the transformation is suffering from multiple challenges as they quickly become interlinked and can cause other issues. It's crucial to call out the elephant in the room and take an honest look at the transformation.

Additionally, opening and maintaining clear dialogue with the transformation team and key stakeholders will be highly valuable and appreciated. People tend to recognize when a transformation is not going well although they may choose not to actively voice this opinion. Clear, regular communication avoids gossip and rumour from running rife whilst also boosting confidence and opening collaboration opportunities to share positive ideas to rescue the transformation.

However, in any instance, recognizing the situation and naming the challenges experienced will reveal root causes and suggest sensible reinvigoration actions.

Fresh energy to reinvigorate the transformation

To help reinvigorate a transformation, a permanent or temporary change of personnel can help shift the dynamic and bring new energy and new perspective. Fresh eyes can raise questions or take a second look at the transformation to ensure that it's focused on the right problem and approaching it in the best way.

There is no historical baggage or emotional ties to the work so they can think differently and are not weighted down by the background. Equally, stakeholders can be more open to sharing their true thoughts around what's happening and where the best opportunities lie. However, be careful to ensure existing knowledge is captured and shared to avoid losing it forever as well as going around in circles or needless backtracking.

However, new people can cause conflict or negative feelings among the original transformation team, especially if they harbour real or perceived ownership for causing the breakdown. This natural reaction is again highly connected to our primal brain and the triggers of failure, existential threats and a general fear of the unknown. Mixing up the team involved will reset progress for Tuckman's Forming, Storming, Norming, Performing model, as discussed in Chapter 10.

Holding workshops to review through the fundamentals of the change can be massively rewarding. By starting at the beginning, new team members are brought up to speed and highlight a multitude of opportunities in several areas.

However, not all businesses have the luxury of talented transformation professionals waiting around to help rescue transformations, so bringing in external consultants or advisors can be a prudent and quick step, especially if you're looking to reinvigorate, not replace, the existing team.

Jump starting to reinvigorate

With new energy to help investigate and reinvigorate the transformation, the main focus should be on testing the viability of the transformation and restarting momentum.

Testing viability ensures it's still the right business decision to continue with the transformation and that the reward for delivering to completion is still worth the effort and risk. This is especially true if there are multiple transformation initiatives vying for prioritization of scarce resources. Do not guarantee that the change is still viable, as a primary reason for the breakdown maybe due to a lack of feasibility.

Assuming that the transformation is still worth saving, it's important to focus on quick wins to start building momentum. These may be genuine quick wins to deliver some benefit to the company, colleagues or customers. Or they may be more metaphorical quick wins to show that there is new energy to create tangible change; examples include workshops, a new transformation strategy or other demonstration that things will be different this time. Reviewing short-term milestones is another way to build momentum, giving near-term objectives which can motivate and give a sense of achievement.

Finally, it's crucial to communicate with stakeholders that the transformation is re-energized. It is usually quite apparent to those near the transformation that there were challenges. Communicating and demonstrating what's different and proving that the transformation is progressing forwards is a key aim as you look to rebuild trust with the promoters and champions of the change.

Pausing for another day

Depending on the cause of the breakdown and findings from the initial investigation, it may make sense to put the initiative on pause. Perhaps a challenge needs deep work in the background, perhaps a dependency needs waiting time or maybe other initiatives hold a greater priority right now.

Pausing a transformation is a valid strategy, but to ensure it can be restarted in the future, valuable information must be recorded. Debriefing the team helps clarify the latest progress and future direction. This can be done as a series of interviews which can be recorded, and should include walkthroughs of relevant information, documents or findings. Consider this a virtual handover of the project as it's entirely feasible that when the transformation restarts, a different group of people will be assigned for various reasons.

All relevant information, documents and handover notes or interviews should be clearly archived with guidance about what's stored and how to use it. This should be shared with a variety of relevant people so that it doesn't get lost in the company's file storage warp or email inboxes.

Like taking a diversion, this news should be communicated to relevant parties along with the reasoning and any implications to the wider organization, including pausing or cancelling scheduled tasks or workload.

The final stage of pausing a transformation is to schedule a review meeting with key stakeholders for a sensible point in the future to consider restarting the work.

Writing off the transformation

In some instances, despite the best rescue efforts, it may be necessary to fully stop a transformation. It's important to know when enough is enough and when it's time to 'stop throwing good money (and resources) after bad.'

When the transformation cannot be resuscitated or repaired, and there is no perceived value in pausing, the transformation should stop. It doesn't make sense to keep a transformation going, almost for the sake of it, when deep down, everyone knows there is little or no benefit or likelihood of it happening. Keeping a zero-value initiative alive as an 'undead' transformation serves no purpose other than distracting and consuming the organization's resources and headspace.

In these occasions, the team must capture any valuable lessons from the experience, go through the mourning process and move on, embracing the failure and ignoring the stigma, as discussed in Chapter 14.

The death of a transformation may affect other parts of the organization and ecosystem too, so ensure that this news is communicated, understood and actioned, including sharing the valuable lessons learned by the experience. These lessons may form crucial guidance or recommendations for future transformation initiatives.

However, a broader group of stakeholders may also need to be involved depending on the progress made to date. The transformation effort, and any assets produced so far, may need to be written off financially. HR implications could exist as individuals may face changing roles, contract termination or face redundancy. Commercial, Purchasing and Legal teams may be involved to discuss and agree implications for cancelling or severing contracts with external parties. And finally, PR and Investor Relations may play a part, depending on the external visibility of the change effort and the broader business impact.

When you declare a transformation as dead, it is natural to feel bad, even if it's the best decision for the company. However, failure does not define us as individuals and the experiences will make us stronger for the next journey of transformation we take.

What we've covered

- ▷ Many different aspects could cause a transformation to breakdown.

- ▷ New individuals can provide a fresh pair of eyes and renew energy levels to reinvigorate an initiative.

- ▷ Breakdowns can also be a good time to intentionally pause or stop the transformation in the best interests of the business, colleagues and customers. Be sure to take learnings in these instances.

Acknowledgements

L ike transformation, writing a book is a journey and relies on the encouragement, support and acumen of many people.

First, my deepest gratitude goes to my wife, Sarah, whose continual encouragement, support, patience and energy have been a constant driving force throughout this venture, and in life. Thank you to my children, Thomas and Rachel, for cheering me on and for all of their creative help in turning this book into reality.

My professional journey has been shaped by numerous mentors and colleagues who have guided me, challenged me and developed my understanding of this industry and topic. A special mention to Vishal Bansal, Rachel Goldberg, Peter Bowrey and Steph Tranter, whose influence has been particularly profound. I offer huge appreciation to countless other colleagues I've been fortunate to work with, as well as those from the broader retail industry who share their experiences and insights with me.

To my clients, whose trust enabled me to play a role in their incredible transformation journeys and who provided the platform of real-world application for the concepts in this book, thank you for allowing me to be part of your success.

I am immensely grateful to Tracey Clements, not only for her insightful foreword but also for her role in inspiring and driving the retail industry. Her leadership plays a pivotal role in propelling businesses forward.

Special thanks are due to those who have generously given their time and expertise for interviews, reviewing early drafts of the manuscript and offering candid feedback to improve the final product. In alphabetical order: Ben Armstrong, Carl Boutet, Claire Lewis, Dan McGrath, Darren Kay, Doug Nesbit, Freddie Banks, Gary Newbury, Holly Steele, Ian Shepherd, Janice Southway, Joe Murray, Laura Ross, Martin Newman, Michael Grange, Mike Doherty, Miya Knights, Natalie Berg, Paula Bobbett, Ricardo Belmar, Sarah Friswell and Steve Dennis. Your insights were invaluable. I am immensely grateful for your time and wisdom.

Last but by no means least, I would like to extend my deepest appreciation to Alison Jones and the team at Practical Inspiration Publishing. Your expertise and advice have been crucial in shaping and crafting this book into what I hope will be received as a notable and meaningful publication.

To everyone who played a part in this journey, I offer my genuine and heartfelt thanks. This book stands as a testament to all your contributions, and I am forever grateful.

References and notes

[1] Ritchie, Hannah, and Roser, Max (2019) [accessed 30 June 2023] *Urbanisation*, Our World in Data. https://ourworldindata.orgurbanization#how-many-people-will-live-in-urban-areas-in-the-future

[2] United Nations (2019) [accessed 30 June 2023] *World Urbanization Prospects 2018*, United Nations. https://population.un.org/wup/publications/Files/WUP2018-Highlights.pdf

[3] Global Wellness Institute (2021) [accessed 11 August 2023] *The Global Wellness Economy: Looking Beyond Covid*, Global Wellness Institute. https://globalwellnessinstitute.org/wp-content/uploads/2021/11/GWI-WE-Monitor-2021_final-digital.pdf

[4] Garcia, Jon (2022) [accessed 30 June 2023] *Common Pitfalls in Transformations*, McKinsey & Company. www.mckinsey.com/capabilities/transformation/our-insights/common-pitfalls-in-transformations-a-conversation-with-jon-garcia

[5] Von Walter, Amy via Rittenhouse, Lindsay (2017) [accessed 17 August 2023] *Toys 'R' Us is Nearing its End These 3 Signs Reveal*, The Street. www.thestreet.com/investing/stocks/these-3-signs-reveal-that-toys-quot-r-quot-us-is-nearing-its-end-14297112

[6] Bezos, Jeff (1997) [accessed 17 August 2023] *Letter to Shareholders, 1997 Annual Report*, Amazon. https://s2.q4cdn.com/299287126/files/doc_financials/annual/Shareholderletter98.pdf

[7] Blockbuster Inc (2008) [accessed 17 August 2023] *Form 10-K*, US Securities and Exchange Commission. www.sec.gov/Archives/edgar/data/1085734/000119312508048757/d10k.htm

[8] Covey, Stephen (1989) *The 7 Habits of Highly Effective People*, Free Press.

[9] Walmart [accessed 30 June 2023] *Grilled Chicken*, Walmart. www.walmart.com/search?q=grilled%20chicken

[10] Walmart [accessed 30 June 2023] *Replacement Truck Grilles*, Walmart. www.walmart.com/ip/Volvo-VNL-2018-Truck-Replacement-Chrome-Grille-w-Bug-Screen-V-Emblem/178783050

[11] Amazon [accessed 30 June 2023] *4000+ Electric Toothbrushes*, Amazon. www.amazon.co.uk/b?node=3012128031&ref=nb_sb_noss

[12] Newman, Martin (2021) *The Power of Customer Experience*, Kogan Page.

[13] Ross, Ashley (2016) [accessed 30 June 2023] *The Surprising Way a Supermarket Changed the World*, Time. https://time.com/4480303/supermarkets-history/

[14] Brown, Derrick (2023) [accessed 30 June 2023] *The Birth of the Barcode*, British Computer Society. www.bcs.org/articles-opinion-and-research/the-birth-of-the-barcode/

[15] Amazon (2018) [accessed 30 June 2023] *1-Click*, Amazon. www.about amazon.co.uk/news/innovation/1-click

[16] Maslow, Abraham (1943) *A Theory of Human Motivation*, Wilder Publications.

[17] Hobbs, Andrew (2023) [accessed 16 August 2023] *EMEIA Board Priorities 2023: How to Shape Tomorrow's Board Agenda Today*, EY. www.ey.com/en_uk/board-matters/emeia-board-priorities-2023-how-to-shape-tomorrows-board-agenda-today

[18] Sanders, Melanie, Cheris, Aaron, Unnikrishnan, Shyam, and Kwok, Connie (2023) [accessed 15 August 2023] *How Engine 2 Expansion Can Power the Future of Retail*, Bain

& Company. www.bain.com/insights/how-engine-2-expansion-can-power-the-future-of-retail/

[19] Bezos, Jeff via Shick, Michael (2010) [accessed 11 August 2023] *Jeff Bezos – 'What's Dangerous is Not to Evolve'*, Fast Company. www.fastcompany.com/1569357/jeff-bezos-whats-dangerous-not-evolve

[20] Oncken Jr, William, and Wass, Donald (1999) [accessed 30 June 2023] *Management Time: Who's Got the Monkey?* Harvard Business Review. https://hbr.org/1999/11/management-time-whos-got-the-monkey/

[21] Cannon, Walter (1915) *Bodily Changes in Pain, Hunger, Fear*, Appleton & Co.

[22] Fisher, Jon (2012) [accessed 30 June 2023] *The Process of Transition*, Business Balls. www.businessballs.com/freepdfmaterials/fisher-transition-curve-2012bb.pdf

[23] Welch, Jack (2005) *Winning*, Harper Business.

[24] New York-Presbyterian (2018) [accessed 20 August 2023] *It Happened Here: The Apgar Score*, Health Matters. https://healthmatters.nyp.org/apgar-score/

[25] Heath, Chip, and Heath, Dan (2006) *Made to Stick: Why Some Ideas Take Hold and Others Come Unstuck*, Harrow.

[26] Pietrangelo, Ann (2019) [accessed 30 June 2023] *Understanding the Baader-Meinhof Phenomenon*, Healthline. www.healthline.com/health/baader-meinhof-phenomenon

[27] Dewar, Carolyn, Keller, Scott, and Malhotra, Vikram (2022) *CEO Excellence: The Six Mindsets that Distinguish the Best Leaders from the Rest*, Nicholas Brealey Publishing.

[28] Hammond, Richard (2019) *Friction/Reward: Be Your Customer's First Choice*, Pearson.

[29] Bloomberg (2018) [accessed 18 August 2023] *Who Knew You Wanted a New Spicy Snickers Bar? Alibaba Did*, Fortune. https://fortune.com/2018/10/24/alibaba-data-mining-unilever-mars-snickers/

[30] Attributed to Buffett, Warren. Gallant, Chris (2022) [accessed 30 June 2023] *How an Economic Moat Provides a Competitive Advantage*, Investopedia. www.investopedia.com/ask/answers/05/economicmoat.asp

[31] Tzu, Sun (2010, revised from circa 500BC) *The Art of War*, Capstone Publishing.

[32] Popular strategy tool to identify strengths, weaknesses, opportunities, threats.

[33] Popular strategy tool to define political, economic, social, technology, legal, and environmental factors.

[34] Popular goal setting tool for objectives and key results.

[35] Bryar, Colin, Barr, Bill (2021) *Working Backwards: Insights, Stories, and Secrets from Inside Amazon*, Macmillan.

[36] Collins, Jim (2011) *Great By Choice*, Harper Business.

[37] Henderson, Simon, Litré, Patrick, Wegener, Rasmus, and Capeless, Mark (2022) [accessed 30 June 2023] *Building A Better Transformation*, Bain & Company. www.bain.com/insights/building-a-better-transformation-infographic/

[38] Amazon (2012–2023) [accessed 30 June 2023] *Leadership Values*, Amazon. www.amazon.jobs/content/en/our-workplace/leadership-principles

[39] Often attributed to Drucker, Peter but no evidence.

[40] McDonnell, Fiona (2021) *Two Mirrors and a Cheetah*, Double Magpie.

[41] Matthias, Gruber, Bernard, Gelman, and Charan, Ranganath (2014) *States of Curiosity Modulate Hippocampus-Dependent Learning via the Dopaminergic Circuit*, Neuron.

[42] Collins, Jim (2001) *Good to Great: Why Some Companies Make the Leap... and Others Don't*, Harper Business.

43 Tuckman, Bruce (1965) [accessed 30 June 2023] 'Developmental sequence in small groups', *Psychological Bulletin*, 63(6), 384–399. https://doi.org/10.1037/h0022100

44 Popular project management tool to confirm who is responsible, accountable, consulted and informed.

45 Tuckman, Bruce, and Jensen, Mary (1977) [accessed 30 June 2023] 'Stages of small-group development revisited', *Group & Organization Studies*, 2(4), 419–427. https://doi.org/10.1177/105960117700200404

46 Collins, Jim, and Porras, Jerry (1994) *Built to Last: Successful Habits of Visionary Companies*, Harper Business.

47 Jaffe, Eric (2013) [accessed 30 June 2023] *Why Wait? The Science Behind Procrastination*, Association for Psychological Science. www.psychologicalscience.org/observer/why-wait-the-science-behind-procrastination

48 Widely referenced, including by Dumaine, Brian (2021) *Bezonomics*, Simon & Schuster UK.

49 Collins, Jim (2001) *Good to Great: Why Some Companies Make the Leap... and Others Don't*, Harper Business.

50 Rumsfeld, Donald (2002) [accessed 30 June 2023] *White House Press conference from 02-Dec-2002*, CNN. www.youtube.com/watch?v=REWeBzGuzCc

51 Williamson, Kirsty (2002) *Research Methods for Students, Academics and Professionals* (Second Edition), Chandos Publishing.

52 Dewar, Carolyn, Keller, Scott, and Malhotra, Vikram (2022) *CEO Excellence: The Six Mindsets That Distinguish the Best Leaders from the Rest*, Nicholas Brealey Publishing.

53 Mulligan, Dr Jackie (2020) [accessed 30 June 2023] *Episode 113: Disruptive Thinking for a Volatile World*, The Retail Transformation Show podcast. https://obandco.uk/113-disruptive-thinking-for-volatile-world/

54 Highsmith, Jim et al (2001) [accessed 30 June 2023] *Agile Manifesto*, Agile Alliance. https://agilemanifesto.org/

55 Frisch, Bob (2012) [accessed 30 June 2023] *If You Think Your Team Makes Decisions, Think Again*, Harvard Business Review. https://hbr.org/2012/04/the-illusion-of-decision-makin

56 Healy, Patrick (2016) [accessed 30 June 2023] *Confirmation Bias: How it Affects Your Organization and How to Overcome it*, Harvard Business School. https://online.hbs.edu/blog/post/confirmation-bias-how-it-affects-your-organization-and-how-to-overcome-it

57 Heskett, James (2004) [accessed 30 June 2023] *Leadership: A Matter of Sustaining or Eliminating Groupthink?* Harvard Business School. https://hbswk.hbs.edu/item/leadership-a-matter-of-sustaining-or-eliminating-groupthink

58 Sharot, Tali (2011) [accessed 30 June 2023] *The Optimism Bias*, Science Direct. www.sciencedirect.com/science/article/pii/S0960982211011912

59 Kahneman, Daniel, Sibony, Olivier, and Sunstein, Cass (2021) *Noise: A Flaw in Human Judgement*, William Collins.

60 Northcote Parkinson, Cyril (1958) *Parkinson's Law, or the Pursuit of Progress*, John Murray Publishers.

61 Galinato, Melissa (2022) [accessed 30 June 2023] *Attention and Focus*, BrainFacts.org & Society for Neuroscience. www.brainfacts.org/thinking-sensing-and-behaving/thinking-and-awareness/2022/attention-and-focus-082922

62 MacNeilage, Peter, Rogers, Lesley, and Vallortigara, Giorgio (2009) [accessed 30 June 2023] *Evolutionary Origins of Your Right and Left Brain*, Scientific American. www.scientificamerican.com/article/evolutionary-origins-of-your-right-and-left-brain/

Index

Page numbers in *italics* indicate figures and tables.